W9-CND-022

BUYER BEWARE

A Home Encyclopedia

How to Avoid Cons,
Swindles, Frauds, and
Other Trickeries

By BARRY MINKOW

with Tony Jaime

DOVE
BOOKS

DEDICATION

To my wife Teresa,
who personifies the meaning of the word *grace*—
God giving you something that you don't deserve.

Copyright © 1997 by Dove Audio, Inc.

All rights reserved. No part of this book may be reproduced or transmitted in any
form or by any means, electronic or mechanical, including photocopying, recording,
or by any information storage and retrieval system, without permission in writing
from the publisher.

ISBN 0-7871-1292-5

Printed in the United States of America

Dove Entertainment
8955 Beverly Boulevard
Los Angeles, CA 90048
(310) 786-1600

Join Dove on the World Wide Web at: www.doveaudio.com/dove/

Text design and layout by Jonathan Wills/Frank Loose Design
Cover design by Rick Penn-Kraus

Distributed by Penguin USA

First Printing: May 1997

10 9 8 7 6 5 4 3 2 1

ACKNOWLEDGMENTS

Many people deserve recognition for the content of this book. The first is Tony Jaime, the producer of our nationally syndicated radio show. He spent hours constructing, editing, and researching the many topics covered in *Buyer Beware*. Additionally, Gary Almond from the Better Business Bureau was a great source of information. He was always there, providing both materials and advice on content. Paul Palladino also deserves recognition. His investigative skills and compilation of data made the book more user-friendly for the consumer.

I would also like to acknowledge the materials I received from the Federal Trade Commission, the United States Postal Inspector, the Florida Attorney General, and other law enforcement agencies that have made educating the public their number one priority. In some cases I simply pass along their advice and do not attempt to improve upon it. Finally, I would like to thank Lee Montgomery and Mary Aarons from Dove Entertainment. It was their prompting and direction that inspired me to write. They wanted a book that would make a difference in the $400-billion-a-year problem of consumer fraud. I only hope that I did not let them down.

Contents

Foreword

Okay, picture this. You walk into your house after a long day at the office. You're tired, a little irritated about the drive-home traffic and the topic on your favorite talk radio show. You set down your coat and briefcase and notice the light blinking on the answering machine. You're late for your son's high school soccer game so you think twice about retrieving the message.

Convinced that it's the boss with some last-minute demands for tomorrow's meeting, you decide to play back the message.

"This is Bill from the college. Your daughter has been in a terrible accident. Please call us immediately at 809-555-6363." Thoughts race through your head. Anxiety, worry, and the thought of your daughter's well-being flood your mind. Without hesitating, you pick up the phone and call the school. The area code is different from the one you usually use, but area codes change daily as phone service demand increases. Besides, *your daughter's health is at issue!*

A man with an accent answers the phone and transfers you to another department. You're on hold for seven minutes before someone else answers. You're transferred a few more times, and fifteen minutes pass before you realize that you have not reached your daughter's college. You hang up, check the number, and frantically call again—but achieve the same result.

Finally, you call the number of your daughter's dorm. She answers the phone—healthy, happy, and glad to receive the unexpected call. You explain the message and convince yourself that the person who called probably got the wrong number—until you receive your phone bill at the end of the month with a charge of $100 for two calls to an unidentified "809" number. You have become the latest victim of the variation on the 900 number scam.

It is because of scams and frauds such as these that I felt compelled to write this book. Perpetrators are preying on the American consumer more now than ever before. In fact, according to a recently released three-year study by the Association of Certified Fraud Examiners, consumer fraud costs Americans over $400 *billion* dollars a year. That figure will easily double over the next four years if the public does not learn how to think about consumer issues.

But before I go any further, I think something needs to be said (or disclosed) about my unique qualifications to write this type of book. In 1988 I was convicted of fifty-seven counts of stock, bank, and mail fraud in connection with ZZZZ Best, a company that I started out of my garage at the age of sixteen. Much to my shame, I was guilty of perpetrating a fraud that victimized financial institutions and stockholders. I offer no excuses for my crime and actually served eighty-seven months in federal prison.

Most of that sentence was served in maximum- and medium-security facilities, and I ended up doing more time in custody than Milken, Boesky, and Leona Helmsley combined. I say that only to let you know that I paid a heavy price for my crimes. I quickly learned that once you squeeze the toothpaste out of the tube, you can't get it back in.

That simply means that although I can't change the past, I *can* try to make an impact on the future. Rather than giving up and believing that false notion that states "once a con, always a con," I decided to take the road less traveled and face my victims and the community, admit I made a mistake, and try to make restitution for my crimes.

Since my release from prison I have worked steadily for law enforcement—including the FBI and much of corporate America—teaching the techniques con men use to deceive their victims. Not only do I appeal to my experiences at ZZZZ Best, but I also integrate the eighty-seven months in prison, where I met many of the country's biggest white-collar criminals. I was a sponge in prison—constantly asking questions—trying to learn the *how* and the *why* behind white-collar crime.

I also host a nationally syndicated radio show where consumers can call in *before* they put their money into a particular business opportunity or send out that check for the sweepstakes offer. The radio show has been a great platform for educating the public about the latest in consumer fraud. And with a $400-billion-a-year problem, we never run out of fresh material.

It is my goal that after reading this book you will do two things. The first is become aware of the significance of the problem. It never ceases to amaze me how many people turn a deaf ear to this situation.

Not long ago, while I was speaking at a fraud seminar in Los Angeles, a man tried to refute my statistics on the regularity of fraud. I responded by challenging him to simply read the "Business" and "Metro" sections of the *L.A. Times* for thirty days and count how many white-collar crimes were reported. Although I never heard from him again, over fifteen frauds were uncovered, totaling more than $100 million, in that thirty-day period alone. In fact, had I thought to open the paper for that day, I could have shown him three frauds—all of which had a victim impact of over $1 million.

The second thing that I would like you to walk away with after reading this book is what I call the think/feel dichotomy. Simply stated, that means I want you to *think* and not *feel* when it comes to making consumer and investment decisions. You might be surprised to learn that in polling victims of white-collar crimes I have learned that many give the same response to the "How were you fooled?" question.

"I felt so good about the deal," or "He was so nice." These answers are far too common and reveal our propensity to allow the subjective to outweigh the objective. I would like to challenge you to use your head and not your heart when making decisions about the issues described in this book. I have arranged this book in such a way that it will be easy for you to follow. It is by no means an exhaustive study on the subject of fraud, but it is a user-friendly manual on everything from fraud on the Internet to the latest scams that come cleverly disguised in your mailbox.

There is one more thing I want you to know, and it goes to my motive for writing this book. I make no apologies for being a Christian. Now I know you are probably thinking that I'm another one of those "born again until you're out again Christians," but that is not the case. I have been out of prison for over two years and continue to try to live a life that is consistent with my beliefs. You need to know that although the crimes of ZZZZ Best were my responsibility, I have served my time. ZZZZ Best is not the unforgivable sin.

If this book helps just a few people avoid becoming victims of the next ZZZZ Best, then it will have served its purpose.

What Makes a Fraud?

"Fraud is the skin of the truth stuffed with a lie," I said to the FBI agent who asked me to define the term at a fraud prevention seminar. "At ZZZZ Best we really did have 1,300 employees in twenty-three locations. We really did clean carpets. But that was the skin of the truth. The 'stuffed with a lie part' was telling Wall Street that ZZZZ Best was doing $50 million a year in revenue when in actuality we were doing approximately $5 million."

Whenever I speak on the topic of fraud, especially to law enforcement agencies and CPAs, they are, more often than not, reluctant to use the word *fraud* in describing a shady business deal. "Fraud is a legal conclusion about a person or set of facts that must be proved in a court of law," a partner in a large CPA firm once said to me. "I can't call something a fraud just because it appears to be fraudulent."

To which I responded, "Why not?"

Webster rightly defines the term *fraud* as "deceit or trickery perpetrated for profit or to gain some unfair or dishonest advantage." Note the word *trickery*. According to this definition, no legal conclusion is necessary to slap the fraud label on a deserving perpetrator. In fact, most of the fraudulent business activities explored in this book are openly advertised in many national magazines and newspapers. Perhaps they are more subtle than the blatant ZZZZ Best fraud, but, as I will conclusively prove in this book, they are no less dangerous. Their victims range from the elderly widow on Social Security to the young entrepreneur seeking his or her first business opportunity. The modus operandi for the crime *never* changes: Prey on the uninformed consumer for profit by the use of trickery and deceit. In *Buyer Beware,* I analyze a variety of fraudulent business activities by first identifying three characteristics, or techniques, that are inherent in them.

The first of these three techniques is what I call *failure to disclose material facts.* The definition of fraud I gave earlier was "the skin of the truth stuffed with a lie"—that is, fraud perpetrators, and fraudulent schemes in particular, only present half-truths. At ZZZZ Best, stockholders invested their money in our company based on my representations that we were earning $50 million a year in gross revenues. But imagine if I had disclosed the *real* truth about the company. Do you think people would have invested in ZZZZ Best if they had known up front that 86 percent of the earnings I was claiming were fictitious? Or that I had secret, undisclosed loan relationships with members of organized crime? I think not. Every fraudulent business enterprise begins with the perpetrator knowingly and willingly failing to disclose material facts.

One of the most startling things I learned during my years on Wall Street is that the Securities and Exchange Commission (SEC) does not care if a company loses money. They take no enforcement action against a company that goes public and never makes a profit. However, if a company loses money and *fails to disclose that fact* to stockholders, thus preventing them from making a fair investment decision, that is when the SEC is forced to take action. Much to my shame, this was the case with ZZZZ Best.

The second technique is what I call *diversion*. Craig and Carla Missos, two California residents, fell victim to this technique when they invested $11,790 in a greeting card distributing business. Their story was reported in an article by Roha Ronaleen in *Kiplinger's Personal Finance Magazine.*

Carla had wanted to start a family, so she quit her job and began searching for the perfect home-based business that would allow her to be with her children and still contribute financially to the household budget. While listening to the radio one summer day in 1992, Carla heard a commercial that caught her attention. For a modest investment, the ad proclaimed, she could earn $50,000 a year working only part-time, simply by servicing greeting card display racks in her area. The business opportunity looked too good to be true (they usually do—and are). Carla told her husband, Craig, and he called Gold Coast Distributors, the marketing arm of the greeting card publisher, Jordan Ashley Galleries. Over the phone, the Gold Coast salesman gave articulate and reasoned answers to Craig's questions and sent him a packet of information that included sample cards.

The cards cost 40 cents and sold for $1.95, which meant a gross profit of more than 225 percent on each item. According to the company business plan, the retailer would get 65 cents per card, leaving a profit of 90 cents on each item sold. With their investment, Carla and Craig would be given an exclusive geographical area to service. The obvious question that any thinking person would ask is, "How many cards can I expect to sell each day?"

When Craig asked that question, he was directed to charts that were contained in the packet. These charts showed the profit potential based on sales of four to twenty cards per day and carried a disclaimer that stated, "These numbers are not guaranteed." Craig, a purchasing agent for a school district, realized the circular nature of the company's response to his question about earnings: "How do I know I will make money in *your* business venture? Because *you* told me I will."

Craig decided that the only way to get independent corroboration was to talk to other Gold Coast distributors. This was where the technique of diversion came in. At first the salesman balked at his request, but then produced two hand-picked references, one in Baltimore and the other in Chicago. As the couple later found out, what the salesman was actually doing was *diverting* their attention away from the many dissatisfied distributors (several of whom were located right in their supposedly *exclusive* area) and instead provided a limited sample of two satisfied distributors.

The goal was simple and often imitated by perpetrators—*divert* the investors' focus away from the frauds of the selling of "exclusive" distributorships to more than one person, and false claims about potential earnings, and direct it toward the hand-picked portions of the business that can hold up to scrutiny. The Federal Trade Commission ultimately shut down Gold Coast Distributors and Jordan Ashley in June of 1993—but not before they took thousands from Craig and Carla and many others.

The third technique inherent in most frauds is *drawing big conclusions from little evidence.* I call it the Oprah Winfrey factor. I have learned over the years that people have the propensity to believe what they see on television and what they read about in magazines and newspapers. For example, one of the things I did to lure investors into ZZZZ Best was to send them a press kit that included clippings of all the articles written about me and a video of my various television appearances. Like it or not, there seems to be an implied due diligence associated with those who receive positive publicity. This is also true for companies that advertise on television or in national magazines. The rationale goes something like this: "Only legitimate businesses have the money to pay for big-budget advertising."

I used this type of thinking to my advantage during the ZZZZ Best era. I boasted of earning more than $50 million a year in revenues (that's the big conclusion), and the evidence I provided to substantiate that claim was my appearances on television and coverage in the newspapers (that's the little evidence). Con men must rely on this type of subjective analysis, because the one thing we fear most is critical thinking. If the perpetrator can get you to accept little or no evidence for claims relating to the investment or opportunity, then the perpetrator is free to draw whatever conclusions he or she wants.

Consider the story of John G. Bennett, Jr., and New Era Philanthropy. A former adviser to nonprofit organizations on fund-raising and money management, Bennett became popular in Philadelphia's philanthropic and cultural circles before founding New Era Philanthropy in 1989. His "big conclusions from little evidence" scam worked like this: Bennett promised organizations (mostly nonprofit Christian organizations) and individuals 100 percent return on their contributions within six months, thanks to donors who he claimed *must remain anonymous.*

What made his scheme prosper were the people who invested early. They proclaimed how, in just six short months, they doubled their money. So, when new investors, skeptical of the 100 percent return in six months, asked questions and sought to perform due diligence by asking for the names and phone numbers of the anonymous donors, Bennett simply used the "big conclusions with little evidence" technique. Instead of disclosing the anonymous donors (which he could not do because they did not exist), Bennett gave the names of the people at the top of the pyramid—those few satisfied investors who had received 100 percent return on their money because they were lucky enough to have invested early in the fraud.

That is drawing a big conclusion (my deal is legitimate even though I have erected a wall between you, the investor, and due diligence) from little evidence (a small number of satisfied customers). At last count, the New Era fraud had cost investors over $400 million!

There they are, the three ingredients of fraud: failing to disclose material facts, diversion, and drawing big conclusions from little evidence. With that foundation laid, we are ready to look at *Buyer Beware*.

CHAPTER 1

The "A"
Advertising Fraud

Fraud costs consumers $400 billion annually in this country. The schemers hurt consumers by using unfair business practices that range from using disingenuous promotions to attract customers to overcharging on advertised discounted items. Deceptive advertising takes on a variety of forms, which we will evaluate looking at some of the most often-used gimmicks.

Most people are familiar with the term *bait and switch*. Advertisers offer unrealistically low prices on certain items—the bait—only to claim those items are unavailable and lead consumers to higher-priced items—the switch. Among many businesses employing this classic scheme are appliance stores, retailers, and now even national department chains.

A friend of mine saw an ad from a local chain store selling Levi's 501 jeans for $19.95. Normally Levi's 501 jeans start at about $29.99. Wanting to take advantage of the sale and knowing it would generate a lot of customers, my friend got to the store right before the doors opened to make sure he got his jeans. His pants size was quite common, but to his amazement the store did not have his size. He checked with the clerk to see if this was the first day of the sale, and it was. He thought this was odd, so he looked at the sizes that were available and noticed that they seemed to be either very large or very small. He again checked with the clerk, but this time the clerk directed him to another department, where the prewashed Levi's 501 jeans were. These jeans were selling for $34.99. The only difference in the two types of jeans was the prewashing. This is an obvious case of bait and switch because the store really wanted to sell the more expensive jeans. It is clear that the store was not even stocked to sell the jeans that were on sale. The bait in this case was the Levi's 501 jeans priced at $19.95 and the switch was the Levi's 501 prewashed jeans priced at $34.99.

Many auto dealerships advertise in the paper an extremely low price on a vehicle only to claim that, once you have arrived on the lot, the model has been sold out. If they do actually have the advertised model, they usually only stock one on the lot, and by the time you arrive, it has been sold. This is a classic case of if-it-sounds-too-good-to-be-true-it-probably-is. Many times the advertised car in the paper is only a stock car. A stock car is a basic car without the extras: bumpers, electric windows, air conditioning, airbags, antilock brakes, upholstery options, and more. The idea is to get you on the lot, at which point a pushy salesman will try to sell you a full-price car with all the options. This usually adds at least a couple thousand extra dollars to the base price tag. Call ahead of time and make sure that the advertised items are still available. Get as much information over the phone as possible. This is not a surefire way of not wasting a trip, but it is basic due diligence.

Beware of stores that have perpetual sales. These aren't true sales promotions but marketing ploys. Often so-called sales items are always sold at that same price. I remember seeing an ad for

FIGURE 1. Deceptive going-out-of-business ad taken from the *Penny Saver,* April 3, 1996.

years that said, "Going out of business sale." They must have been in the process of going out of business for more than four years. Phony price comparisons often go hand in hand with stores that have perpetual sales. The advertiser creates a false impression with a sign that reads, WAS $59.99, ON SALE THIS WEEK FOR ONLY $29.99, when in fact the product has had the same price all year long. Some of the most frequent violators are car dealerships, jewelers, and home furnishing businesses.

There are other methods businesses use to make it appear as though a great sale is taking place. The ad in FIGURE 1 reads, "We're not going out of business." Technically, this ad is not illegal, but it is using trickery and deceit to gain an unfair advantage. At first glance, the average consumer would read this as a going-out-of-business sale. The deception occurs with the words "We're not," which is one-third the size of "going out of business" and is in a different font. This is a commonplace tactic during difficult economic times such as those we face today. Ads may claim "Court-ordered liquidation sale" or "Lost our lease" when the store or chains have no intention of closing their doors.

FIGURE 2 displays a perfect example of an advertiser trying to give the appearance of low prices. Liquidation sales usually mean that the business must sell. This ad has been in the *Penny Saver* for at least one year, and it always says the same thing. This is definitely not a true liquidation sale. This is an attempt to make the consumer believe that prices are radically reduced, to make the consumer buy now before the doors close. It is difficult to go into any store and not find some kind of sale sign of one form or another. I am not against sale signs or going-out-of-business promotions as long as they make a true statement. A sale by defini-tion is a bargain-based price. Often the advertiser wants us to believe that bargains can be

FIGURE 2. Year-old "liquidation sale" ad taken from the *Penny Saver,* April 3, 1996.

found in its store when the fact of the matter is, no bargain is intended. I am amazed that every supermarket claims to have the lowest prices in town. Basic logic (the law of noncontradic-tion) tells us that two contradictory views can't both be true. Only one supermarket can have the lowest prices.

Perception is everything, and deceptive advertisers like to display their products as top-of-the-line when in fact the man-ufacturing of the product is inferior. I call this product B sold as product A. Many times advertisers promote their products as takeoffs of popular products. Many items such as watches, clothing, foods, and appliances are replicas of famous name-brand products and are often sold sight unseen. The only thing the consumer has to go by is a picture or a written description. You might be familiar with the phrase, "Don't believe every-thing you hear." Well, I am here to tell you to believe only half of what you see.

Pictures often make products look just like the real thing, but the manufacturing of the rip-off product is often inferior to that of a name-brand product. As soon as you receive the product in the mail and examine it, you know you've been deceived by slick marketing. Many of the products advertised on radio, on TV, and in newspapers, coupons, and magazines do not come from top stores.

Whenever I see gold jewelry advertised under market value, I know something is not right. Some of the ads I see tell me that if I bought all of the store's gold chains and went to a coin or precious metal dealer, I could make a killing on the conver-sion alone. The gold itself is worth more than the sale price of the jewelry. Now I know this can't be true (I should stop writ-ing and get into the jewelry business).

Other ads are not so flagrant. Clothing is a huge violator of false information. The feel, cut, style, durability, and fit of clothing are so important, yet I see ads all the time comparing their clothing to top-name brands. Radios, televisions, VCRs, and other electronic equipment drastically differ in price and quality. Representing product B as product A, as you can see, is a major deception. Remember, the definition of *fraud* is the use of trickery and deceit to gain an unfair advantage.

Sale items with a catch fill our newspapers and mailboxes. Go through any newspaper and you will see such ads. I saw one that was promoting airline tickets at a reduced price. The price of the tickets was about half the normal value. The catch was that the plane would be making a four-hour stop halfway through the flight to pick up more passengers. This extra stop obviously made the plane trip longer. These details are usually given in small print at the bottom of the ad. The ad, however, audaciously states that the flight includes a free four-hour stay-over. The idea that you are getting a bonus is what is misleading. Note the term *stayover* instead of *layover*. Do you get the idea that somebody is trying to hide something? I don't know about you, but I don't consider a four-hour layover a bargain.

I also noticed a video ad with the classic "buy one, get one free" promotion, which normally I have no problem with. The problem is the fine print, which says the promotion is good Monday through Thursday only. I couldn't even read the print without my glasses! I get these types of ads in my mailbox all the time. Buying one item and receiving the second item for free is a good deal. The problem comes when you read the disclaimer. "Buy one, get one free" is always in big, bold letters, while the disclaimer is small and obscure. The disclaimer or restriction can change the value of the promotion. Most video rentals are made Friday through Sunday. I felt both stupid and cheated when I went to the video store on Friday and the deal was not valid. I hadn't noticed the hidden disclaimer.

Some of the worst examples of hidden costs are found in cellular phone and pager ads. Look at FIGURE 3. Motorola's Micro Tac Lite II phone is advertised for $1. Note the asterisk. As the tiny copy at the bottom of the ad indicates, this offer does *not* include the required service activation fee and minimum service commitment on a selected value plan. Your $1 phone will really cost about $100 for activation and at least $30 a month for service. Whatever "value" plan you choose will also

* Phone offers require service activation and a minimum service commitment on a selected value plan.
State requires sales tax to be calculated on non-activated phone price. **Ask for details.

FIGURE 3. Cellular phone ad taken from the *Los Angeles Times,* May 6, 1996. The true cost of getting the phone is hidden in the fine print.

add to the bill. The ad also features two other cellular phones, the Nokia 232 for $3 and the Ericsson AH 320 for $5. Both of these phones have the same disclaimer as the Motorola $1 phone. The most important part of the ad is the asterisk. To find out what the double asterisks mean, you must call the company for details. On this one 6 x 10 ad I counted eight asterisks. You must read the entire ad, especially when you see an asterisk. The problem with most of these outrageous bargains and free claims is that it ends up costing more to get a deal than to buy at full price.

Coupon promotions are notorious for having hidden

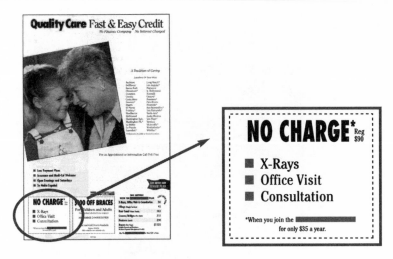

FIGURE 4. Dental care ad from a direct-mail piece.

catches. Often I see the word *FREE* in big letters followed by the little phrase "with purchase of." What you must purchase in order to receive the deal is the hidden catch. Another expression for *free* is *no charge.* In the dental ad in FIGURE 4, the coupon is a no-charge offer. However, the asterisk indicates, "When you join for only $35 a year." How can this be a no-charge coupon when you must pay a $35 fee? I see these ads all the time. Remember, always read the fine print.

Auto service advertisements are often loaded with low prices on brakes, oil changes, transmissions, and tune-ups, only to sport disclaimers that add to the cost of the service.

Let us look at the tune-up special for $24.95 in the ad in FIGURE 5. The disclaimer indicates that there is an additional charge for parts and service. So is the tune-up really $24.95? No! The brake special is even worse. The first disclaimer says parts and service are extra, just like the tune-up. The second disclaimer adds an extra charge for four-wheel-drives and semi-metallic pads. I can't even imagine how much more this would cost. The ad also says that the prices are only valid with "most cars." What does that mean? The "most cars" disclaimer simply allows the business to back out of any deal. When David Solomon, author of *The Automotive Panic Button,* was a guest on my radio show, he said, "Never go to a shop that would advertise in this manner." I've seen oil changes advertised for $9.95 that did not even include the new oil. Please don't expect an honest mechanic to compete with these fraudulent advertisements. The tragedy is that these advertisements create a false perception of fair market value for maintenance and repair services. Your car is usually your second-largest investment next to a house.

FIGURE 5. This ad, with its disclaimers, gives a false perception of fair market value for auto maintenance service.

Don't be so quick to chase a false hope. Maintenance on a vehicle is unfortunately an expensive but necessary evil.

Trickery and deceit in advertising fill customers with false hopes and expectations. I see so many ads featuring beautiful men and women with perfect bodies trying to appeal to my envious desire to look just like them. Athletes and movie and television stars often endorse a product, which gives us the impression that we can be just like them if we use the products they use. Appealing to the consumer's emotions rather than the quality of the product is deceptive. The goal? Get you to feel, not think. Remember the Wheaties commercial with Michael Jordan? The theme song in the commercial went, "If I could be like Mike . . ." The implication is that although we all want to play basketball as well as Michael Jordan, we know we cannot. The one thing we can do, however, is eat the same cereal as Mike. The idea that we are like Mike if we use his endorsed product is exactly what the marketers wanted to portray. We can also join Ted Danson, of "Cheers" fame, in fighting ocean pollution if we contribute to the environmental organization he endorses. We can feel "close" to our friend Ted if we are part of the same cause.

The papers are filled with before and after pictures of how products successfully transform bald heads into hairy heads, wrinkles into no wrinkles, and fat into muscles. One ad I saw proclaimed, "Erase wrinkles and years with new laser method." Before and after pictures of an elderly lady are shown. Of course, in the before picture she is not wearing any makeup and her hair is not brushed, unlike in the after picture. The problem is, any good makeover can deliver the same results. Is laser surgery for thousands of dollars really necessary? Price is almost never mentioned in these ads. Why not? The advertiser wants you to make your decision on a picture, not on prices or facts. Don't be deceived; some of the best salesmen are in doctors' offices, though not all doctors are crooks, of course. Beware if it appears you are getting something for nothing.

Let's talk about home improvement–type services that are advertised through newspapers and direct mail. I'd like to use carpet cleaners as an example since I have had some experience in this area. Ads often have low prices for basic cleaning. What is not listed is the cost of the special cleaning that your carpet needs. Let me explain. You're sitting at home looking at

FIGURE 6. Carpet cleaning ad taken from a community coupons direct-mail piece. This coupon was taken directly from my mailbox. The name of the carpet cleaning company has been removed.

your dirty carpet. You would love to buy new carpeting but economic times are tough. You suddenly remember you recently received a coupon special for carpet cleaning in the mail (see FIGURE 6). You know that cleaning the carpet will be much cheaper than buying new carpeting. The ad says you can have two rooms cleaned for $6.95. You quickly count three bedrooms, a dining room, and a den. The ad indicates that you will be spending about $14.95 for five rooms. You call the cleaner for an appointment.

Carpet cleaner or slick salesman? You be the judge. The carpet cleaner comes to your home and surveys the scene. He is sure to point out stains and spots and notifies you that you will need "special cleaning" because the stains are deep. You find out the cost will be minimal, so you agree. He then starts sniffing the air to indicate that you will also need some deodorizer. He asks if you have any pets, knowing that many people do. If you say yes, he indicates that he has some special flea repellent as well, and again you agree. Finally the job is done, except for the special Scotch-Gard treatment, which will prevent any further stains or spots. This is a prime example of how that $14.95 bill turns into a $150 bill. Hopefully, the cleaner is honest enough to at least use the extra products he just sold you. Not only might you get charged more than what you were expecting, but water is sometimes used instead of product. I, to my shame, used to spray water instead of Scotch-Gard on my customers' carpets. My problem is with the ad declaring a professional cleaning for $6.95 for two rooms. You would think getting out pet odors and stains is exactly what carpet cleaning is and should not cost extra. The reality is that the final price will often be twice as much, or more, than the advertised price.

Advertisers realize that the consumer wants high-quality products at low prices. Remember, millions of dollars are spent in marketing meetings that target the consumer's need for products at a good price. The advertiser wants to buy low and sell high, thus increasing his profitability. In some ways consumers expect too much, wanting a Rolex watch for the price of a Timex.

Beware of that greed and don't be gullible. Do your homework and don't be an impulse buyer. Read consumer journals for best quality and price. Nothing is free. Don't expect a "free lunch." When purchasing goods, watch closely at the cash wrap to ensure that the computer indicates the same amount as the advertised price. If you've been victimized, complain. If the sales clerk is not in charge, talk with a supervisor, then put it in writing to the business owner. The Federal Trade Commission (FTC) regulates misleading and deceptive advertising, and so does your local Better Business Bureau.

Advertising can be a legitimate way for a company to expose their products and services to the public. If they have a quality product that is competitively priced and you are a qualified buyer, then it is a "win-win" situation for everyone. Unfortunately, as has been demonstrated, there is a substantial amount of abuse. By not disclosing all the facts through the use

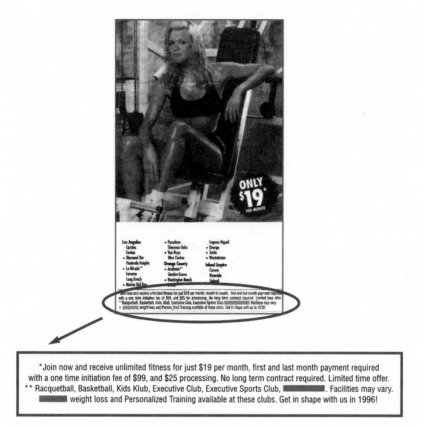

*Join now and receive unlimited fitness for just $19 per month, first and last month payment required with a one time initiation fee of $99, and $25 processing. No long term contract required. Limited time offer.
** Racquetball, Basketball, Kids Klub, Executive Club, Executive Sports Club, ▮▮▮▮▮▮▮. Facilities may vary.
▮▮▮▮▮▮ weight loss and Personalized Training available at these clubs. Get in shape with us in 1996!

FIGURE 7. Fitness club ad taken from the *Los Angeles Times*, May 6, 1996.

of trickery and deceit, the company is committing fraud. Whether it is a large chain or a small local business, fraud is fraud. To avoid falling victim to this type of scam, I suggest you follow these four steps, using the ad in FIGURE 7 for practice:

1. Compare prices industrywide. It is unlikely that a quality product or service will differ in price by more than 15 percent. If the price is more than 15 percent lower, it might be a product A versus product B scam. Are most health clubs $19 a month?

2. Always, always read the small print. What does the small print say on our gym ad?

3. Find out if the company guarantees satisfaction. Is there such a guarantee in this ad?

4. Don't be greedy. If it sounds too good to be true, it probably is. Do you really believe a full-service gym charges $19 a month?

CHAPTER 2

The "B"
Bad Credit?
We'll Clean It Up, Guaranteed

In 1992 a posting on the Internet caught the eye of Maryland resident Ronald Thomas. The ad offered to clean up a bad credit record and restore it to good health. Just two years earlier he had been a little lavish, trying to impress his girl-friend—now his wife—by buying $800 worth of jewelry and taking out a $500 loan to help pay off the amount he owed to two jewelry stores. On top of that, he had quit his job in February 1991, thinking he would find something better. He was out of work for sixteen months. By the end of that period, his debts added up to $3,650, including interest, late fees, and lawyer fees. Thomas was deep in debt. Thomas felt frustrated and desperate. The bills and the creditors were starting to annoy him. He needed breathing room, particularly now that he was a new father.

Many times, feelings of frustration and desperation lead people into making poor decisions. I counseled a young man in his mid-twenties who had credit card debt. The overwhelming pressure to pay the debt off caused him to lose his common sense. He was offered a business deal that promised to yield him a profit of $18,000 in a month for a low investment of $2,000. Any straight-thinking person would ask, "If this deal is true, then why isn't everyone doing it?" By the way, the young man lost his $2,000.

Ronald Thomas's plight could have been avoided had he not tried to impress his girlfriend. Trying to impress others was the beginning of my own downfall. I made three major mistakes in running ZZZZ Best Carpet. These three mistakes caused me to make poor decisions. Many people who get defrauded make these same mistakes.

The first mistake I made was trying to impress others. As a student at Cleveland High School in Southern California's San Fernando Valley, I had aspirations of being popular. At my high school, and yours, too, I'm sure, in order to impress a girl, you had to have a nice car, be the best, or be the best-looking. Since I did not possess any of those "qualities," I chose to gain popularity by making money. Like Ronald Thomas, I wanted to impress others with money.

The second mistake I made was pride. The definition of pride is autonomy—I'm in charge. Too often we think too highly of ourselves. I thought that I was invincible. When I was lying to stockholders on Wall Street, I never thought I could get caught. I also believed that whatever I did would work out in the end. When people borrow money or use their credit card, they are borrowing against their future earnings. Thomas quit his job thinking he could find something better but went jobless for sixteen months. At ZZZZ Best I always believed that in the future I would be making enough money to pay back all my creditors. An underlying principle of pride is that prideful people think they are too smart. I thought I was smarter than the investors, the customers, the FBI, even the judge and jury. Having confidence in yourself is admirable, but thinking that you are invincible is dangerous.

Third, I made the early mistake of taking shortcuts. Get-rich-quick scams prey on people who take shortcuts. Shortcuts seem so innocent and simple, yet their consequences can be long-lasting and complex. My shortcuts cost me seven years of my life and $26 million.

Ronald Thomas lost his objectivity when he bought the idea that his bad credit could be restored so easily. If restoring bad credit was easy, wouldn't everyone do it?

"The ad hit me at the right point," Thomas, now twenty-five, recalls. "It was a point of frustration where I felt, 'If I could just pay off the creditors I'd be OK.'"

The credit repair company asked for $125 up front. Fortunately, Thomas still had a grain of sense left. He thought the deal sounded fishy and decided against it.

The FTC has reported that firms have charged between $500 and $1,200 to clean up errors in credit card records. A $125 to $300 fee is a fairly standard fee to restore bad credit.

"If it sounds suspicious, more than likely it is," says David Medine, associate director of credit practices for the FTC. Remember, if it sounds like a duck, walks like a duck, quacks like a duck, and swims like a duck, it probably is a duck.

At a time when we have moved from being a cash-dependent society to a credit-dependent one and pre-approved credit offers bombard consumers, unscrupulous businesses are flourishing as they prey on people who have succumbed to credit dependency, drive themselves into a sea of debt, and lack the wherewithal to get out. The potential for these businesses is great. A 1994 survey by the National Foundation for Consumer

Credit found that nearly eighteen million U.S. households need some form of help in dealing with their debt.

Although many agencies that offer credit or debt *counseling* are legitimate, some agencies that offer to *repair* credit and *change* credit histories are operating illegally. "There is nothing wrong with providing assistance to consumers with debt problems," says Medine. "The problem with credit repair is that some of these companies make promises on things they can't deliver."

Sometimes, as consumers, we exercise more due diligence in the produce section of our supermarket than in investigating the validity of companies we spend hundreds and thousands of dollars with. We get so busy counting the pennies that we forget to guard our dollars.

Credit repair scams have become such a thorn in the side of state law enforcement agencies and the credit industry that in November 1995, state attorneys general, creditors, representatives of the three major credit reporting agencies, public interest groups, and members of the FTC held a summit in Washington to discuss ways to eliminate the growing problem. At that time, the FTC announced that it had reached a settlement with Chase Consulting that included a permanent injunction prohibiting Chase from engaging in deceptive practices that violate the Federal Trade Commission Act. The FTC accused the Sacramento, California–based company of using America Online to advertise credit repair services and to provide new identities to consumers, Medine says. The company is one of a dozen such businesses the FTC has taken legal action against.

Remember, just because you are dealing with a big consulting company doesn't mean you should stop practicing due diligence. Many times these companies hide their deceptive practices behind slick advertising campaigns. Dave Mooney, spokesman for Equifax, Inc., one of the three major credit reporting bureaus, says the alleged illegal businesses, whose bold, boastful ads imply that they can make the most tarnished credit record spotless, are easy to recognize. Many are located in one state and conduct business in states other than the one they're located in. The ones that operate in the same state in which they offer their services frequently change the name, location, and phone number of their operation. In a Washington and suburban Maryland 1994–95 phone book, eight of the twenty-seven businesses I called under credit and debt counseling had disconnected phone lines.

Under a tough telemarketing law passed by Congress in 1994 and implemented at the beginning of 1996, it is illegal for a credit repair firm to collect any money until six months after it delivers the services promised. Most fly-by-night firms do not operate under these rules, however.

The methods of operation are common, and some are not illegal, just annoying to creditors. Some companies ask for up-front fees, charging from $100 to $1,500 for their services. Then they bombard the credit reporting agencies with letters disputing everything on the consumer's credit report, whether the information is true or false. These services operate under the premise that they can wear out the agencies with letters on every item and get each item removed.

But the point is, if the dispute is legitimate, any consumer can mail continuous letters to a creditor without the services of an agency. The cost to handle the issue on your own would be pennies on the dollar. In fact, the only cost would be that of postage and letterhead.

Credit reporting bureaus are required to respond within thirty days to disputes in a credit report. The investigation must be completed within those thirty days, or the item in question must be removed. Equifax and other credit bureaus can now E-mail information on disputed items to creditors. Previously, file review requests were made by mail. The faster response reduces the likelihood that the items in question will have to be removed. No matter what credit repair clinics say, accurate information cannot be removed, whether it's a loan default, a bankruptcy, or a host of overdue payments. Overdue payments can stay on your record for seven years, bankruptcies for ten years. As for false information, credit bureaus are far from infallible and frequently mix up files.

Stop and think for a second. Doesn't it make sense that, if you have legitimately defaulted on a loan or had a bankruptcy or a host of overdue payments, your credit would be affected? I'm amazed at the lack of personal accountability. People want to do the crime but they don't want to do the time. It has become too easy to run up high charges on credit cards and walk away from mortgage loan obligations. You can't honestly expect not to pay some kind of consequence for these types of actions.

Medine says the FTC received complaints on about 5,000 to 8,000 files regarding incorrect credit reports in 1991 and 1992. Of course, many other incorrect files go unnoticed. The credit bureaus argue that they maintain files on 180 million Americans and make 2 billion updates on those files every month. "It would be foolish to say that all are correct," says Norm Magnuson, a spokesman for Associated Credit Bureaus, a group that represents the nation's 800 credit reporting agencies. But, Magnuson claims, saying that 20 percent of credit files contain errors is incorrect. "Any error in a credit file concerns us," he notes. "The only value [a file] has is the integrity of the information. The erroneous report that the errors are rampant and furious is just not so."

For individuals, correcting an inaccurate record can be time-consuming, even costly. Sending certified letters to all three major credit bureaus and the creditor is a first step to clearing up the problem. A growing tactic used by repair clinics is called file segregation, in which they promise to give those with tarnished credit a new identity. This entails giving the person an employer identification number, which resembles a Social Security number but is used in general by businesses to report information to the Internal Revenue Service or the Social Security Administration. The repair clinics tell the client to use this number instead of his or her Social Security number when applying for credit. The consumer as well as the credit repair clinic could face federal charges for improper use of this number.

The National Consumers League (NCL) says to beware of ads that say, "Bad credit? No credit? No problem!" and offer 900 or 976 numbers to call. These are toll calls and can add up quickly. Always beware of a 900 or 976 number because calls usually last five to nine minutes at $2.95 a minute. The quick math says that each time you speak to them it will cost you $14.75 for a five-minute call. Most consumers would never pay $14.75 to call an insurance agent to get a quote over the phone. Would you pay any company $14.75 to give you basic information?

The NCL also says to watch for one-shot credit cards. The credit repair business makes the false pitch that the card, issued at a cost of about $50, will help re-establish your good credit. The restoration of your credit is based on the idea that you now have an active credit card. Generally the card is good only for one store or catalog sales outlet that may offer nothing of interest to the consumer. One-shot credit cards are a clever marketing ploy to get you to spend money where you normally would not. The credit company receives $50 while the store gets your business. After your one-shot purchase you are still left with no credit and with merchandise you really couldn't afford.

Another credit repair scam to look out for is giving out your checking account number. NEVER give your checking account number to anyone who asks for it over the telephone. The consumer is often asked to give his or her checking account number as part of the verification process. Some repair companies will use this to withdraw money directly from the individual's account.

One caller to my radio show described how a local printer and an accountant teamed up to print phony checks. After getting account numbers, the two would print checks with the numbers on colored paper and pass them off as the real thing. Tracing the checks led only to the unknowing person who held the account number. NEVER give your account number to anyone.

To find a reputable counselor, check with the state consumer affairs office, the state attorney general, or the local Better Business Bureau. Check to see if any complaints have been registered against the credit repair business. Also, check to see if the business is licensed or bonded, as is required by law in many states. Consider nonprofit rather than for-profit counselors. There are benefits and disadvantages to both. Most nonprofit organizations offer free services or require a minimal charge. If it is more than $50, start walking. The FTC and NCL recommend Consumer Credit Counseling Services, a nonprofit group offering low-cost or free service at 1,100 offices across the country. To find the office nearest you, call 1-800-388-2227.

After nixing the first credit repair clinic, Ronald Thomas went to Consumer Credit Counseling Services, and the results were fabulous. They were immediately able to work out an agreement with Thomas's creditors to pay off all three cards at a total of $94 a month. About a month after paying off his debt, Thomas was shown how to reduce other costs in his budget. His car payment was reduced by $100 and he and his wife purchased a $139,500 house on their combined income of $43,500. Fortunately, Thomas put his pride aside and sought the wise counsel of others. Too often when consumers find themselves in trouble, they seek the easy way out.

The FTC says consumers can clean up their own credit without having to resort to credit counselors. The key is creating awareness through consumer education. In dealing with debt, here are seven practical steps in handling credit problems. And since I succeeded in accumulating $26 million in debt, I'm an expert on the subject!

1. As soon as you realize that you have credit problems, contact a credit bureau to make sure your credit report is accurate. If you have been wrongly denied credit within the past sixty days, ask for a copy of your report. You can call TRW Consumer Assistance (1-800-682-7654), Equifax (1-800-685-1111), or Trans Union (1-800-851-2674). Find out exactly what your situation is; never assume. Visa offers consumers "Credit Cards: An Owner's Manual," with budget worksheets and a financial fitness quiz. To get a free copy, call 1-800-847-2511.

2. Send the agency an explanation in writing of what your accurate information is. The agency will delete any information that does not belong on your record.

3. If you have a legitimate, irreconcilable discrepancy with a creditor, ask the agency to include your version, in writing, of the dispute in your file in the event the investigation fails to resolve the matter. Your version is limited to 100 words.

4. Work with your creditors. Try to negotiate a reasonable payment plan. They might waive late fees or offer a lower interest rate. Be honest and sincere with the people you owe money to.

5. Contact a legitimate credit counselor such as Consumer Credit Counseling Services. Don't try to fix all your problems on your own. Seek the counsel of people who are wiser than you. Have some personal accountability. Swallow your pride and admit your problem.

6. Make a personal resolution to work your way out of debt. Whatever the payment, big or small, begin today. All problems can be resolved by taking the next step now. It is never too late to turn things around! MasterCard offers a brochure, "In the Red," which offers advice and resources for managing debt. To get a free copy, call 1-800-633-1185.

7. Avoid firms and agencies that promise quick fixes for credit problems. There is little or nothing they can do that you can't do for yourself.

Let me ask you a question. If somebody owed you money, wouldn't you want your money back? Why do we sometimes expect big companies, who are in business to make money off credit card users, to forgive us our debt? Why should we expect them to allow us to spend money with another credit card company before our debt with them is retired? Our greed and gullibility are the two main components that cause us to be defrauded as consumers.

CHAPTER 3

The "C"
Credit Card Fraud

Imagine that you have just walked out of the shopping mall. You go out to the parking lot and notice your car is missing. You can't believe what has happened. All of a sudden, you remember that you gave your car keys to a stranger before you entered the mall. He seemed honest and trustworthy. He politely asked you for your car keys so you handed them over to him.

Get real, you say. You would never give a stranger the keys to your car. Not if you care about your Mercedes or, in my case, a 1979 Nissan Sentra known as the Dentmobile.

Yet some people unwittingly give their credit card number away without a second thought. A thief who has your card or card number and expiration date can charge thousands of dollars to your account in a matter of minutes.

Credit card fraud is a serious problem. It causes an estimated $1.5 billion each year in losses in the United States. The consumer pays for the fraud by way of higher finance charges, annual fees, and costly high-tech security measures. But did you know that it's also one of the most preventable forms of robbery, if you take precautions?

How does credit card fraud work? It can start with cards lost by or stolen from the cardholder, new cards stolen from mailboxes, or credit card billing errors. Thieves can get your credit cards by stealing your wallet or by burglarizing your home. Pickpockets are loose in our streets, and believe it or not, they would rather have credit cards than cash.

In his book *Scam!,* Don Wright documents America's con artist clans. These clans are better known as "Travelers." There are more than 8,000 of these "families" in America who are professional thieves. These thieves thrive on everything from shoplifting to stealing cars to credit card fraud. Credit card fraud for a Traveler usually begins with home intrusion. A Traveler, posing as a handyman or door-to-door salesman, will enter a house with the intention of stealing. Cash is always a favorite, but he will steal anything that he can sell quickly. A Traveler will steal a credit card and run up charges on it immediately. He will then return the purchased items for cash refunds. Whether it is a Traveler or a local pickpocket, the scam is the same. Guard your credit cards as if you were literally carrying a lot of cash in your wallet.

"It took that thief less than twenty minutes to grab my card and use it," said Pam W., a Florida resident. She had just been served lunch at a restaurant when she realized her purse, placed on the floor next to her chair, had been stolen. She rushed to a phone to call her credit card issuer and found to her amazement that the card had already been used by the thief.

Credit card crooks also steal cards from mailboxes or mail centers before you even receive them. Today our streets are filled with workers for flyer companies who walk up to houses and leave advertisements for local businesses. It is not uncommon for this to happen four out of seven days of the week. This means that people are constantly approaching your house. It takes only seconds to reach into your mailbox and steal your mail, and this type of theft is rising at an alarming rate. Remember, credit card thieves do not have to have the card itself to rob your account. All they need is your account number and expiration date.

In upstate New York, Paul B. left on a two-week vacation. When he returned, he found a charge for a $1,300 computer he hadn't ordered on his next credit card bill. He later discovered that the annually reissued card had been stolen from his mailbox while he was gone. The rest is history.

The worst kind of home intrusion is the modern-day telemarketer. Crooked telemarketers may call you to make tantalizing offers of discounted merchandise or to tell you that you've won a prize. They'll ask for a credit card number for "shipping and handling charges" or some other phony reason. They may send you shoddy products worth much less than what they've charged you, or they may charge your credit card account without sending you anything at all.

At ZZZZ Best I committed credit card fraud by creating billing errors. I knew that credit card slips could be written out by hand and did not have to be imprinted. With so many crews in the field, it would have been impossible to give each one an imprinter. As long as the customer signed the credit card slip, the bank agreed to accept the deposit. I realized that if I used the names and numbers of my legitimate customers to make up additional slips in large amounts and forged their signatures, I could raise immediate cash. Of course, the customers would later dispute the charges, but the process would take months. In the meantime, I'd have free use of their money. I could easily take an $89 bill and change it to $890 by creating bogus credit card slips and forging the signatures. Now, the laws have been tightened so that dishonest merchants cannot get away with such blatant acts of fraud.

Thieves also search through store and restaurant trash cans for carbons from credit card transactions so they can copy the numbers and use them. Carlos P. of Arizona returned a radio to an electronics store for credit but accidentally left the credit card receipt on the counter. When his account statement arrived weeks later, he discovered hundreds of dollars of unauthorized charges and realized that someone had picked up the receipt and used the card number.

Sometimes crooks listen in while you dictate your account number over a public phone, and copy it down to use later. Or they'll monitor cellular and cordless phone conversations, hoping to overhear a credit card transaction.

Here are some ways that you can protect yourself.

1. Protect your cards as you would protect your cash. A credit card could have a limit of $5,000, all of which can be charged at any time. Whatever your card limit is, treat your card as though you are carrying the $2,500 or $5,000 in cash!

2. Carry only one or two cards with you. If you lose them or are robbed, you have fewer to report missing. Again, how much cash would you carry with you?

3. Never leave your purse or wallet out in public and walk away. It takes a thief only a few seconds to grab it. Keep an eye out for pickpockets, especially when you are in a crowd. Malls and sporting events are filled with pickpockets.

4. Always check your card when you get it back in a

restaurant or store. It's easy for servers or salespeople to give you the wrong card if they're in a rush.

5. At home, keep all cards you don't carry with you in a safe place that won't be obvious to burglars. According to Don Wright, the most popular room in which to hide things is the bedroom, but that is the *first* place a thief looks.

6. Always sign your card in ink as soon as you receive it.

7. Keep in mind that when you add the names of other people, such as your children, to your credit card account, you will be held responsible for any of the charges that they make. This is also true in the case of divorce.

8. Never lend your card to anyone! If you want to put someone else's purchases on your card, handle the transaction over the phone, or go to the store yourself.

9. Keep track of when new and reissued cards are due to arrive, and call the credit card issuer if they don't come on time.

10. Make sure your mailbox is secure and that only you and the postal carrier have access to it. You may need to purchase a new mailbox, but it is worth the investment.

11. If you want to send your credit card back to the issuer to close your account, cut the card in half, then mail one half with your request.

12. Don't leave correspondence, receipts, or statements with your credit card number lying around your

office or place of business for someone else to read. Know when you're due to receive a statement, and call your credit card issuer if it doesn't arrive on time. A thief who has stolen your statement can use your credit card number at his own free will. If you throw your statements away, you might want to buy a shredder to shred them first.

13. Keep a complete list of all your credit card numbers in a safe place (never carry the list in your wallet). This list will make it easier for you to quickly report a lost or stolen card.

14. Maintain receipts from all credit card purchases. Always check your monthly statements against the receipts, and look for charges you didn't make. This is the best way of making sure that no one is making unauthorized purchases with your card.

15. Never write your card number on a postcard or on the outside of an envelope. Guard and protect your number from public view.

16. If you're making a purchase by personal check, don't let merchants write down your card number as confirmation on the check. It is illegal in many states for merchants to require credit cards as identification when you pay by check. You can always have the merchant call your bank to see if there are sufficient funds available.

17. Many people use their credit card as an ATM card. Memorize your personal identification number (PIN). Don't write it down in your wallet or on the

back of the card. Keep a copy of the number safe at home. Don't designate the same PIN for all your cards, and don't use a number, such as your birthdate, that can be found easily in your wallet.

18. If someone calls claiming to be a bank representative and asks for your PIN, don't give it. Immediately report the call to the card issuer and the police.

19. Always destroy credit card carbons. Do it yourself; don't expect a busy cashier or server to do it for you. Also, tear up copies of airline tickets or itineraries from travel agencies that contain credit card numbers.

20. Shield your credit card or calling card when you make a long-distance call from a public pay phone. Also, shield the telephone's buttons if you're asked to enter your card number. Be sure nobody can overhear you when you read your card number to an operator.

Protecting your card numbers is essential in preventing credit card fraud from happening to you. Keeping your number safe from the dangerous hands of the criminal will shield you from unwanted harm. With your number they can even order a new credit card in your name. Never give your credit card number to strangers who call you, no matter how legitimate their business may sound. You can never be sure that an unknown telemarketer is honest. Don't give your card number unless you initiated the call.

Visa International and MasterCard International filed a $95 million lawsuit on April 15, 1996, alleging that "a nationwide network of telemarketing fraud operations have bilked consumers and banks out of millions of dollars through phony offers of low-interest credit cards." The civil lawsuit seeks damages based on allegations of trademark infringement, fraud, unlawful business practices, and violation of federal racketeering laws.

Perhaps you have been solicited or possibly victimized by these "boiler room" operations. The most common method used in this scam is a simple postcard. The message reads something like: "Due to your excellent credit record, you have been selected to receive a low-interest credit card with an interest rate of 11.88%." The postcard lists an 800 or a 900 number to call for more information. When you call, you are greeted by a high-pressure salesman offering to issue or help you obtain a low-interest Visa or MasterCard for a fee ranging from $70 to $200. If you fell for the pitch, you would have ended up receiving only a small booklet listing a few banks offering low-interest-rate cards. The promise of an 11.88 percent Visa or MasterCard being issued to you was fraudulent, and you're out only $70 if you're lucky. Some consumers are solicited over the phone by telemarketers making cold calls using the same sales pitch.

Unfortunately, credit cards do get lost or stolen. What are you to do when this happens to you? Fast action is critical. Please expect the worst. Remember Murphy's Law—anything bad that can happen will happen. I am also reminded of the motto of the Boy Scouts of America: Be Prepared. Keep the phone numbers of your card issuers at the office or in an address book you carry with you, as well as at home. If you don't have the numbers with you, don't wait until you get home; call directory assistance at 1-800-555-1212 for the card issuer's toll-free number.

To protect your rights, you must report the loss or theft of your card as soon as you realize the card is gone or has been used fraudulently. Federal law limits the amount of money that you can lose as a result of fraudulent use of your credit card. If you notify the card issuer before the card has been used, you will not be liable for unauthorized charges. If the card has been used fraudulently before you notify the card issuer, you may be required to pay up to $50 per card for those charges. If your account number but not the card itself was used illegally, you're not liable for any amount.

Do not use your credit card number after you have reported your card lost or stolen. This really confuses the issuer, and if the thief uses the card you may be liable for the full amount. After you've called to report the problem, follow up with a letter to the issuer. This paper record of your notification can also limit your liability.

Since we are in an era of fax machines and mass communication between cardholder and issuer, don't hesitate to call your credit card issuer if you see anything suspicious on your bill. You could uncover fraud—and save yourself from paying unauthorized charges.

I came across an article in Credentials Services International's newsletter, written by Bruce W. Frazier. He is right on the money with his awareness and vigilance in keeping track of your credit. The article read as follows: "My identity was stolen by a wanted felon from Florida. Once he came to Arizona, met my mom and learned about me, he put his plan into effect.

"He obtained my birth certificate rather easily, simply by writing and requesting it. Also, he obtained a Social Security card in my name, simply by writing and requesting one. He obtained a driver's license by going to the DMV and filling out their forms. Once armed with items in my name, the criminal began living as me. He purchased a house, opened bank accounts, obtained credit cards, bought a new four-wheel-drive pick-up truck, a motorcycle, furniture, carpet, ceiling fans for his house; all in all, just about whatever he felt like buying.

"How was he able to do this? My wife and I had not bought anything on credit for several years, and felt there was no reason to check our credit, until we needed it . . . WRONG! All totaled, the career criminal charged approximately $110,000 in my name.

"Our experience has been extremely time-consuming: twenty months so far, and over $10,000 of our own money. Frustrating is an understatement. Stopping a career criminal after he has entrenched himself in your identity makes it difficult to know even where to start fixing the situation.

"We have both learned that vigilance is very important when it comes to your credit. We have had 'fraud victim statements' placed on our credit reports, and plan on checking our credit at least twice a year. . . .

"After twenty months our persistence has paid off. We are happy to say that the career criminal who stole my identity and ruined my credit is now serving a seventeen-month sentence in a federal prison. After that he will serve four years in the Arizona State Prison system.

"My wife and I have both learned a very expensive and valuable lesson, one which we will never forget: Your credit report is valuable."

As credit card use becomes more common than cash, it is important to be aware of the many forms of credit card fraud. The Better Business Bureau (BBB) publishes a hot sheet of frauds and scams relating to credit card fraud ranging from divorced couples charging up bills to family members stealing numbers. Call your local BBB office for more information.

Much to my shame, I stole from my grandmother once. This is to show you that desperate people do desperate things. Be cautious with your cards and numbers because if they fall into the wrong hands, the results can be devastating.

CHAPTER 4

The "D"
Direct-Mail Fraud

SWEEPSTAKES: NO HARMLESS HOBBY was the headline of Dear Abby's October 12, 1994, column. "I am an attorney," a correspondent writes, "in the field of real estate and elder law, and not a week goes by that I do not get a call from an older person who needs to speak to me privately. . . . One 83-year-old woman had just built a two-car garage onto her home to accommodate the new Jaguar she was told she had won. Another woman had three shopping bags full of canceled checks she had sent to various agencies to 'win' some kind of contest. In two years, she had spent more than $175,000. All her checks were for $3 and $5."

Sweepstakes, elder fraud, and deceptive advertising are all part of the growing problem of direct-mail fraud. In 1991 direct-mail advertising increased 282 percent, more than doubling any other form of advertising. The study was done by the Direct Mail Association in conjunction with the University of Minnesota. Why the big jump? Because it works! The reason for direct mail increases are as follows:

1. Target marketing. This allows a company to mail only to its prospects; for example, a pool company can mail to people who have pools. The amount of information these companies have enables them to be as specific as they want. If they so desire, they can mail to all blond-haired, blue-eyed, left-handed men who drive Hondas and own homes worth $200,000 or more.

2. 100-percent saturation. This allows a company to gain complete saturation of a specific area. Unlike TV, radio, or newspapers, direct mail can reach every home.

3. 100-percent attention. A direct-mail piece gets into your hands whether you like it or not. With TV and radio, a consumer can always change the channel.

4. Cost. A direct-mail piece can reach a home for as little as a penny apiece. Compare a penny to the price of a full-page ad in the *New York Times* or a prime-time spot on TV.

Direct-mail advertising is a wonderful way to promote a business as long as trickery and deceit are not used. I have a problem with direct-mail pieces that intentionally target consumers using deceptive wording to gain an unfair advantage.

There is a six-part formula that outlines deceptive direct-mail pieces:

1. Official, legal, quasi-governmental appearance.

2. Extensive, almost incantatory use of personalization.

3. State-of-the-art direct-mail technology.

4. Brilliantly crafted double-talk.

5. A cynicism-busting protest of authenticity.

6. A seemingly off-handed, low-key request for a small fee.

First, an outer envelope that says, "Official Documents . . . Documents Requiring Signature . . . Very Important Papers" is an example of a legal, quasi-governmental direct-mail piece. Most people open these letters out of fear of being penalized by the government or bank which they believe is sending the piece.

James R. Rosenfield wrote an article in *Direct Mail Marketing* on "sleazestakes" which, through fraudulent direct mailings, suck money out of consumers every day. Rosenfield's own seventy-two-year-old mother has an astonishing junk-mail pile. One little masterpiece declares "Audited Delivery" on the outer envelope. What on earth does that mean? Also indicated is "Important: The enclosed notification pertains to a large cash sum and is time-sensitive including a deadline. Deliver immediately and only to the person named." Above the name and address window: "Official notification of guaranteed cash availability. . . . The information contained herein has been authorized, verified, and fully guaranteed by internal regulations."

Sound familiar? Of course it does. Our mailboxes are bombarded with these types of pieces all the time. Today I received a piece that said, "Confidential: Immediate Response Requested." This "confidential" piece was mailed to me bulk rate, as well as to thousands of other preferred customers, asking me to sign up for some insurance plan.

Extensive, almost incantatory use of personalization is used in the direct-mail industry. Only friends and business associates know your name, right? Wrong! Almost any name and address can be obtained through mailing-list companies. Short letters in direct-mail pieces often use the consumer's name several times. In one direct-mail piece I received, my name appeared twenty-one times on two pages. Personalizing the letter often breaks down the barrier that many people have with direct mail. Marketing departments and psychologists spend hours crafting these letters in order to get consumers to open and respond.

State-of-the-art direct-mail technology is used to target and mass-mail potential victims. It is amazing how documents can be laser-printed to look official or even made to look like type-written letters. Often I receive checks that look more official than my own. The graphic design that goes into these pieces is fantastic. Full-color envelopes and photos make the packet look very professional and legitimate. I get certificates that look good enough to frame.

Don't be fooled. This is serious business—and you are the target.

Brilliantly crafted double-talk can confuse even a college graduate like myself. Rosenfield's mother received a piece that read, "The $12,000.00 Cash Certified Check will be forwarded to your home at 5698 Oakbrook Ave., Cincinnati, OH 45237, via Official U.S.P.S. uniformed courier within 10 working days, if you complete the Prize Delivery Data sheet below, and return it along with the winning claim number to my office before the deadline." "U.S.P.S. uniformed courier? That's the mailman, for Pete's sake!" writes Rosenfield.

I love the checks I get in the mail that would cost me more money to cash than to throw away. The last check I received was for $20. The whole letter described how the $20 was a free gift. The check is good and can be cashed at any time. What is hidden in two pages of wordy information is the fact that cashing the check automatically starts your membership with their services. Oh, the monthly fee is $69, but since you received a

$20 check, it will only cost you $49. Nowhere on the check is this indicated.

Another common mailing piece gives me a complimentary gift and introductory membership. Implied in the sentence is that both gift and membership are free. The small print reads as follows: "Yes! I'll try _____ for three months at no charge. Unless I notify you to discontinue my membership before the expiration of my three-month trial period, I authorize _____ to charge the $49 yearly membership fee to my account." If I continue and pay the $49 yearly membership fee, then did I really get three months free? Also notice that you will be charged *unless* you notify them. What are the chances of you remembering to notify them when your three months are up?

Then there is the cynicism-busting protest of authenticity. Most people will ask, "What is the catch?" so the company answers the question before you ask it: "This letter is no joke. The $12,000.00 cash will definitely be awarded. Failure on your part to reply before the deadline will result in immediate forfeiture of any and all of the prize." The whole package is designed to gain credibility. From the full-color images to the personalization of the letters, the goal is to gain your confidence.

When you hear "Trust me," run. I am always perplexed when someone looks me in the eye and says, "Let me be honest with you." Does that mean everything they said up to that point was a lie?

A seemingly off-handed, low-key request for a small fee is always a warning sign. I usually advise not to pay for services until they have been rendered, especially when you, the consumer, are approached. If they are seeking your business, hold off payment until you have satisfaction.

Companies usually ask for money in this way: "To cover overhead, processing, filing, and other related costs, a fee of

$5.95 is required." The price seems low, but don't give in. If they are legitimate, they can wait. Rosenfield's mother received a letter with a cash prize of $10,000. All she had to do was mail in the top copy of her notice with $5 for the judging fee. I would have said, "Why don't you take my $5 judging fee out of my prize and send me $9,995?!"

Sometimes money isn't what the direct mailer is going for at all. Many companies desire information more than money. They try to obtain driver's license and credit card numbers, birth certificate information, passport ID numbers, Social Security numbers, and more. This information will be used to sucker consumers at a later date with a different catch and a different product. I refer to this list as the "Idiot List." Based on the mail I get, I must be first on that list.

What about the law? Doesn't the government protect us against these sharks? The government does protect us in many ways through the U.S. Post Office as it pertains to mail fraud. Remember, though: A fraud is not necessarily illegal. The letter of the law doesn't always represent the spirit of the law.

Direct mail has not slowed down, and you will continue to see more and more of it in your mailbox. Don't expect that to change. As soon as you know that you have an *un*OFFICIAL mail piece, throw it away. These companies are designed to beat Uncle Sam legally and you financially.

CHAPTER 5

The "E" Education

Teddy Stallard's fifth-grade teacher, Mrs. Thompson, didn't like him. He was one of those kids who always looked like an unmade bed. His hair was messy, his clothes were wrinkled, and he had a musty smell about him. Plus, he seemed to ignore Mrs. Thompson, which offended her. In class, he would just stare off into space and pay no attention to her instruction.

That's why, whenever Teddy turned in his test papers, she took great pleasure in marking, with big red Xs, the incorrect answers; that is, until she ran across the file containing his educational history. It read something like this:

First Grade: Teddy is a good boy with a good attitude but he has some problems at home.

Second Grade: Teddy is a hard worker and a good boy but is deeply troubled. His mother is terminally ill.

Third Grade: Teddy is falling far behind. He is totally preoccupied and unresponsive. His mother died this year. His father shows no interest in Teddy.

Fourth Grade: Teddy is deeply troubled and will flunk without some kind of assistance.

Christmas arrived, and all the students brought beautifully wrapped gifts to Mrs. Thompson. Much to her surprise, Teddy also brought a gift. It was wrapped in a wrinkled brown paper bag. When she opened the gift in front of the class, out fell an old broken bracelet and a half-full bottle of perfume. The class started to laugh, but Mrs. Thompson was quick on her feet—she put some perfume on each wrist. The class stopped laughing.

At the end of the day, after the other students had left, Teddy remained behind. He went up to his teacher and said, "Mrs. Thompson, you smell just like my mother did when she wore that perfume, and her bracelet looks nice on you, too. I'm glad you liked my gifts." He turned and walked out of the class. Mrs. Thompson dropped to her knees and prayed for God's forgiveness.

When she returned to school the next day, she was a changed woman. No longer would she be like many teachers who simply dictated lessons by rote to whomever would listen. Mrs. Thompson resolved to make a difference in the lives of these kids, a difference that would live on long after she died. Her journey began with Teddy. She worked with him after school and provided him with the extra-special attention he so desperately needed. By the end of the year, he had caught up with the rest of the students and was prepared to move on.

Several years later, Mrs. Thompson received a letter that read something like this:

Dear Mrs. Thompson,
I'm graduating second in my class and I wanted you to
be the first to know.

                              Love, Teddy Stallard

Four years later she received a second letter that read:

Dear Mrs. Thompson,
I wanted you to be the first to know that I'm graduating
first in my class. The university was tough, but I endured.
                                        Love, Teddy

Four years after that, she received another which read:

Dear Mrs. Thompson,
As of today I am Theodore J. Stallard, M.D. How about
that! I'm going to be married on July 27th of this year
and I want you to come to the wedding and sit at the
table where my mother would have sat. You're the only
family I have left now. Dad died last year.
                                        Love, Teddy

Whenever I tell this story, taken from a video lecture of Dr. Tony Campola, I still cry. This story represents not only how a teacher made a difference in one student's life but also how she and others before her had dropped the ball and allowed needy children like Teddy to fall through the cracks.

Are the teachers of today like the old Mrs. Thompson or the changed Mrs. Thompson? It seems as though the only time we hear from teachers is when they go on strike. Nearly seven out of ten high school seniors in the L. A. Unified School District do not graduate. California, my home state, is ranked last in the country in reading skills. How can this be? Where does the blame lie? Teachers? Parents? Curriculum? Is it because we as a nation don't spend enough money on education? In this chapter we will look at some of the misconceptions we have of our educational system.

The American educational system today must contend with problems of a scope unparalleled in other industrialized nations. Whereas most national school systems can teach standard curricula to the same type of students, American educators must accommodate a wide diversity of students. Without a clear national curriculum or a student body that can easily be held to a single standard of performance, American schools are struggling to find direction. Despite persistent efforts at reform since the late 1970s, no lasting solution has yet been found.

In fact, the past thirty years have witnessed a marked decline in student achievement. The results of various performance tests, national and international, reveal an unmistakable trend: In 1972 more than 116,000 students scored above 600 on the verbal portion of the SAT (Scholastic Aptitude Test); ten years later, fewer than 71,000 scored as high, even though many more students took the exam. International math and science exams consistently show American students losing ground to their European and Asian counterparts. This steady deterioration is reflected in the weakness of today's high school curricula. In "Education Adrift," Alex Zarkaras says that in 1990 only 30 percent of American children graduated from high school having taken even the most fundamental courses.

What is really going on in our schools?

The schools, to put it bluntly, are failing at best and perpetrating fraud at worst. Despite rising school expenditures in the last half century (doubling every twenty years), survey after survey demonstrates that students who have been through the public schools cannot accomplish relatively simple tasks. Not only do they have trouble with reading and arithmetic, but they are appallingly ignorant of history and geography.

Part of the rationale of the public schools is to make children good citizens with a strong sense of American heritage.

Thus it is interesting to note that in a 1989 survey by the National Endowment for the Humanities, nearly one quarter of college seniors thought the words "from each according to his abilities, to each according to his needs" were found in the U.S. Constitution! (They are actually from Karl Marx's *Critique of the Gotha Program,* written in 1875.)

Senator Edward M. Kennedy's office once issued a paper stating that the literacy rate in Massachusetts had never been as high as it was before compulsory schooling was instituted. Before 1850, when Massachusetts became the first state in the United States to force children to go to school, the literacy rate was 98 percent. When Kennedy's office released the paper, the rate was 91 percent, although if the "functional illiterates" were removed, it would have been much lower.

The implications of this statement are earth-shaking. Schools are, at the very least, supposed to teach children to read. If, after nearly 150 years of compulsory government schooling, the literacy rate is lower than it was when parents freely saw to their children's education, what has been the point of "public education"? What happened to the billions of dollars spent and all the promises made to parents? Should we accept another promise from, or tolerate the allocation of another penny to, what can only be regarded as nothing less than a stupendous fraud?

According to Sheldon Richman in "Why the State Took Control of 'Education,'" none of this has deterred the advocates of public schooling from demanding more money from the taxpayers, sending the unsubtle message that it is the people's lack of funding that has kept the system from delivering on its extravagant promises. The fact of the matter is, we spend approximately $360 billion on education in this country and around $340 billion on defense. Lack of money is not the problem.

Richman tells of one high school teacher in Fairfax County, Virginia, one of the richest counties in the nation, who writes that boredom is the predominant undertone of school. "Instead of quality teaching," he explains, "schools are obsessed with time and regimentation. Such a concern would be justifiable if it produced results, but what it produces is a feeling among students that if they show up and shut up, everything will be fine." The curriculum, and in some cases, poor teaching, is the problem, not the funding.

At the elementary and secondary levels, revenues per student have increased substantially since the early 1980s, a sign that even under the strain of slower economic growth, our nation is willing to continue supporting its schools. Yet revenues per student vary widely across states: State governments are responsible for funding education, and they vary in their capacity and willingness to do so. In addition, there is considerable variation within states because states delegate authority for operating and funding schools to local school districts. For instance, one estimate is that the wealthiest districts have about 16 percent more cost-of-living adjusted revenue per student than the poorest districts. However, other factors such as the educational needs of the students require consideration before disparities in the allocation of education resources can be adequately measured. Districts with a large percentage of school-age children under the poverty level do receive a much larger share of their revenue from federal and state sources than from local governments. Even though inner-city schools receive more funding, they remain the lowest in test scoring nationwide.

Expenditures per student are often used as a proxy measure of the quality of education. But this can only be considered a crude measure, because the results of hundreds of studies that examine the relationship between spending and outcomes are mixed. Neither a strong nor a consistent relationship is found. However, no one can deny the importance of money to build schools, hire teachers, and buy textbooks, as well as the importance of having dedicated teachers, principals, and parents who create the learning environment.

In a statement from "The Condition of Education 1995," posted on the Internet, the Commissioner of Education Statistics says that the average teacher's salary in public schools was higher in 1994 than in 1960, although most of the gain since 1981 only recouped losses incurred during the 1970s. As most elementary and secondary teachers are women, and labor market opportunities for women have improved over the last two decades, these increases in salary may have been necessary in order to encourage teachers to stay in the field and to encourage college graduates to choose teaching as a career. Nevertheless, teacher earnings are relatively low compared to those of many other professions open to college students.

The idea that teachers are underpaid is a modern-day misconception. In the L.A. Unified School District, the average teacher's salary is $44,000 a year. Remember, a teacher's year includes three months' summer vacation, winter break, spring break, and every other holiday known to mankind. The average work year for a teacher is 180 days, while for most of the rest of us it is 240. Also, health benefits and sick days are included in their salaries. Don't forget, nobody forced these people to become teachers. This is the profession they chose. Although their salary was never intended to make anyone rich, $44,000 is certainly a decent living wage.

But let's look at other factors teachers must deal with today. How have the conditions facing the schools changed?

First, schools are facing a period of rising enrollment after a long period of decline. These increases affect school budgets as well as policies of teacher recruitment and retention. Second, many more disabled students, particularly those with learning disabilities, are receiving special services. This has major financial implications for school districts. Evidence suggests that serving special education students costs as much as 2.3 times that of serving regular students. Third, many more students speak a language other than English at home and have difficulty speaking English, a likely indication that many of them may have difficulty reading and writing. By law, school systems nationwide must provide services for children from non-English-language backgrounds. These students are disproportionately concentrated in California, Texas, New Mexico, Arizona, and New York.

Fourth, many children live in poverty (22 percent, or 14.6 million), and these children typically live in the same neighborhoods and attend the same schools. Fifth, crime in the schools remains a problem. Violence in and around schools directly affects educators and students by reducing school effectiveness and inhibiting students' learning. According to the commissioner's statement, in 1993 more than one in five high school seniors had been threatened at school.

I realize that rooms full of kids chewing bubble gum and speaking out of turn are "dream" classrooms to the modern-day teacher, but the fact remains that we do spend good money to provide children the opportunity to become productive adults in society. But do we realize what we are truly teaching our children? It seems the true agenda is not teaching; otherwise we would practice reading until our students knew how to read, and we would add until our students knew how to add. Once we had a grasp of that, then and only then would we start studying history. After all, how can we learn if we can't read?

But instead of reading and math, we are teaching self-esteem and condom use. In Simi Valley, California, report cards for those in grades one through three no longer measure performance by A, B, C, D, and F because if a student should fail, a letter grade would lower his or her self-worth. Shouldn't these things be taught at home? Isn't school supposed to teach you "how" to think and not "what" to think?

Additionally, a new morality is being taught: There is no real right or wrong; whatever works for you is fine. This is not accurately defined as personal values. It is more accurately defined as anarchy. We don't want any problems from the children, so we don't even grade them on performance. We don't want to ruin their self-esteem. The best lesson to be learned from school is failure. A bad grade can be overcome only by working harder. Sitting around feeling sorry for yourself will not get the job done in the classroom or the work force. We are not helping our students by giving them grades or by not grading them at all. Take it from an ex-convict, who learned it the hard way: *Life is about discipline.*

Our schools have become nothing more than glorified babysitters. Teachers watch over the crowd to make sure the kids don't kill each other. If that goal is achieved, then the day was a success. Public education has become public indoctrination. We as taxpayers are being cheated! David Boaz, vice president of Cato Institute, points out that the record of the public schools is revealed in the following facts: "Twenty-five percent of U.S. college freshmen take remedial math courses, 21 percent take remedial writing courses, and 16 percent take remedial reading courses. Meanwhile, a recent survey of 200 major corporations has found that 22 percent of them teach employees reading, 41 percent teach writing, and 31 percent teach mathematical skills. The American Society for Training and Development projects that 93 percent of the nation's biggest companies will be teaching their workers basic skills within the next three years."

Surely, kids are no more stupid today than they were in the past. So what is the problem? Nowadays students who would rather talk and play than listen are diagnosed as having attention deficit hyperactivity disorder (ADHD). These students are prescribed a potent drug called Ritalin. By the way, there is no medical or scientific evidence that ADHD is a proven physical illness. In fact, *Newsweek*'s March 1996 issue ran an article detailing the extent of use of Ritalin. Dr. Shaeffer of Johns Hopkins University School of Medicine calculates that out of America's 38 million children, 3.3 million take Ritalin regularly. This so-called proven illness is primarily an American phenomenon. American children use five times more Ritalin than the rest of the world. No doctor could give a testable or provable diagnosis for the disease. It seems that our schools would rather label a child than teach him or her self-control and discipline.

The solution to the education crisis is the complete separation of school and state. The public schools should be sold to the highest bidder, school taxes scrapped, and compulsory attendance laws repealed. Anyone should be free to start any kind of school, profit or nonprofit, religious or secular. There should be no government requirements for curricula or textbooks. Parents should be free to send their children to any kind of school, or school them at home. Laws regarding child apprenticeships should be scrapped. All restrictions on home schooling should be abolished.

Richman's article quotes John Holt as saying that this would not only liberate parents and children, but it would also revive the dying teaching profession. "Only when all parents, not just the rich ones, have a truly free choice in education, when they can take their children out of a school they don't like, and have a choice of many others to send them to, or the possibility of starting their own, or of educating their children outside of school altogether—only then will we teachers begin to stop being what most of us still are, and if we are honest, we can admit we are jailers, babysitters, cops, and begin to be professionals, freely exercising an important, valued and honored skill and art."

If public school had stockholders to answer to, one of two things would happen. Either the company would go out of business or it would have to change its ways. Public schools have done nothing but deceive taxpayers into believing that they are providing quality education. I got twenty-five years for a similar deception.

I began this chapter with the story of Teddy Stallard and Mrs. Thompson. For a while Mrs. Thompson was merely going through the motions. It is not up to our students to reach out for help. Our teachers are paid to *teach*! And if we evaluate all the variables, they are paid well. Mrs. Thompson didn't need computers or money to make a difference; she needed a change of heart. Likewise, our country needs a change of heart when it comes to the education of our young ones. They are the future of our country. Every American is affected by the educational system either directly or indirectly. Part of the reason why so many Americans are scammed is because they have not learned the basic educational skills to prevent themselves from being taken advantage of. On the flip side, many uneducated, desperate Americans are scamming others because they have never learned the basic skill of discipline to hold down a respectable job. In the past, when times got tough in school, students worked and studied hard, and a good grade was given to them. Now, when times get tough, they simply "take" what they need . . . and a whole lot more.

CHAPTER 6

The "F"
Financial Planning

Bob worked for a prestigious brokerage firm and had a long list of wealthy clients. On an average day, he would trade hundreds of thousands of dollars' worth of securities on behalf of doctors, lawyers, bank presidents, and even a few federal judges. Bob was an aggressive, charismatic man who worked no less than fourteen hours a day. He had a reputation of always doing his homework before investing his clients' funds. He would spend hours researching and analyzing a company's past, present, and future growth plans, financial statements, and management before deciding whether or not the stock was worthy of consideration.

Such preparation and due diligence paid off. The investment portfolios he managed were earning no less than 30 percent annually (on average). It wasn't long before people from all over the country were opening accounts at his firm just so he would be their investment adviser. Even some Wall Street analysts called him for advice. Bob was a competitor who wanted to be the best. At the end of each month, he would call several of his stockbroker friends and compare volume, profits, and commissions. He enjoyed outperforming his contemporaries and being recognized as "the best of the bunch."

Then it happened. Bob received a tip from a usually reliable source about a possible merger between two companies. At first he paid little attention to the lead, but as the weeks passed, he realized his volume and profits were not up to their usual record-breaking level. Fearing possible defeat, Bob decided to risk a large percentage of his portfolio on one of the companies. The thought of not being the best broker—even for only thirty days—scared him more than anything else.

According to an agreement he had with his clients, Bob was not permitted to invest more than 5 percent of their money in any one deal without their prior approval. But those were the rules for brokers who had lost their clients' money, not for successful brokers like Bob, whose track record was impeccable. Time was running out. Because he needed to keep up with the competition, there was no time to solicit client approval.

The tip he received appeared to be good information. Two companies were about to merge, and, because of the market's anticipation of the acquisition, both stocks slowly began to climb. Bob had the opportunity to sell his position and make an adequate profit, but he decided against it. He reasoned that to keep his title of "best of the bunch," he would need a "big score"—the kind a "superstar" stockpicker makes only a few times in his career. He watched his computer carefully, waiting for official announcement of the merger.

Then tragedy struck. Instead of the stock continuing to go up, it began to go down. At first it was only off three-eighths, but by the end of the trading day it was down three and a half points. Bob was in shock. Desperate, he called his source, who had always been so reliable in the past. When he finally reached him, the market had already closed. He learned that at the last minute one of the companies had backed out of the deal. The merger was off, and within hours everyone would know it. The following day Bob tried to liquidate his position, but there were hundreds of orders ahead of his. By the time he got out of the stock, he had lost 70 percent of his portfolio.

Fearing the possibility of criminal charges and the peer pressure that accompanied failure, Jim decided to try to recover the funds by putting the remainder of his portfolio in the risky futures market. That didn't work either, and within a ten-day period he had lost all of his clients' money. Rather than face his many angry investors, he prepared a video in which he explained what had happened and delivered a copy to each client. He was ultimately indicted for his crimes and eventually pled guilty to various securities-related charges.

Unfortunately, this is an almost daily occurrence on Wall Street: well-meaning brokers with big egos risking it all to salvage or make up for a previous bad trade. Financial planners are usually viewed by clients as either their best friend or their worst enemy. A good, honest financial planner can be worth his or her weight in gold. Planning for the future is so important, yet few Americans rely on anything more than Social Security and Medicare. You must be able to trust and confide in your financial planner. In fact, the whole industry is based on trust. Unfortunately, there are many scam artists who pose as financial planners. In this chapter I list some tips to help you choose a reputable planner.

In June 1996, "60 Minutes" ran a story on Prudential, a company well known because of its reputation and television commercials ("Get a piece of the rock"). Unfortunately, thousands of Americans were lied to and millions of dollars were lost. Prudential's investment department had defrauded its investors into purchasing guaranteed investments. The offer would normally have sounded "too good to be true" were it not for the fact that the company was Prudential. The salespersons for Prudential were selling it to family members and friends with the belief that the investment was truly guaranteed.

Do you really need a financial planner? Not if you are up to date with all the current tax laws and investments. Since most of us do not fall into that category, a financial planner is a worthy consideration. Managing your money can determine the quality of your future life. By having a financial plan, you can provide for your family for years to come. Learning how to budget your monthly expenditures as well as making your money grow is essential in understanding what financial planning is. However, there is a right way and a wrong way. Today, too many people are taking the shortcut. Both the investor and the planner are too greedy.

According to the Better Business Bureau, under existing federal law (the Investment Advisors Act of 1940), anyone who offers to furnish, for a fee, advice on the purchase and sale of securities is considered an investment adviser and is required to register with the Securities and Exchange Commission (SEC). Some states also have adopted legislation requiring investment advisers to be licensed at the state level and, in some cases, to meet certain testing requirements.

Financial planners generally have varied backgrounds and may hold a variety of degrees and licenses attesting to their education and expertise. Finding a good planner takes time and due diligence.

How do we separate a good adviser from a bad one? Anyone can open a business and call himself or herself a financial planner. Insurance and mutual-fund salespersons, stockbrokers, accountants, attorneys, and bankers all may call themselves financial planners. Usually these types of professions work on commission. Commission-only planners earn a commission on the investment products they sell. The so-called advantage is that the customer would have to pay a commission no matter where the product was purchased. Commission-only planners also charge a planning fee. The claimed advantage is that the fee is usually lower than that charged by fee-only planners. Instead, seek planners who charge flat fees, hourly fees, a percentage of assets, a project fee, or a percentage of income. Fee-only planners charge either an annual fee based on assets and investment activity or an hourly fee of $50 to $200 or more. Basically, they offer a financial plan and then refer clients to others who sell financial products such as stocks or mutual funds. Payment is required whether or not you choose to implement the suggested plan. This protects the investor from a potential conflict of interest or unnecessary commission-based investments.

The first step in choosing the right financial planner is to start with professionals who have one or more of these designations: Certified Financial Planner, Chartered Financial Consultant, Master of Science in Financial Services, Master's Degree in Business Administration, or Registry of Financial Planning Practitioners. Let's briefly look at each of these in turn.

Certified Financial Planner (CFP). The International Board of Standards and Practices for Certified Financial Planners, Inc., accredits qualified colleges and universities to teach and test students to qualify for CFP certification. The CFP course, which usually takes two or three academic years to complete, consists of six sections covering the following subjects: introduction to financial planning, risk management (insurance), investments, tax planning and management, retirement planning and employee benefits, and real estate planning. A single comprehensive examination is given after completion of all required courses of study. In addition to the examination, candidates for certification must meet experience requirements in financial-planning-related work, which vary according to educational background. CFP licensees are also subject to continuing education requirements to maintain their certification.

Chartered Financial Consultant (ChFC). This program, an outgrowth of the Chartered Life Underwriter course for insurance agents given by the American College in Bryn Mawr, Pennsylvania, is a correspondence program with eight required courses and two electives. Graduates must have three years of qualifying business experience and meet ethical standards.

Master of Science in Financial Services (MSFS). Granted by the American College, this degree is awarded to those who complete graduate-level courses in financial planning. Degree requirements include thirteen courses and a research paper.

Master's Degree in Business Administration (MBA). An MBA can be earned at the graduate level in colleges and universities. Many schools offer courses specializing in financial planning or family financial planning.

Registry of Financial Planning Practitioners. Sponsored by the International Association for Financial Planning, registry members must have three years of full-time practice as a financial planner and have a CFP, ChFC, CPA, law, or business degree. They are also required to pass an examination and meet certain other requirements. Financial planners who are admitted to the Registry of Financial Planning Practitioners, or who hold the designation CFP or ChFC, or who are members of the National Association of Personal Financial Advisors, have codes on ethics, honesty, and conflicts of interest that they are obligated to uphold. Violations of these standards may result in the financial planner losing his or her membership in the association and/or his or her designation.

Accountability is the key in choosing a good financial adviser. Titles don't guarantee performance, but at least you know that behind these titles is a code of ethics and honesty. Get referrals from trusted friends and interview a handful of planners. This also provides some accountability. Most financial planners offer a free thirty-minute or one-hour consultation.

Robert Detterman, a certified financial planner for Bo-Gin Financial in Westlake Village, California, says, "If they won't answer questions, stand up and walk away."

Barbara Roper, director of investor protection at the Consumer Federation of America in Washington, D.C., suggests that fee-only planners are more objective. Because they don't benefit from pushing you into a certain investment, they tend to give you advice that is best for you.

"You can't generalize that commissioned planners won't look out for your best interest, but fee-only planners have a better leg to stand on," says Mike Wilson, spokesman for the College for Financial Planning in Denver.

Be careful to distinguish between fee-only and fee-based or fee-offset planners. Fee-based and fee-offset actually means the planner is paid through *both* commission and fees, according to the National Association of Personal Financial Advisors, a fee-only professional group in Buffalo Grove, Illinois.

A good financial planner should give you unbiased help in budgeting your money toward investments. A planner should be able to give you a customized plan that is appropriate for your specific needs. Begin your search with family and friends. Choose your referrals wisely, as many of your family and friends have different portfolios. Keep in mind that individual planners have different strengths depending on certain income levels. Always ask for random referrals. Don't rely solely on "hand-picked" referrals. Consult local organizations such as the

Chamber of Commerce for additional names. According to "Fraud and Abuse in the Financial Planning Industry," an article on the Internet, more than 6,000 Chicago-area investors are believed to have lost $45 million to a financial planner who is now facing action by the securities department of the Illinois Secretary of State. Investors nearing retirement age were targeted in the scheme, which involved a complex web of trust and 350 real estate limited partnerships. Investors who attended the promoter's four-night seminar program were promised that they could earn more money retiring than they were making while working. The state found that investor funds had been diverted into the financial planner's purchase of three homes, a 26-foot boat, aircraft, an airport hangar, and motor vehicles. All this was made possible by fraudulent "hand-picked" referrals.

Once you have the names of several prospects, the Better Business Bureau says you should check with:

- Your state securities division. A background check can reveal any noncompliance with state federal laws.

- The SEC. Your planner should be registered with the SEC or registered under state laws dealing with investment advisers.

- The Better Business Bureau. Ask for a reliability report on the planner.

Your next step is to schedule interviews with the prospects. There is usually no charge for these appointments, but ask about fees before scheduling. At the meeting, ask the following questions:

- What is the planner's professional background? Look for a strong track record of education and job experience covering a broad spectrum of financial planning needs. Ask whether the planner is continuing education and training.

* How long has she or he been a financial planner? Look for three or more years of experience and several more years of prior experience as a broker, insurance agent, accountant, or lawyer. Yes, there are some honest lawyers out there!

* How long has she or he been in the community? Choose a planner you know personally or can check out through reliable references.

* Will the planner provide references? Get the names and phone numbers of three or more clients whom the planner has counseled for at least two years. Ask the clients about their level of satisfaction, their investment returns, and the planner's integrity.

* Ask for examples of plans and monitoring reports the planner has drawn up for other investors.

* Pay attention to the frequency and quality of the monitoring reports, since these updates will be vital to reviewing and recharting your financial objectives.

* Will you be dealing with the planner or with an associate? If the planner will be turning over all or most of the day-to-day work on your financial plan to an associate, take the time to check out that individual as well.

* What professional organizations does the planner belong to? Call the organizations to verify the planner's membership. Remember, membership in an

organization and initials after a name do not guarantee competence or integrity.

* What specific experience does the planner have in the areas that concern you? Determine whether the planner's area of specialty matches your specific goals. Ask if the planner refers clients to another source of assistance if the need arises for services outside his or her areas of expertise.

A planner should ask you these basic questions:

* Do you intend to stay with your job?

* Is your spouse going to continue to work?

* Do you like your home or want a larger one, perhaps even a vacation home?

* Do you have anyone who may become dependent on you in the future?

* Do you intend to put your children through college?

Avoid planners who pressure you into making quick investments without showing a track record of proven success. According to the National Association of Securities Dealers in Washington, D.C., good reasons to dump an adviser include the promise of spectacular profit, such as "your money will double in six months," guarantees that you won't lose money on an investment, and a high level of transactions in your account that generates more commissions for your adviser but has no clear benefit to you.

Ask for an estimate of the planner's bill before you commit yourself. The bill generally should not exceed 3 percent of your annual income or investment base, regardless of whether compensation comes from fees or commissions. No matter what kind of fee arrangement, you should receive the following services:

- A clearly written financial plan that includes a balance sheet of assets versus liabilities; a projected cash flow statement for at least one year; and a precise definition of your financial goals and the steps you will need to take to achieve them.

- A discussion of the amount of risk you are willing to assume.

- Specific suggestions for improving your personal cash management.

- Projections for shifts in the rate of interest, inflation, and other factors that will affect your plan.

- Options and alternatives that provide a range of investment choices, with a list of the pros and cons of each.

- A plan for liquidation in the event of an emergency, outlining ways to obtain cash with the least possible cost and disruption.

- Suggested sources of advice from other professionals such as an accountant, attorney, insurance agent, or stockbroker.

- A specific schedule for monitoring your financial plan and periodically reviewing its performance and objectives.

Be on the alert for financial-planning fraud and abuse. It is essential to know as much information as possible regarding your planner. You can never be too safe. Check to see if your planner has a criminal record or a history of securities-related complaints or disciplinary action taken. To investigate any CFP, call the local SEC or the Certified Financial Planner Board of Standards at 1-888-CFP-MARK (toll-free). Above all, make sure your planner's name isn't Barry Minkow!

Be on guard for possible Ponzi schemes. In 1919 Charles Ponzi became infamous for his attractive "high rate" of return investments. Ponzi schemes are the rich man's version of the old pyramid scheme (see FIGURE 8; for more information, see chapter 16). A Ponzi scheme involves a few initial investors who are paid interest out of the proceeds from later investors, who in turn end up with nothing when the gig is up. Ponzi schemes masquerade as tax shelters, precious metals, commodities, high-tech stocks, and other new investment vehicles.

Four common characteristics of Ponzi schemes are:

1. The business cannot sustain itself and therefore must rely on outside sources to function.

2. The investor money is not used according to the stated purpose. Some of the investor money is used to pay the returns promised to earlier investors.

3. The business enterprise lacks profits sufficient to provide the promised return.

4. The basic flaw in the Ponzi promoter psyche is that investment capital is viewed as "earnings" to be spent, not as equity to serve as a foundation to generate revenue and profits.

To investigate a possible Ponzi scheme, you must do three things:

PYRAMID SCHEME

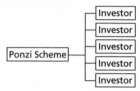

PONZI SCHEME

FIGURE 8. Diagrams of pyramid and Ponzi schemes. In our discussions about Ponzi schemes, have we mentioned the need to have a multi-level sales organization to promote them? No! In fact, my experience is that most Ponzi schemes don't rely on a multi-level sales organization to promote the scheme, but rather on word of mouth of the satisfied investors.

1. Determine that the outside investor money represents a primary source of capital to fund the business.

2. Prepare a cash flow analysis that traces the disposition of funds received from investors. In those instances where cash is commingled with cash from other sources, a comparison of total sources with total uses must be made. A determination is needed as to whether total monies received from investors exceed total monies disbursed for the purposes disclosed to the investors. This falls under the *failure to disclose material facts* ingredient of fraud.

3. Prepare an analysis of the "real" income-producing activity and determine whether or not it is sufficient to assure the promised return to investors. The focus of this step should be on the revenues

generated and the levels of inventory in relation to the investment activity.

On my radio show I interviewed a woman who was cheated out of $500,000 by her financial planner. Her planner used a few referrals, who were at the front end of the Ponzi scheme, to gain the confidence of future investors. He promised that there was "no risk" for the principal money that was invested. The sad part of this story is that her planner was her brother. He used not only his sister but other members of his family, including his mother, as well. His whole plan was to use other people's money to accumulate wealth. The "no risk" promise is the number one sign of a possible Ponzi rip-off.

Avoid financial planners who use high-pressure tactics to get you to make quick decisions. It may be a warning sign that your adviser is leading you toward a fraudulent scheme. Beware of planners who run a one-man show. If they use only a P.O. box as an address, that is a bad sign. If they can move operations out of town quickly and easily, you don't want to do business with them.

Finally, I can't stress the accountability issue enough. Once you have completed your due diligence, continue to keep your eyes and ears open. Most businesses don't begin with the intent to commit fraud. Constantly check to see if your planner is aboveboard. Build a monthly list of referrals and contacts. Let him know that you are checking up on him or her. If your planner knows that someone is watching, he or she will be less likely to defraud clients.

You never know to what extent a criminal will go to perpetrate a crime. The Internet article "Fraud and Abuse in the Financial Planning Industry" names the following examples. A Richmond, Virginia, financial planner was sentenced in

September 1987 to 222 years in prison for a phony investment pool scheme in which he was accused by the Virginia Division of Securities and Retail Franchising of stealing $1.3 million from investors in eight states, including $20,000 taken from his grandmother-in-law. A so-called pastor was sentenced to five years in federal prison for swindling investors out of $226,000 in a "consumer savings certificate" scam. The financial planner–pastor promised 15 to 18 percent annual interest returns on high-yield investments that were never made.

If your planner seems to be unbelievably honest and successful or seems to be struggling, both should send up a red flag. Fraud specialist Jim Ratley's 80/20 rule says that 80 percent of con men will buy that dream car or boat. By contrast, a struggling planner may feel pressure to gamble in order to get a big payoff. Don't think that your past due diligence is a lifetime guarantee. You make yourself susceptible to becoming a victim by failing to follow up.

When Sam Minyard (a fictitious name to protect the families), a stockbroker from Bateman Eichler, Hill Richards, called longtime client Helen Dickman (also a fictitious name), he believed he had a hot tip. The company had three years of audited financial statements that showed constant and steady growth. The management was articulate and confident and the stock had already increased by 100 percent.

"I'd put at least seventy thousand in the company," Sam said. Not wanting to pass up such a great opportunity, Helen followed his suggestion. Within days the stock almost doubled in value. "I'd hang on to it," Sam advised. Helen trusted Sam and believed that he did his homework on all the companies. She decided to hold on to the stock.

Days later she received the phone call. "It's a fraud," Sam cried. "I swear I didn't know!" Helen lost all her money. The company was ZZZZ Best.

Although the above case was fraud on the part of the company, neither the broker nor the investor took the time to investigate the investment. Don't let that be the case for you!

CHAPTER 7

The "G"
Gambling

~

If this were a book on ethics, I would probably approach the topic of gambling differently. I believe Paul, the old Jewish apostle of the New Testament, said it best when he wrote, "If any would not work, neither should he eat." That's really the issue here. The appeal of gambling is that it provides monetary rewards for no work. It appeals to the consumer in the same way fraud appealed to me. It's a shortcut: I can achieve financial prosperity by somehow circumventing the "work" process. Sure, we can gift-wrap gambling with fallacious synonyms such as "entertainment" or "recreational fun," but for most of its loyal patrons, it is nothing more than a cleverly disguised shortcut.

Ronald A. Reno, a research associate in the public policy division of Focus on the Family, reported on the gambling industry in an article in the *Policy Review*. In 1996, Americans legally wagered more money—some $500 billion—than they spent on groceries. That represents a 3,000 percent increase since 1976. Utah and Hawaii are the only states that prohibit all forms of gambling, although Hawaii is now considering casinos.

Casinos are legal in about half of the states and constitute nearly half of total gambling revenues, which are growing at the rate of 15 percent annually.

There is no question that gambling is on the rise every day. The question is whether or not consumers have a fighting chance! The truth about gambling is that it's a game of stakes, that is, failure to disclose all material facts. The chances of winning are very low. Gambling is perceived as a game of luck or chance, but in reality consumers have very little chance, and luck loses in the long run.

While in prison I was one of the few people who was truly guilty. Not many of my fellow inmates would admit that they broke the law. I often hear a similar statement from people who gamble; they say, "Nobody loses! Everyone either breaks even or wins." If that were the case, then casinos would not be in business. The fact of the matter is that cities like Las Vegas are building new casinos even as we speak.

Over the last decade, the gambling industry has sold itself as the economic booster for strapped communities. Inflated promises of jobs, tourism, and additional tax monies have seduced politicians and citizens in dozens of states and communities. But as Americans become more aware of the societal devastation brought on by legalized gambling, the industry is finding it increasingly difficult, and ever more expensive, to peddle its product.

This is a typical example of failing to disclose key material facts. Obviously a casino or gambling hall would bring additional jobs, but are these well-paying jobs? And how many will be available? Every city has dreams of having a tourist industry. Unfortunately, generating that kind of an atmosphere is difficult. It takes a lot more than a gambling hall to bring tourists in. Many waterfront cities are tricked into believing that all their city needs is a casino to boost tourism. It is true that the gambling industry generates a lot of money. Reno notes in his article that in 1994 our government received $1.4 billion from casinos alone and $10 billion from lotteries, but at what price? The California Council on Compulsive Gambling reports that the Maryland State Task Force on Gambling Addiction determined that the estimated 50,000 adult gambling addicts in Maryland alone cost the state $1.5 billion in lost work productivity, monies stolen and embezzled, bad checks, and unpaid taxes. This figure increased significantly when related costs for social services, health care, bankruptcies, and legal and correctional fees were considered. The simple math shows that Maryland alone loses $1.5 billion compared to the $1.4 billion that the U.S. government receives from the taxes paid by the gambling industry.

Something else the gambling industry doesn't want communities to know is that gambling breeds crime. Three years after the arrival of casinos, Atlantic City rose from fiftieth to first in the nation in per capita crime. Nevada, home to Las Vegas, continually ranks near the top of the same list.

In prison I met a lawyer, Jim Carrol, who was the financial trustee for a nonprofit charity organization. He began his gambling endeavors innocently enough—a bet on a game here and there and an occasional trip to Las Vegas. Before long, however, he became addicted to gambling. He began to steal money from the organization he worked for in order to support his habit. He never thought he'd lose all the money because he always felt that "lucky" streak was right around the corner, but it never came. Jim was indicted for misappropriation of funds and sent to prison. He was one of the few men I met in prison who was sorry for what he had done. To this day Jim says gambling "promises like a god and pays like a devil."

Reno reports that in Deadwood, South Dakota, only five

years after allowing limited-stakes casinos in their community, serious crimes rose 93 percent. Mississippi's Gulf Coast permitted casinos in August of 1992 and after one year, bank robberies had increased from one to thirteen, and armed robberies tripled. In Ledyard, Connecticut, rape, robbery, car theft, and larceny all increased more than 400 percent in the first three years after Foxwoods, the nation's richest casino, opened.

Dr. Durand Jacobs, a guest on my national radio show, detailed some of the specific crimes committed by compulsive gamblers. He queried 190 adult male compulsive gamblers about which kinds of illegal activities they had engaged in to gamble or to pay gambling debts. Illegal activities were grouped under two categories: white-collar crime and commonplace crime. The kinds of white-collar crime they admitted to were as follows:

* Civil loan fraud (getting multiple loans from different sources on the same collateral) (41%)
* Embezzlement and employer theft (38%)
* Check forgery (33%)
* Noncheck forgery (18%)
* Tax evasion (28%)
* Tax fraud (18%)

The incidence of commonplace crimes was much lower:

* Simple larceny (21%)
* Burglary (15%)
* Fencing stolen goods (14%)
* Selling drugs (9%)
* Pimping (2%)

Massachusetts Attorney General Scott Harshbarger says, "The fact is, in every city that casinos have been introduced in any significant way, crime in the streets has gone up." Maryland attorney general J. Joseph Curran, Jr., issued a notable report on the gambling-crime link. Curran concluded: "Casinos would bring a substantial increase in crime to our state. There would be more violent crime, more crimes against property, more insurance fraud, more white-collar crime, more juvenile crime, more drug and alcohol-related crime, more domestic violence and child abuse, and more organized crime."

The gambling industry claims that these increases are due only to the fact that more people are visiting the communities. They are trying to say that an area like Los Angeles County, which contains some 8 million people, will always have more crime than Spokane, Washington, which has only about 250,000 people. What they fail to disclose is that per capita is based on *ratios* of crimes to *number* of people. Los Angeles has about thirty-two times more people than Spokane. For every crime in Spokane, Los Angeles is allowed thirty-two. If Spokane had three robberies to Los Angeles's thirty, Spokane would have more robberies per capita.

Reno also reports that in Jefferson City, Missouri, voters approved casino riverboats in 1992, then voted them out in November 1996. States such as Louisiana and Wisconsin are also trying to repeal legalized gambling.

Joe Koslowski is one of thousands who fall prey to the gambling bug every year. At sixteen Joe began gambling as many young Americans do: by joining college and pro football pools or weekend poker games. Flush with money he had just won in a bowling tournament, Joe invited some friends to celebrate with him in Atlantic City. Joe and all his buddies were able to gamble despite the age limit of 21. Joe's good fortune continued as he parlayed his bowling winnings into a couple of thousand dollars. After his initial success, Joe returned to the casinos frequently. His winning streak eventually ended, but his taste for the thrill of gambling did not. Once he was out of cash, he opened credit card accounts under his family members' names and took out cash advances using the credit cards.

The whole scheme finally came crashing down on Joe in 1995 after he had amassed $20,000 in debt. At age twenty, Joe, who had no prior criminal record, is serving time in a Pennsylvania federal prison for credit card fraud.

Reno writes that in 1995, University of Minnesota researchers reported that more than half of underage Minnesota teens surveyed had participated in some form of legalized gambling. An earlier survey of Atlantic City high school students revealed that nearly two-thirds had gambled at the city's casinos.

Is gambling an innocent game, or is it a scam? Gambling masquerades as a fun recreational activity. For many people it is just that. I have heard two questions asked repeatedly: Is gambling gambling if you don't lose? and, Is gambling gambling if it doesn't matter if you win? To which I answer, the end does not justify the means. Some try to justify their gambling problem by saying that the end result of winning is what matters. The temporary end of winning does not justify the possible addiction of gambling. As long as there is a chance or risk of losing, it is gambling. A reminder: Fraud is not a legal conclusion.

There is a huge misconception when it comes to gambling. Gambling is associated with fun and games, as Joe believed. For many people, losing some money isn't a problem if you can afford it. The problem is that most people cannot afford to lose the money that they commit to their gambling endeavors. The true "fun" is provided by the environment of the casinos. The gambling industry uses deliberate deception to distract consumers. Whether they are on a beautiful riverboat or on the glittering strip of Las Vegas, casinos are designed to do one thing:

bring in customers. The goal of the casino is to provide an environment in which people will not mind giving their money away. Caught up in the scenery and the excitement of being in the center of all the glitz and glamour, normal reasoning skills vanish. Everything from the complimentary drinks and inexpensive meals to the cigar and cigarette hawkers is a strategic maneuver. People who usually keep a tight rein on their purse strings all of a sudden relax and let their guard down. Make no mistake about it: Everyone in the casino is out for one thing—themselves! The house wants to win, and the people you are gambling against want to win. Of course, the house gets a percentage of the winnings from all the tables. And the tables are often full of professional gamblers. My question is, is it really fun to lose money?

Gambling preys on people's fantasies of becoming wealthy or making an easy buck. Everyone dreams of winning the lottery, but only a few see that dream come true. Most people have made the resolution that they might not win the lottery, but winning a couple hundred or thousand dollars at the casino is certainly possible. The problem is that both have about the same odds.

The biggest misconception about gambling is that it's not addictive. The gambling industry knows that many people lose control or get addicted, whichever you prefer. Like most businesses, they know that their most difficult task is getting new customers. Once they influence people to come for the entertainment, the seed of addiction has been planted.

Richard Rosenthal of UCLA's School of Medicine defines pathological gambling as "a progressive disorder characterized by a continuous or periodic loss of control over gambling; a preoccupation with gambling and with obtaining money with which to gamble; irrational thinking; and a continuation of the behavior despite adverse consequences."

The California Council on Compulsive Gambling indicates that more than 800,000 California adults and over 50,000 California juveniles already are experiencing serious gambling-related problems.

Gambling is much the same as any other addiction. Although the physical signs may be lacking, the social effects may be similar and in some ways much worse. Addictive behaviors cause us to neglect our responsibilities and our financial obligations to others, even our families. Gambling has a set of problems all its own, however. People who suffer from substance abuse are restricted by physical limitations; there is only so much alcohol a person can consume. But there is no limit to the amount of money a person can spend gambling. Gambling has few physical barriers to control its abuse. Our only limitation is the amount of money we have, borrow, or in many cases steal!

Friends and families of gamblers feel the effects in the form of strained personal relationships and financial hardship. People who are addicted to gambling will often neglect paying their bills and will spend money they don't have. They may lose their home, car, or any number of personal items. The California Council on Compulsive Gambling revealed some of the effects gambling has on families:

- Children of problem gamblers had higher levels of use for tobacco, alcohol, illicit drugs, and overeating during the previous twelve months than did their classroom peers.

- Seventy-five percent of problem gamblers' children reported their first gambling experience before eleven years of age, compared to 34 percent of their classmates.

❧ Children of problem gamblers experienced almost twice the incidence of homes broken by separation, divorce, or death of a parent before they had reached the age of fifteen (37% to 20%).

❧ When compared to their classmates, children of problem gamblers rated themselves as more insecure, emotionally down, and "unhappy with life and myself." They also reported poorer school and work performance.

❧ Underscoring the combined family, health, and personal adjustment problems faced by children whose parents gambled excessively was the finding that they acknowledged suicide attempts at twice the rate of their classmates (12% to 6%).

On the average, it can take eight years to progress from a recreational gambler to a compulsive gambler. Predisposing factors may include childhood trauma, abuse, and unresolved grief issues. Compulsive gambling is the so-called hidden illness because there is no smell of liquor on the breath, no drunken stumbling, and no slurring of speech.

Ask yourself the following questions if you feel you may have a problem with gambling. They are the Twenty Questions of Gamblers Anonymous:

1. Do you lose time from work due to gambling?

2. Does gambling make your home life unhappy?

3. Does gambling affect your reputation?

4. Do you ever feel remorse after gambling?

5. Do you ever gamble to get money with which to pay debts or otherwise solve financial difficulties?

6. Does gambling cause a decrease in your ambition or efficiency?

7. After losing, do you have a strong urge to return and win more?

8. After a win, do you have a strong urge to return and win more?

9. Do you often gamble until your last dollar is gone?

10. Do you ever borrow to finance your gambling?

11. Do you ever sell anything to finance gambling?

12. Are you reluctant to use "gambling money" for normal expenditures?

13. Does gambling make you careless about the welfare of your family?

14. Do you ever gamble longer than you planned?

15. Do you ever gamble to escape worry or trouble?

16. Do you ever commit, or consider committing, an illegal act to finance your gambling?

17. Does gambling cause you to have difficulty sleeping?

18. Do arguments, disappointments, or frustrations create within you an urge to gamble?

19. Do you have an urge to celebrate good fortune by a few hours of gambling?

20. Do you ever consider self-destruction as result of
    your gambling?

In his article, Reno describes a family from Ohio. In August
1993, Mike and Sharon James (not their real names) and their
two preschool children left a successful business in East
Liverpool, Ohio, for promising prospects in Charleston, South
Carolina. The couple had been in Charleston one month when
Sharon received an overdrawn notice from the bank. She knew
she and Mike had several thousand dollars in their checking
account set aside for a down payment on a house. Puzzled, she
contacted the bank.

Sharon discovered that Mike, her husband of ten years, had
made several withdrawals in recent weeks, many in the neighborhood of $1,000. When she questioned him, she learned he
had spent the money on South Carolina's ubiquitous video
poker machines. Despite Sharon's pleas and Mike's attempts at
treatment, Mike couldn't kick the habit. He squandered the
family's remaining savings, hocked many of their possessions,
and even cashed in the children's savings bonds, leaving the
family $20,000 in debt. Finally, Sharon filed for divorce. Mike
wound up in the county jail for delinquency in child support
payments and for writing bad checks.

"This man was a wonderful person, a very caring father,"
says Sharon. "I really believe he didn't realize what he was
doing, because he was never like that before. This addiction just
grabs you and twists you. It destroyed him and us."

In 1995 the Illinois Council on Compulsive Gambling surveyed nearly 200 Gamblers Anonymous members and found
that 16 had divorced because of their gambling addictions;
another 10 percent had separated as a result. An earlier study of
spouses of compulsive gamblers discovered that 78 percent had

threatened separation or divorce, and half had carried through on their threats. A survey of 850 high school students in Southern California found that children of compulsive gamblers were almost twice as likely to experience the trauma of a broken home. In Harrison County, Mississippi, the hub of the state's casino industry, the number of divorces rose from 440 in 1992 to nearly 1,100 in 1993, the first full year after gambling had been legalized. Judge William Stewart, who has served for seventeen years, says he knows gambling to be a factor in about a third of the divorce cases he oversees.

Spousal and child abuse and neglect are other problems attendant to gambling addictions, according to reports from social service agencies in gambling communities. The Gulf Coast Women's Center in Biloxi, Mississippi, has averaged 400 additional crisis calls per month since the advent of casinos there.

Gambling is not fun and games. Wherever gambling flourishes, so does misery and crime. Thousands of people have fallen so far that they cannot stop gambling despite massive cash losses. The Surgeon General issues warnings on cigarette packages and advertisements that cigarettes may be harmful to your health. Maybe we should have similar warnings in casinos regarding gambling.

In prison there were three things every inmate avoided to stay out of trouble. The first was dealing or using drugs. The second was involvement in homosexual activity. The third was gambling. In my experience, more people died in prison over unpaid gambling debts than anything else. I am willing to "bet" that the same is true in the free world as well. By the way, I've never met an addicted gambler who didn't make that first, very innocent, bet!

CHAPTER 8

The "H"
HMOs

We all know about the enrollment increase in health maintenance organizations (HMOs) and the growth in the number of
new HMOs and other forms of managed care. Their philosophy
is to cut the fat and control patient visits and care. According to
the *Wall Street Journal*, U.S. Healthcare reduced the cost to its
subscribers from a 12 percent increase in 1993 to a 3 percent
increase in 1994, and projected a zero percent increase in 1995.

How did the company do it? By reducing the length of hospital stays by 11 percent; by reducing payment to physicians by
12 to 23 percent; and by implementing incentive programs to
encourage physicians to do such things as immunize children,
perform mammographies for women over forty, and have open
clinics at night for patients' convenience.

That's admirable, and for the most part it has made a difference in service and cost control. But, in addition, the company told doctors that if they reduced the number of patient
referrals to specialists and the number of high-tech tests, the
doctors would receive a bonus. In other words, they would

profit by reducing the amount of care provided to patients. Unless such care is not necessary, that, in the opinion of a medical professional, is unethical.

Simultaneously, U.S. Healthcare takes 30 cents of every premium dollar and puts it into administration, advertising, and dividends. The company also paid its chief executive officer more than $20 million in salary, stock options, and dividends. Although I have no objection to a CEO earning a high salary (that's the incentive and payoff for hard work), I do object when it comes at the expense of quality care.

In July 1996, the *Los Angeles Times* reported that to cut costs, HMOs have employed rules limiting what doctors, nurses, and other health care providers may tell patients about treatment options. At this writing, doctors do not have to disclose that they have a financial advantage in not sending patients to a specialist for further care.

State legislators are trying to change that. AB 2649, a California bill, would require your HMO to tell you what incentive plans it uses and describe to you the financial risks your physicians face if they tell you all available treatment options. It includes clear and specific disclosure requirements for HMOs. Another bill, SB 1064, leaves it up to the HMO to disclose what its incentive plans are and puts the burden on the consumer to contact the HMO for details.

I have a problem with three key material facts that health insurance policies fail to disclose:

1. Incentives for not giving full treatment.

2. Disparity in payment of claims—corporate plans versus individual plans.

3. Nonmedical staff known as "claim screeners" giving

treatment advice to qualified medical doctors just because they write the check.

The general understanding of health insurance is that if something unforeseen happens to you or your family member, then you have protection to pay for the expenses. The protection should cover any type of injury and illness and should also cover births. Today, health care costs have skyrocketed. Even a simple doctor's visit for a flu shot can run over a hundred dollars. The cost of having a baby in many cases begins at $10,000 as long as there are no complications.

The purpose of this chapter is not to advocate "what should be" in a health policy but rather "what we should know about." I want full disclosure in health insurance policies that the layperson can read in five minutes without having to use a microscope to read the fine print. There is no reason why our policies can't fully disclose all of our benefits along with any incentives doctors might have in providing more or less treatment. I know having the best insurance policy in the world can't guarantee good health, but anyone who has paid for health insurance should be given full treatment to be restored back into the best possible health, no matter what the cost!

Created in the 1920s, HMOs, or prepaid group practices, have become popular over the past decade because of their success at making high-quality health care more available and less costly. Every HMO is different, and with nearly 600 HMOs nationwide, it may be difficult to find the perfect one for you. According to a 1996 *Newsweek* article, 53.3 million Americans currently use HMOs.

HMOs provide access to services from basic office visits to life-threatening conditions. The services they provide include

X rays; laboratory tests; rehabilitation therapy; physician, hospital and out-patient services; mental health care; and more. Some HMOs even offer prescription drugs as part of the plan. And, as I learned the hard way, few provide fertility services.

Unlike traditional insurance, in which patients are charged every time they receive medical attention, HMOs provide health coverage for a fixed monthly premium that is usually much lower than the cost of traditional insurance. Whereas traditional insurance commonly covers only 80 percent of many medical expenses, HMOs usually have minimal or no copayments without a deductible. These practices not only save consumers money, but also remove financial limitations that generally keep people from seeking early or preventive treatment. By definition, health maintenance organizations take special care in helping their members stay healthy. HMOs offer health education classes on nutrition, stress management, smoking addictions, parenting, CPR, and first aid. Screening for cancer and other diseases is also available. Many HMOs even offer discounts at health clubs and fitness centers.

Some people say that HMO stands for "higher malpractice occurrence." HMOs have basically shifted the job of the insurance claims adjuster to the doctor who is providing the medical service. Under traditional health insurance plans, the doctor is given essentially free rein to treat the patient and ensure his or her recovery. As long as the doctor does not engage in unnecessary treatment, the insurance plan pays most or all of the patient's bills after the patient pays the deductible. The doctor thus has the incentive to fully diagnose and treat the patient, even if some testing or treatment later proves unnecessary. Although this system definitely results in higher health insurance costs, it ensures better treatment for patients.

HMOs do things differently. They pay a given doctor, called

the primary care physician (PCP), a set fee per patient per month. This fee is quite small, as low as $5. The PCP must have numerous patients on the patient rolls to meet his or her overhead. The PCP receives the same fee no matter how often he or she treats the patient or what procedures he or she uses on the patient. That is, the PCP receives $5 for the healthy patient he never sees, and he or she also receives $5 for the cancer-stricken patient who needs constant care.

The PCP profits at the end of the year when he or she is given a "bonus" for prescribing the "least" amount of referrals to specialists, and also when he or she never sees the patient or when the patient sees him or her as seldom as possible. This is the opposite of the traditional health insurance plan, in which doctors profit only when providing full and complete service. Under HMOs, doctors show profit only for patients whom they never or rarely see. Doctors actually lose money on patients they have to see often, because the doctor has to spend time and office resources treating and retreating the same patient.

This system removes a valuable part of free market competition. An HMO doctor really doesn't have to be good—he just has to be fast. In fact, 29 percent of HMO users say that they don't have a choice of doctors because they have a company plan. This means doctors should worry more about landing a contract from a company than providing full and complete service. HMO plans allow for more opportunities to take shortcuts at the expense of patients because the doctors are not really accountable to their patients.

Each HMO varies as to whether it provides specialist care. Some HMOs are cooperative, whereas others will not pay extra for a patient who needs a referral to a specialist. Some will even charge the PCP if the patient's specialist care exceeds a set minimum. Of course, the HMO decrees to whom a PCP can refer a patient for a given specialty, and the specialists are under the same set fee bonuses as the PCP.

According to Blue Shield, surveys have found that 15 to 25 percent of HMO members express overall dissatisfaction with their access to specialist care. With roughly 12 million Californians belonging to HMOs, that means up to 3 million dissatisfied people in California alone. In a bold move, Blue Shield is attempting to waive the specialist referral process. This will allow members to go directly to a specialist instead of having to go through their primary physician. This should save not only time in processing but money as well, because the primary doctor visit is bypassed. Under the Blue Shield plan, patients can refer themselves to a specialist by making a $30 copayment to the doctor. That's $20 more than Blue Shield's usual $10 copayment.

The way the system is set up now, HMO doctors help soothe economic tensions by cutting back on care and doing only what is absolutely necessary. So-called second opinions used to be quite common in medicine ten years ago but are increasingly less common today. In essence, PCPs have become merely nurses of sorts, choosing more extensive care only for those whose symptoms cannot be questioned, and often denying necessary care to other patients whose symptoms are less severe, for fear of being punished economically.

Robert F. Brennan, an experienced attorney in malpractice cases, gives some helpful hints that patients can use to protect themselves from poor service.

Get it in writing. If the doctor refuses what you believe to be a necessary treatment, or if the doctor refuses to refer you to a specialist, make the doctor write down that he or she is refusing the treatment, and why. If the doctor won't put it in writing, go home and send a letter to the doctor confirming that he or she refused to do so.

If your condition doesn't improve, insist on more tests or treatment. More and more patients are being sent home today with the bland assertion that nothing is the matter. It is best to ignore this platitude and listen to your own body. If, indeed, you get better, leave the doctor alone. However, if you don't, make another appointment right away. Insist on more treatment. Insist on more tests, particularly the tests that the doctor refused to administer at your last visit. Remember, the doctors themselves usually have to pay specialists and technicians to run many of these tests; the HMO provides a disincentive to administer what are often considered necessary tests. Don't accept that "nothing is the matter," because nowadays doctors have a positive economic incentive to tell you this.

Learn about your symptoms and about the tests that are used to diagnose your symptoms. In any library or on the Internet, there are lots of resources about what a given symptom might mean, especially when combined with other symptoms. It is actually not too difficult to learn the medical significance of most symptoms or to learn what tests should be used to diagnose or rule out conditions associated with those symptoms. It's your body and your life. Call the local or state medical board and get references to study up on your symptoms. For example, if you have acute chest pains and the doctor refuses to give you an electrocardiogram (EKG), something is terribly wrong. You will know this only if you've done your due diligence or homework. Take the time to educate yourself. It might save you or a family member.

Involve the HMO in any decision to deny testing or treatment. This is the most important preventive step currently available to HMO patients. HMOs hate getting sued and will often yield to your will if threatened with anything even remotely resembling a lawsuit. If you are denied treatment or testing that you feel is reasonably necessary, don't just write a letter to your doctor confirming this. Write the HMO. Use the magical phrase, "I believe Dr. Smith's denial of further testing for my chest pains is a bad faith denial of my right to medical coverage under your health maintenance organization. If you do not immediately approve additional funds for these tests, I will contact a lawyer." I mean it: Use those very words. The pen is mightier than the sword. If you are insured through your employer, go directly to the HMO but be sure to send a copy to the personnel office.

Involve a lawyer early and often. States such as California have the California Medical Board, which oversees the conduct of doctors throughout the state. The board does respond to complaints, although sometimes not as aggressively or as quickly as you may wish.

As in most frauds, many times the victims forget that they can't win if they don't fight. Often the fight begins with due diligence, which basically means doing your homework. Most people review their insurance policy only when something has gone wrong. We must educate ourselves about the things that matter in our lives before the problem arises.

Because of the constant interference with medical practice and economics by policy makers and social engineers, most physicians have been aware of the problem for a long time but are afraid to speak out for fear that they might lose their livelihoods. Social and government pressures have served to undermine the ethics that have been the bedrock of American medicine. Once health care planners successfully switched the American public from thinking of their individual health care needs and responsibilities to a mind-set of "health care dollars," "providers" instead of doctors became inevitable.

In 1994, after twenty-three years as a practicing obstetrician-gynecologist in Fairfield, Connecticut, a doctor concluded that he could not practice in an ethical manner in a managed care environment and closed his practice. The following, taken from the January 22, 1996, issue of *Time*, is from a letter he sent out to all his patients:

"The truth of the matter is that the economic and regulatory climate in which medicine must now be practiced has made my personalized style and type of practice, in which I take great pride, extremely difficult. Employers shift their workers (my patients) around from doctor to doctor, thinking only of how 'cheap' a group insurance plan is and giving no thought at all to the physician-patient relationship. Insurance companies appropriate to themselves, under the guise of the term 'managed care,' the right to refuse necessary care to patients in order to enhance their own profits. Medically untrained lay persons, reading words they cannot pronounce from pre-programmed computer screens, tell physicians how to practice medicine."

These words continue to ring true every day, and the situation is getting worse. Some HMO committees meet daily to make such decisions as: Patients over age seventy-two are "too old" to qualify for coronary bypass surgery, and aggressive cancer chemotherapy is "not economically justifiable" in patients over age seventy-five. This is contrary to the very basis of American liberty and individualism. Unfortunately, there is nothing new about managed care, managed competition, managed trade, or any other such policy creation. It is called corporatism. If we start denying care to people over seventy-five, where do we stop? Will the mentally ill or handicapped be next? What about smokers or overweight or ugly people—will they someday be excluded? We saw this type of discrimination with Hitler and the Jews, which began because of Germany's economic hardship from World War I retributions. Today the Chinese government, because of economics, allows each family only one child.

For a doctor to join a small number of managed care plans in order to enhance the survival of his practice until things can be fixed is probably acceptable, even necessary, in today's climate. But to join as many plans as he or she can get into, to accept whatever reimbursement is offered by the managed care firm, and to fail to defend a patient's right to the best possible care for fear of being "deselected" from the companies' provider panels is inexcusable collaboration. We stand at a dangerous crossroads in American medicine today. Let us not cross over the threshold into unethical and inhumane care.

The battle for control goes beyond denying a health claim. It's actually a conspiracy to take away the consumer's freedom to choose! Is the new, bigger HMO better? According to a briefing note on the Internet from Karen Davis in January of 1996, studies say no! After conducting six case studies of health plans in Boston, Los Angeles, and Philadelphia and an analysis of each of the three markets, it was concluded that "size and growth" may be more important for plan survival than "quality" of patient care and services. Plans with relatively poorer quality reputations appear to be growing and expanding. The case studies point to the lack of objective information on how plans perform in terms of quality of care, and to the critical need to develop quality measures and standards and policies to hold plans accountable as they restructure in a dynamic market. With a combined annual growth rate of more than 11 percent, independent practice associations (IPAs) and network model plans now enroll nearly two-thirds of all new HMO members. IPAs operate through contracts with individual physicians, while network model HMOs contract with multiple physician groups.

Although the figures don't lie, we know that liars can figure. Sure, HMOs have a high growth rate because businesses that employ hundreds and thousands of employees are joining every year to save money. Growth is not necessarily a reflection of good medical care. If contracts are being made with physician groups and HMOs, the accountability is where? We are given the skin of the truth—HMOs are rapidly growing—stuffed with an implied lie: They are growing because they give quality care and service.

Davis also reports that the Boston, L.A., and Philadelphia study revealed interesting information as to what the patients think. Here is how patients compared HMOs with fee-for-service (FFS) plans:

- Overall, HMO members are more likely to rate their plan as fair or poor (21%) than are FFS users (14%).

- Fifteen percent of HMO members rate the quality of health care services they receive as fair or poor, compared with 6 percent of FFS members.

- HMO users are far more likely than FFS users to rate their plans as fair or poor for access to services, including specialty care (23% v. 8%).

- HMO members are much less satisfied than FFS enrollees with their plans' ease of changing doctors (25% v. 6%), choice of doctors (25% v. 5%), and quality of doctors (17% v. 4%).

- Twenty-nine percent of HMO enrollees report that they had *no choice* regarding their type of plan.

- Almost half (45%) of all insured adults report being enrolled in their current plan for less than three years. Nearly three-quarters of those adults who changed plans in the past three years did so voluntarily, usually because their employer changed plans.

⚡ The perception that HMOs provide full coverage is misleading. Roughly equal numbers of adults and their families in both FFS (50%) and HMO (55%) plans spent between $1 and $500 out-of-pocket last year on medical bills that were not covered by insurance. Equal numbers of HMO and FFS enrollees did not receive these preventive services in the last year: pap smear (25% v. 24%); pelvic exam (25% v. 24%); mammogram (31% v. 31%); blood pressure reading (14% v. 12%); screening for prostate cancer (46% v. 48%); complete physical exam (36% v. 37%).

If consumers are so unhappy, why are HMOs thriving? The California Medical Association's (CMA) report on all California HMOs demonstrates that as much as 25 percent of each health care dollar paid by businesses and consumers goes toward profit, paperwork, advertising, and executives' salaries. The CMA report also includes a three-year comparison for 1994 to 1996 that shows an overall trend toward increased profits and administrative costs for California HMOs (see *TABLE 1*).

HMOs are thriving at the expense of consumers. Always follow the "money trail." The HMOs' real customers are the

Profit for HMOs

Company	Administration (%)	Profit (%)
PacifiCare of CA	11.0	4.9
FHP/Takecare, Inc.	12.3	3.9
Cigna Health Care of CA	13.7	3.1
Prudential	15.5	2.9
Health Net	12.86	6.79
California Care	16.34	10.63

TABLE 1. Percent of HMO revenues that go toward administration and profit.

physicians and businesses that they are providing the service to, not the patients. As long as they are able to keep costs down for businesses, their number one customer is happy. User satisfaction isn't important.

Although no plan is perfect, I do believe in having some kind of insurance plan. This chapter is intended to alert you to some of the fallacies and abuses in the HMO industry. Don't mistake that with perfection. No company is perfect—I only wish that companies would fully disclose some of the following important questions. When considering which health plan is best for you, follow these tips from the Better Business Bureau:

1. Does the policy cover everyone in your immediate family? To what age are children insured?

2. Can the policy be canceled, and if so, under what circumstances or conditions?

3. What is the policy's effective date?

4. How long is the waiting period before benefits begin?

5. Are surgical benefits in line with surgeon's fees in the area where you live?

6. What conditions are not covered?

7. What is the maximum amount paid under major medical? How large is the deductible? After recovery from an illness, will the maximum amount of benefits again be available?

8. Did you compute the total amount of funds your family can obtain from all sources if your income should increase, before acquiring disability insurance?

9. Was the loss of income policy reviewed carefully for the exact definition of "total disability"?

10. How reliable is your agent and the company he or she represents? Is the company licensed to do business in your state?

11. Did you fall prey to high-pressure tactics by an insurance agent or glowing promises made in an advertisement? Did you consult other policyholders about their experiences with the company?

12. Was the policy studied with special care before you signed it?

Choosing the HMO or other health insurance plan is only the beginning. You must also choose a doctor. For most of us, our doctor is chosen for us. Many plans, though, offer consumers a choice. Dr. Dwight McNeill, vice president of AccessHealth in Rancho Cordova, California, thinks it's ridiculous that we demand every conceivable statistic on a baseball player, but when it comes to open-heart surgery, we often don't know the first thing about our doctor. "Most people pick a doctor like they do a dry cleaner," says McNeill. "Whoever is closest to your home is the right one!" Here's how to find out more about your doctor:

 * **Dig for data.** Turn to some key sources of public information. In a few states, information on whether a doctor has been sued or has had his license suspended is available from the state's medical-licensing boards. The Public Citizen's Health Research Group publishes a book called *13,012 Questionable Doctors.*

- **Knock on the HMO's door.** Any health plan accred-ited by the National Committee for Quality Assurance should be able to tell you which of its doctors admit patients to teaching or community hospitals. A doctor with admitting privileges to both is best.

- **Ask the quality cops.** Most big HMOs have quality assurance departments designed to monitor customer service, and many compile patient satisfaction surveys on doctors.

- **Survey the Ivory Towers.** Doctors who teach as well as practice medicine have usually earned the respect of colleagues and are familiar with the latest develop-ments in the field.

- **Bug the boss.** While HMOs might give short shrift to an individual member requesting information, they'd find it difficult to ignore an employer who's channel-ing hundreds of thousands of health care dollars into their coffers each year.

Back in 1892, there was a managed health care problem similar to the problem we have today. The Bunker Hill Mining Company of Idaho took a dollar a month out of every employee's paycheck and used the funds to build a hospital. When the miners realized it was costing the company only a few cents out of each dollar to run the hospital, they protested. In fact, they blew up the company's main smelter. It was the first violent protest against managed health care, according to an Internet article by Dr. M. Roy Schwarz of the American Medical Association. (For the record, I don't advocate this kind of violence.)

Someday, physicians will organize and go to the employers and say: "We can cut out the middleman—HMOs—and provide your employees with better care for less." There really is no reason why a private practice can't set this system up now. The only way to bring costs down, have quality service, and be able to choose your own doctor is to cut out the HMO. It's too bad an ex-convict had to be the one to say it.

CHAPTER 9

The "I"
Infomercials and Internet Fraud

What looks like a TV show, sounds like a TV show, but isn't a TV show? It's the infomercial, the latest innovation in advertising. You've seen them on Saturday mornings—everything from Don Lupre's 900 numbers to cooking shows. Movie stars or athletes get in on the act, including Victoria Principal or Cher hawking skin care or hair care products, or Bruce Jenner promoting exercise equipment.

My concern is twofold: First, I am concerned with the get-rich-quick philosophy, and second, I am worried that consumers are being manipulated, usually by celebrities, by the thousands.

Don Lupre has made a fortune advertising 900 numbers in newspapers throughout the country. He spends his whole infomercial appealing to the greed of those who watch and want to be just like him. It concerns me that the success of a few businessmen can make the multitudes believe that they, too, can get rich quick. Most business opportunities take time, effort, and money. I'm sure if you followed Don's techniques you, too, might be successful, but the infomercial makes it look too fast and too easy. Lupre's infomercial is a perfect example of hype built on a one-sided story.

My personal favorite is the Anthony Robbins infomercial. This is what I believe to be the granddaddy of celebrity infomercials because so many are used in different capacities. The infomercial is about Anthony Robbins (for the record, I don't have anything bad to say about Anthony Robbins's materials; I am only using the format of his infomercials), a celebrity in his own right. His co-host is Hall of Fame quarterback Fran Tarkenton. The voice-over announcer for the show is radio show personality Rick Dees. The other announcer is Leeza Gibbons, a TV talk show host. To add to his credibility, Robbins highlights how he has helped NBA teams such as the San Antonio Spurs, focusing on star center David Robinson. Ironically, Anthony Robbins, who is one of the best, if not the best speaker in the world, also trains top salespeople globally! Does a consumer have a fighting chance when faced by the best?

Seen increasingly on cable and independent television stations, many commercials have the look, feel, and duration of real TV programs, often imitating the format of genuine talk shows or investigative consumer news programs. Does this fall under the category of trickery and deceit? The product being sold is often discussed as part of the program and touted by paid "experts," "moderators," or "reporters." The shows range in length from fifteen to thirty minutes long and may even be interrupted by realistic-looking advertisements for the product with ordering information. Consumers may find it difficult to tell the difference between an infomercial and an independent TV program, in which the content of the show and the advertisements are separately developed and paid for.

Most physical fitness products use so-called experts. I say so-called because we have abused the term *expert* in this country.

Anyone with a degree is considered an expert in his or her field. I drive a car every day, but that doesn't make me an expert at driving. One infomercial called the AbTrainer claims to have the trainer who trains the trainers. This, then, is the expert of experts, right? My question would be, who trained *him*?

As part of its job of monitoring national advertising, the Federal Trade Commission (FTC) investigates infomercials that do not disclose their true advertising nature. The FTC has already accused one company of misrepresenting itself as a TV consumer news program.

There is nothing illegal about advertisers paying for infomercials to sell products. It is important to remember, however, that product claims made on such programs are those of the biased advertiser. I am all for capitalism and business opportunities, but not at the expense of failing to disclose all facts to the consumer. I'm concerned that these infomercials are made to look like consumer help programs, not the commercials that they are.

Here are some tips on how to spot a paid advertisement.

1. Look for commercials similar to the program content. Infomercials always have a segment that tells how to purchase their product. Some programs display an 800 number on the screen throughout the show. Most consumer help programs do not provide ordering opportunities through their program.

2. Check for sponsor identification at the beginning or end of the show. The Federal Communications Commission requires television stations to disclose who is paying for the infomercial.

3. Be careful in evaluating health claims or get-rich-quick claims in infomercials. These ads usually promise great

results and give just enough information to get you to call. TV does not validate a business. Remember, ZZZZ Best advertised on TV.

4. Be aware that celebrities and experts who endorse a product are often being paid by the advertiser. This is an obvious conflict of interest in the objectivity of the expert or celebrity.

If you decide to purchase a product advertised on an infomercial, you have certain protections under the law if you make your purchase by credit card or if you make your order or payment by mail.

Make sure that there is a specific shipping and handling period. Most order forms say something like, "Add $4.95 for shipping and handling and allow thirty days for arrival." By law, a company should ship your order within the time stated in its ads. If no time is promised, the company should ship your order within thirty days after receiving payment. If the company is unable to ship within the promised time, the company must give you an option notice. This notice gives you the choice of agreeing to the delay or canceling your order and receiving a prompt refund. There is one exception to the thirty-day rule: If a company doesn't promise a shipping time and you are applying for credit to pay for your purchase, the company has fifty days after receiving your order to ship.

If you charge an item on a credit card by either telephone or mail, the Fair Credit Billing Act may offer you some added protection. For example, if you disagree with a charge on your monthly credit card bill (such as a wrong amount), send the credit card issuer a letter right away using the special "billing error address" given on your monthly statement or credit card contract. Include your name and account number; the date, type, and dollar amount of the charge you question; and why you think there was a mistake. The credit card company must respond to your letter and either correct the mistake or explain why the bill is believed to be correct. Send your letter as soon as possible. It must reach the creditor within sixty days after the first bill containing the error was mailed to you. The creditor must acknowledge your complaint in writing within thirty days after receiving it, unless the problem has been resolved. The creditor must resolve the dispute within two billing cycles (but not more than ninety days) after receiving your letter.

Mistakes do happen, so always check your monthly credit card statement to make sure the charges add up. Sometimes the mistakes are an intentional ploy to cheat people out of money.

If you bought an unsatisfactory product, you also may dispute the charge for that product and withhold payment on the disputed amount while the matter is being investigated. You must pay for any part of the bill that is not being disputed, including finance charges on the undisputed amount.

There are a few other rules regarding protection. First, if you have bought the item in your home state or within a hundred miles of your current billing address and the product cost more than $50, you have protection. Second, if you make a good faith effort first to resolve the dispute with the seller, then you are not required to use any special procedure. There are some exceptions. The dollar and distance limitations don't apply if the seller is also the card issuer or if a special business relationship exists between the seller and card issuer. Unfortunately, this may not be the case with most sales from infomercials.

The infomercial is a glorified sales pitch. The first deception takes place through the format, which is designed to trick people into believing that the infomercial is not a commercial. The nature of the program is disingenuous from the start. The whole goal of the infomercial is to point out all the benefits of the product by eliminating all the objections. Of course, these infomercials don't come under the careful scrutiny of an investigative reporter. It seems as though all the questions are being asked and answered, but the reality is that they deceptively skirt the real issue: Is the product really what it claims to be?

Weight-loss products are notorious for advertising through infomercials. The benefit to these companies is that they don't have to answer the tough questions given by a Barbara Walters or a Diane Sawyer. Are there any side effects from the product? Do they have any unhappy customers? What is the success rate of weight loss from the product? It can't possibly work for everyone. It is pretty easy to find six happy customers with any business or product. We don't get those simple questions answered on an infomercial.

Some slick infomercials use nothing but the best technology, starting with the use of the television medium itself. People look beautiful and happy and life is perfect in these infomercials. Is this really what life is like? The implication is that if you buy their products, it will be. All of the representatives on infomercials, whether or not they are celebrities, use the best makeup, lighting, and clothing to enhance their appearance. We really have no idea what they truly look like.

Think about buying a piece of fruit at the grocery store. First, you look at the fruit to make sure it looks OK. Then, you feel the fruit to verify that it feels like it should. Next, we smell the fruit to make sure it's fresh.

When we make purchases on sight alone, there are clear limits on the due diligence we can exercise. Instead, we must rely on slick visual production. We can't touch the product to make sure it truly is good quality. We can't smell the product through the television.

Most people don't make it a habit of purchasing items from strangers who live on the other side of the country. Yet that is exactly what we are doing when we buy from certain infomercials. This new method of selling is as old as the pitchman on the side of the road. The goal for the pitchman is to work the crowd into a frenzy so that people don't think about what they are going to buy based on tangible evidence. The buying pattern is based on emotions and feelings. Infomercials feed off of this "impulse"-type environment. The old pitchman had plants in the crowd who praised the products and were the first to buy. Ever notice the audiences in the infomercials? They're always clapping excitedly over the product. Doesn't it seem logical to conclude that they, like the plants of the pitchman, are paid to react that way?

I want to make it clear that there *are* good products sold through infomercials. The key is to weed out the quality from the con.

Television is not the only medium to be abused by scam artists. Computers and online services have opened up a whole new world of potential fraud.

The Internet is rapidly growing into an exciting new avenue for worldwide communication and commerce. Consumers surfing the Net quickly discover a fascinating array of products and services available around the clock—everyone's open twenty-four hours a day. But one of the Internet's strengths—it's easily accessible to anyone with a computer and a modem—is also its biggest weakness—consumer vulnerability.

The Connecticut Department of Banking reported that a real potential for fraud unfortunately exists in cyberspace. First, the security of Internet business transactions has many

people concerned. In a communication medium characterized by its openness, how can consumers safely and privately
transmit credit card numbers and other confidential information to businesses? Second, the relative anonymity of the
Internet may mask illegitimate business motives. How can
consumers surfing the Net determine whether the "merchant"
behind a flashy home page is someone they can trust or a con
man with a computer?

Dishonest business practices claim victims daily on the
Internet through pyramid schemes, credit card theft, stock fraud,
phony Internet consulting, or any other fraud imaginable.
Internet ScamBusters is a free electronic newsletter that helps consumers protect themselves from Internet scams, misinformation,
and hype. It was born from the painful experience of three people who were scammed in one week. First, one person was
charged $1,000 to register a domain name. Second, a friend got a
proposal to put her company on the Web for "only" $300,000!
(They actually used the word *only*.) Third, a small business owner
paid $40,000 for work that should have cost about $1,500. These
three banded together to start *Internet ScamBusters*.

Almost every scam in this book could have been perpetrated
on the Internet. But in this chapter we will focus primarily on
some of the more popular and documented scams in cyberspace.

In Moorpark, a suburb of Los Angeles, four high school students were arrested in a computer scam. Andrew D. Blechman,
a reporter for the *Los Angeles Times*, reported that sheriff's
deputies arrested the four students on suspicion of illegally
downloading and using credit card numbers. Authorities were
alerted to the computer scam after a substitute teacher found a
student with a list of hundreds of credit card numbers.

"The students obtained the numbers from the Internet and
were using them to set up false America Online accounts, shop

on the Internet for a camcorder, and download pornography and pirated computer games," deputies said.

The students were using computers at both home and school to conduct their illegal activities. Police also suspect that the students were involved in the theft of a $1,900 laptop computer used by a disabled student and a $900 CD-ROM containing yearbook photographs of all students on campus.

Authorities said, "All four of the youths confessed to the crimes and were charged with computer access fraud—a felony—and two students were also charged with theft."

It's amazing how much damage some teenagers are able to do through the use of their home computers. And if high school students are perpetrating fraud over the Internet, we can be sure that highly skilled computer hackers and con men are also taking advantage of the system.

Some of the oldest cons in the book are recycled through the Internet. Pyramid schemes (see chapter 16) have been around for ages and the Web apparently has not been able to avoid them, either. According to the May 30, 1996, *Los Angeles Times,* one scheme advertised on the Internet bilked thousands of investors out of more than $6 million. The scheme's promise of huge investment returns spurred thousands of investors to plunk down anywhere from $250 to $1,750 to join. It is the FTC's largest case to date involving fraud on the worldwide computer network. The FTC obtained a federal court order temporarily halting the scheme, which it said was carried out by the firm Fortuna Alliance of Bellingham, Washington. The FTC also asked the court to issue a permanent injunction that would provide remedies for consumers hurt by the alleged scam.

The Internet has made it possible for these con men to avoid prosecution by the Postal Service by using the Web instead of the U.S. mail. This has given old schemes new life.

When I wanted to create hype for ZZZZ Best, I would utilize television commercials or appear on shows like "The Oprah Winfrey Show." But, for most, advertising is costly, and not everyone can get on Oprah.

Today, however, a small company can create its own hype relatively inexpensively through the Internet. A small company that doesn't have strong financial backing can create hype in its own company, thus raising the price of the stock and giving the company the necessary funds to operate business.

In fact, in the case of Comarator Systems Corp., the hype was extremely blatant. There were thousands of messages coursing through America Online as the stock soared from $36 million to $1 billion in just three days.

During a trading frenzy that set volume records on the NASDAQ stock market, computer chat rooms, bulletin boards, and discussion groups were littered with hundreds of electronic postings on Comparator. One newsgroup said, "Everyone who hasn't gotten in on this stock, get in now. Volume is approximately 25 million . . . share price jumped from 6 cents to 12 cents today!!! Don't miss the boat!!!"

More than 449 million shares changed hands over the next three days, until nervous regulators halted trading and launched investigations that culminated in a sweeping lawsuit filed against the company by the Securities and Exchange Commission.

New Jersey state securities regulators have identified the following as being among the most common investment fraud and abuse problems in the online world today:

Manipulation of obscure, thinly traded stocks. Most commercial bulletin-board services allow individuals to post messages under not only one alias but multiple aliases. Because it is nearly impossible for another subscriber to ascertain the true identity of the individual behind the message (or even if a series of messages are being entered by just one individual under various aliases), there is enormous potential for manipulation of little-known companies that have small float (the number of shares available to be bought and sold). Acting alone or with accomplices, a company insider, broker, public relations executive, or even just a large shareholder can leave numerous messages calculated to spark interest in an obscure stock. Among the most popular targets for cybermanipulation today are Canadian gold, silver, and diamond mining stocks.

Misconduct by phony or unlicensed brokers/investment advisers. Here, states are concerned that brokers may be attempting to drum up new business without approval of their employers and by liberally using illegal assurances about the potential for profit in certain investments. States are also concerned about brokers who may try to rope in new clients without regard for the state's clear interest in keeping individuals with a history of fraud and abuse outside the borders. Remember, if you don't know the people behind the investment, you're investing in the dark.

Undisclosed interests of promoters. The anonymity of cyberspace is exploited to the hilt by schemers who promote fraudulent and abusive investment schemes. In reading a bulletin-board message about a stock, you have no way of knowing if the person involved is a company official, a public relations representative, or an employee of a market-making brokerage firm. Has the person hyping the stock been paid to do so, and, if so, has that fact been disclosed? In some cases, the role of the person involved in the scheme is such that he or she is considered by regulators to be an "agent" of the stock issuer and, as a result, is subject to strict legal requirements regarding public statements, disclosure language, and penalties for international "misrepresentations and omissions" intended to move stock prices.

Promotion of "exotic" scams. Hundreds of messages have been posted in cyberspace promoting a wide variety of highly suspect, unregistered investment deals (e.g., wireless cable television "build-out" schemes, ostrich farming) as well as flat-out rip-offs (e.g., pyramid schemes, chain letters, Ponzi schemes). These so-called exotic securities may pose a greater threat to consumers than other investment-related cyberschemes, because out-and-out scams often appeal to individuals who think they are not sophisticated enough to speculate in legitimate stocks.

The following advertisement came across my desk regarding the booming business of Internet consulting. I've omitted the name of the company. This is how the ad copy went:

> Before I ever learned how to use a computer I had ads making money on the Internet. Over the past two years I've invented a lot of tricks to sell anything on line. NOW nearly everything I put on it EXPLODES!
>
> In 1995, for the first time ever, more computers were sold than TV sets. Recent advancements for Windows 95, America Online, and others have transformed the once complicated Internet into a fun, simple to use, Point and Click process.
>
> For less than one penny I reach over 1,000 people. I've put up ads and in less than 6 minutes gotten orders. Best of all, my fulfillment is done electronically: No postage, No Printing, No Inventory. GM sells cars on the Net, Reebok sells shoes. 15-year-old Luke Sims made $800,000 selling tips on video games. Bob Banks built a $15 million travel agency by offering a newsletter on the Net with 77,000 subscribers. He has no printing or postage cost, he just writes and clicks. Cindy's Bakery makes more money selling bread on the Net than their

14 bakeries combined. Washington's Best Coffees, a small coffee store, nets $15,000 a month from their ads. Beth Voorheis has made $100,000 in her first 6 months selling her hot sauce.

Almost every business and entrepreneur can profit from being on the Internet. So why are so few of them on it? Because they don't know how! And there is no one to show them. This has created an incredible need for Internet Consultants.

Entrepreneur magazine, in its December 1995 issue, ranked Internet Consulting #1, as the hottest business to be in. And you don't even have to know how to operate a computer. This is a business that can be run part-time from home.

I'm looking for trainable people to use my proprietary secrets for making money on the Internet in select territories in the United States and Canada. My first student who became an Internet Consultant is Brett Morgan; he is a full-time airline captain for a major carrier. Working part-time, he has made $50,000 in three months. You'll see him in the next infomercial. Now I'm ready to work with a few more people. If chosen, you will place my highly effective ads in your area as an Internet Consultant.

Ads like this one are very appealing to many investors and entrepreneurs, and although it sounds as though it will make all your dreams come true, I see a few danger signs in reading it. I also called the ad's 800 number for more information. These are the red flags that went up in my mind:

1. **"Before I ever learned how to use a computer."** This statement is to let the prospective consultant know that anyone can conduct this business. Although the

statement regarding use of a computer is true, strong selling skills are required for true success. And nothing about that is said up front.

2. **"Over the past two years I've invented a lot a tricks to sell anything on line."** Honest businesses don't need to rely on tricks for success. Remember, the definition of fraud is the use of trickery to gain an unfair advantage.

3. **"NOW nearly everything I put on it EXPLODES!"** This is a blatant attempt to try to guarantee success without actually guaranteeing success.

4. **"I've put up ads and in less than 6 minutes gotten orders."** Don't expect any business to succeed quickly, as this statement suggests. Notice he doesn't actually say whether he received two orders or 200.

5. **"No Postage, No Printing, No Inventory."** No investment, right? Wrong! When I called this ad's 800 number, I found out that there is a cost to become a consultant. Oh, the cost is a mere $2,500!

6. **"15-year-old Luke Sims made $800,000."** If a kid can make money, certainly you can, too. Now begin the testimonials, which I am sure are true, but do we have all the facts and information behind their success? And my first question is, how many others have failed? Almost every business opportunity has someone who is successful, but that doesn't mean that everyone genuinely has a chance for success.

7. **"*Entrepreneur* magazine ranked Internet Consulting #1."** Name-dropping is one of the most common

tools of the salesman. Notice the magazine doesn't rate this particular company as the hottest or #1, just the area of business it's in. Yet this company takes ownership of the ranking. This statement is supposed to be the icing on the cake by saying this is the best opportunity there is.

8. **"Now I'm ready to work with a few more people."** Let me tell you, *anyone* who pays the fee will be accepted. Don't think that you're getting personal, one-on-one instruction to start your business (which is clearly implied). Be ready to be given a notebook and a bill—and that's called "working with you."

9. **"If chosen . . . "** The pressure to act now is subtle yet present. There are no "ifs" about it—you pay and you become a consultant instantly.

Internet consulting can be a great opportunity, but the variables involved are a little more complicated than merely responding to an ad on a Web site. As in all advertising, the avenue in which you advertise and the cost can make all the difference in the world. We know that the Internet is full of money-making opportunities, but not all sites or servers are gold mines. Remember the fallacy of composition: The whole is not equal to the sum of its parts. Just because many people have been successful in the Internet business doesn't mean that all Internet business is successful.

If you're a shopper on the Internet, don't let technology make you susceptible to fraud. Just because you see a full-color ad on your expensive computer, don't think that those two facts guarantee protection. You must protect yourself. Guard your confidential information. The Internet is a great way to shop for products because its "stores" have the latest merchandise and they never close. Be cautious, though, when you decide to make a purchase. There are some steps you can take to reduce the potential for cyberspace fraud. I advise consumers NOT to give out personal information such as credit card numbers, bank account numbers, and ATM PIN numbers over the Internet. If you want to make a purchase, do it offline.

Remember the story of the Moorpark students I described earlier? They were able to access credit card numbers from purchases made on the Internet. Be sure you can confidently confirm an Internet merchant's business reputation before buying products from them.

Although there are some great advertising opportunities on the Internet, be sure to take the following precautions:

1. Don't buy the hype. Promised results don't mean anything to your business. Get referrals for other businesses who are advertising on the prospective site. Take a look at the current advertisers and call them to see what kind of response they are getting. Don't solely take the salesperson's word for it.

2. Take it easy. Invest slowly when advertising. Don't spend too much money too soon. Salespeople will tell you that in order to maximize your profits, you need to "think big." Every advertisement is a risk, so always conduct a test before committing too much money.

3. The test. Any true marketing plan is a long process, but never commit to a long-term contract without testing the waters first. All reputable companies allow for some kind of testing period. Good companies are not afraid to prove themselves.

4. Go on an information hunt. Gather as much information about the company as you possibly can. Don't rely solely on their advertisement or on a phone conversation. Anyone can look good on paper. Time and effort are always the vindicators of truth. Be patient. Take your time to investigate before handing your money over to someone.

5. Work person to person. Try to deal with a local vendor who has an office nearby. Do business as much as you can with people who can be reached. Doing business over the Internet can be very difficult to track. Find a local company, visit the office, and speak with managers and administrators.

6. Consult the computer geeks. Check computer trade journals and computer stores regarding the credibility or reputation of the site you are going to advertise on.

7. Check for smoke. Always check with the Better Business Bureau, Federal Trade Commission, and attorney general's offices regarding the company you are purchasing advertising from.

In television advertising, there are good channels and bad channels, good time slots and bad time slots. Cyberadvertising is equally competitive and confusing. Here are some final tips on how to protect yourself from some of the Internet scams and investment schemes:

1. Beware of get-rich-quick schemes. The online world is full of good and accurate information to help you make wise investment choices. Unfortunately, it is

also a haven for numerous investment scams and tricks that entice investors out of their money.

2. Online computer servers are not watchdogs. It's your responsibility to check out the companies you are giving your money to. Don't rely on others' due diligence.

3. Don't buy stocks from unknown companies and brokers. These types of stocks are the most susceptible to manipulation and fraud. Don't buy into chat-room hype. Rely on your knowledge of the company and their stock, not some stranger with a computer.

4. Never trust a stranger. What used to be common sense is now a con man's greatest tool. Whether he hides behind a post office box number or a bulletin-board alias or nickname, he is still a stranger. Hidden identity is a con man's dream. Would you trust a stranger at your door?

5. Make sure people you do business with are legitimate. Every business should be registered with the local county, either through a D.B.A. or a corporation.

The Internet is a wonderful vehicle for gathering information. In fact, most of the information in this book came from law enforcement Web sites found on the Net. But as I have stated before, con men exploit opportunity. And because of easy access, no internal controls, and hidden identities, the Internet has been and will continue to be a hotbed for fraud.

CHAPTER 10

The "J"
Job Searches

You're unemployed, with a spouse and two children. You've been searching the classified ads for months. All of a sudden, you find the perfect job. The job description fits your qualifications perfectly and the pay is exactly what you need, so you call and . . .

Unfortunately, from there the story turns into a Stephen King horror novel. Most con men recognize a need and meet it with a scam. Whenever someone is unemployed, the need is now and the need is great. Con men have no mercy, even when it comes to taking money from people who don't have jobs or who are searching for better opportunities.

"I was unemployed, so I called as soon as I saw the ad that guaranteed job interviews," exclaimed George P. of Cleveland. George called the 900 number advertised in a magazine. He heard a tape that repeated some job listings that appeared that same day in his local newspaper's classified advertising. He could have looked up those listings himself for free. Instead, his phone bill showed a $21 charge for that call.

Many jobless people like George are falling victim to job search scams. In fact, my local newspaper has an employment code for the consumer's protection. The *Daily News* Classified Department states that it maintains standards of advertising acceptability, under which "Employment Opportunities" advertisements must conform to the following standards:

1. All advertised statements must be accurate and not designed to mislead the reader.

2. Each advertisement must clearly indicate the type of employment offered.

3. Employment agencies advertising in the "Employment Opportunities" columns must conform to the policies of the *Daily News* and clearly state that they are an employment agency and indicate if the job is "free" or "fee." Any employment agency that refers job applicants to a training program or school that requires a fee must state "unqualified job applicants will be referred to a school; possible fee charged."

4. Advertisements for sales positions must clearly state the type of product or service to be sold. Specific earnings amounts in sales advertisements may be stated if qualified by type of remuneration such as salary, salary and commission, or commission. Earnings claims must be accurate and substantial.

5. Employment advertising for positions that require a training fee, the purchasing of inventory, sales kits, or any deposit, fee, or cost to the applicant of any kind must clearly state the specific requirement.

With fraud running rampant through our country, it's great to see that some publications are taking responsibility for these false ads. I can't tell you how many deceptive ads I see in top business magazines such as *Entrepreneur*. According to the *Denver Post*, forty U.S. newspapers have joined the fight by organizing what they call CatchScam. The participating papers have agreed to fax the Federal Trade Commission any ads that look suspicious. The FTC will then investigate the ads under question.

The back section of *Entrepreneur* is full of classified ads. Under Employment Opportunities, one ad read as follows: GET PAID FOR READING BOOKS! $100 EACH. This looks like a job opportunity, but in fact it is an ad that sells information. When you write or call, as I did, you will find that you need to send $29.95 for information on opportunities that pay for book readers. Even the information you are purchasing for $29.95 doesn't give you the names and numbers of publishers to call for a job. Unfortunately, I see book or information offers that read like job offers all too often.

In September of 1992 the FTC sued two companies advertising jobs using 900 numbers. These companies not only failed to disclose the cost of each call, which ranged between $10 and $18, but they also provided little, if any, information that would lead to a job. Some consumers had to call back several times to write down the recorded information and were billed for each call.

The FTC also sued two other firms that advertised they would find overseas jobs for up-front fees of as much as $600. One of the companies claimed it had information on more than 10,000 currently available overseas jobs and that its customers would be matched with at least three prospective employers. The FTC charged that few, if any, of the company's job seekers received even an interview, much less a job.

Fresh out of high school, a few young men answered an ad for jobs on a cruise ship. To make the proper arrangements, a $600 processing fee was needed to reserve a spot on the ship and arrange air travel. As in so many other cases, the boys lost their $600.

Beware of job opportunity pitches that guarantee placement in a job, claim no experience or special skills are needed, offer too-good-to-be-true wages, or offer overseas employment.

Frequently, a con artist who promotes a job opportunity scheme offers job training in a specific field such as truck driving, oil rigging, or heavy equipment operating at double or triple the applicant's current salary. The pitch assures a successful graduate of work with the same company offering the training. The trainee must pay for the training program, which turns out to be overpriced and often uncertified. Graduates will most likely not be placed in jobs because the company could never have enough positions for each graduate.

Sometimes con artists try to sell you a catalog containing the names of companies supposedly hiring workers for various jobs. Frequently, these jobs are said to be high-paying positions overseas. If you buy the catalog, which often costs $30 or more, you may find that the companies listed are not hiring. Any money-back guarantee that comes with your catalog will often have requirements that may be difficult for you to meet.

Be wary of ads that promise you a job with the U.S. Postal Service. In 1991, the Postal Service began to significantly reduce the number of employees in its work force. In 1992, a reorganization of the Postal Service eliminated tens of thousands of additional positions. The money you spend to obtain information on how to get a postal job may get you only generic information that is already available at no charge from the Postal Service and from some public libraries. Save your money and instead contact your nearest Postal Service employment office to see if postal jobs are available in your area and to obtain the necessary application forms.

The FTC suggests taking the following precautions before you spend money to respond to job ads or sign job-placement contracts.

1. Know what a 900 number call will cost before you make the call. Reputable employment service companies will state these costs up front. If you have a problem with charges on your phone bill for 900 numbers because of calls made to a fraudulent business, contact your telephone company immediately. You can ask your phone company to delete the charges, although the company is not legally obligated to do so. AT&T cannot disconnect your phone for failure to pay. For policy information related to other carriers, call the carrier or the FTC.

2. Realize that employment service firms can only *promise* to help you find a job; they cannot *guarantee* that they will find you a suitable one. There are no guarantees in the job placement industry, period!

3. Check with your local consumer protection agency and the state attorney general's office to see if they have received any complaints about an employment company with whom you intend to sign a contract.

4. Ask the company for references and call them. Asking questions is great, but you must follow through. Make sure the list is not "cherry-picked." Ask for a random reference list, not just the best testimonials. Every company has a few happy customers.

5. Most important, read your contract carefully before you sign it. Nobody reads contracts anymore because of laziness and time. Take the time to read and ask questions to clarify the contract. If need be, you can make changes to the contract as you read it over. If the employment service representative makes claims that are not in the contract, remember that the contract is what counts.

It is becoming too expensive to be trusting nowadays. I read a story in the *Chicago Sun-Times* that reminded me that the reason why we can't trust is because cheating is practiced by almost everybody:

It's OK, Son, Everybody Does It
by Jack Griffin

When Johnny was 6 years old, he was with his father when they were caught speeding. His father handed the officer a twenty-dollar bill with his driver's license. "It's OK, son," his father said as they drove off. "Everybody does it."

When he was 8, he was present at a family council meeting presided over by Uncle George on the surest means to shave points off an income tax return. "It's OK, kid," his uncle said. "Everybody does it."

When he was 9, his mother took him to his first theater production. The box office man couldn't find any seats until his mother discovered an extra $5 in her purse. "It's OK, son," she said. "Everybody does it."

When he was 12, he broke his glasses on the way to school. His aunt Francine persuaded the insurance company that they had been stolen and they collected $75.

"It's OK, kid," she said. "Everybody does it."

When he was 15, he made right guard on the high school football team. His coach showed him how to block and at the same time grab the opposing end by the shirt so the official couldn't see it. "It's OK, kid," the coach said. "Everybody does it."

When he was 16, he took his first summer job at the supermarket. His assignment was to put the overripe strawberries in the bottom of the boxes and the good ones on top so that the nice strawberries would show. "It's OK, kid," the manager said. "Everybody does it."

When he was 18, Johnny and a neighbor applied for a college scholarship. Johnny was a marginal student. His neighbor was in the upper 3% of his class, but he couldn't play right guard. Johnny got the scholarship. "It's OK, son," his parents said. "Everybody does it."

When he was 19, he was approached by an upper-classman who offered test answers for $50. "It's OK, kid," he said. "Everybody does it."

Johnny was caught and sent home in disgrace. "How could you do this to your mother and me?" his father said. "You never learned anything like this at home." His aunt and uncle were also shocked. If there's one thing the adult world can't stand, it's a kid who cheats.

There are a number of resources that you *can* trust and that also happen to be free. If you are looking for a job and want assistance in doing so without spending much money, consider the resources listed below.

1. The classified ad section of your local newspaper lists numerous job opportunities.

2. Your telephone directory can tell you how to contact your local community and social service organizations.

3. State job service offices post job vacancies. They also provide counseling and referrals to other job sources.

4. Local and county human resource offices and information referral services offer placement assistance. They can give you the names of other groups that can help, such as labor unions or federally funded vocational programs.

5. University and college career service offices usually limit their assistance to students and alumni, but some may let you look at their job listings. They may be a good reference for other job sources.

6. Local libraries also can be a helpful source. Ask the librarian for materials that can show you how to write a résumé, conduct yourself in an interview, and compile a list of companies that you might contact about job openings.

In a job search, desperation and impatience come with the territory. Many salesmen sell on the basis of emotion rather than on sound logic or level-headed thinking. Don't let your guard down, even when it seems that someone is trying to help you. When money is involved, your trust should be replaced by detailed examination. Remember, there is a con for every circumstance.

Finally, beware of what kind of job you take. Many innocent people who have taken jobs in telemarketing, advertising, or direct mail find out that the products they were selling either didn't exist or were severely overpriced. None of the 1,300 employees who worked for me at ZZZZ Best knew that 86 percent of our earnings were fraudulent, and they had a hard time explaining such ignorance to law enforcement. Know the company, its management, and the product you are representing before you take the job.

CHAPTER 11

The "K"
Knock, Knock

Knock, knock jokes have always been harmless schoolyard fun. Today, however, the term *knock, knock* has come to symbolize a serious problem plaguing the American people. Frauds and scams have come to our doorstep. Con men and women are walking our streets and knocking on our doors, posing as Social Security workers, termite inspectors, police officers, bank agents, utility workers, and home improvement reps. In writing this chapter, I owe a special thanks to Don Wright, who has been on my radio show, "Consumer Hotline," several times and on whose book *Scam!* we have heavily relied for most of our true stories.

One day Tony Jaime, the producer of my radio show, heard a knocking on his door. When Tony opened the door, he was greeted by a man in his early thirties. "Hello!" the man exclaimed. "You might remember me from last year. I was here last year collecting money for the Los Angeles Mission."

He then showed Tony a folder that looked like it had been pulled out of a dumpster. In the folder he had a couple of pages of typed letters that looked semilegitimate except for the fact that they were torn and crumpled. The man looked as though he had just come from the mission himself! As Tony listened to the pitch, he was told that the best part of making a donation today was that the mission would not be calling him or putting him on a mailing list. "Any loose change or cash you have would gladly be accepted," said the man. Tony smelled trouble, so he politely declined. The man left, talking to himself under his breath.

Solicitors are constantly roaming the streets asking for neighborhood donations. I even heard of a report of con men posing as Boy Scout leaders collecting donations. Knowledgeable, seemingly sophisticated people are defrauded every day by con artists. All it takes is the right scheme, at the right time, by the right operator. Older people, especially women, tend to be most vulnerable. Loneliness, concern about retirement cost, and a basic trustfulness all contribute to older people's vulnerability.

Take notes and beware of the following types of scams that are being perpetrated even as we speak. Alice Carlson (not her real name) was in her seventies. She had lived alone for eight years since her husband died, and although she was in excellent health, she was not physically able to keep her home as well maintained as it had been before her husband passed away. Her sons promised to make repairs for her, but they were busy with their own families. A few days earlier, rainwater had leaked into her kitchen.

It was perfect timing for Paul Burke. When he pulled up into Alice's driveway, she was very happy to see that someone could finally help her. "I was doing some roof repair down the street," he said, "and your neighbors said that you might need some help as well." Burke said that he had some leftover sealer material in his truck and could offer it to her for a great deal.

"How much do you charge?" asked Alice.

"I can do the whole job for ten dollars," responded Burke.

Alice agreed. Burke poured fifty gallons of driveway sealer material into his 200-gallon tank and mixed in 55 gallons of silver paste. He worked about two hours before he came down from the roof.

"Mrs. Carlson, the roof is soaking up the sealer. I want to make sure it's OK to continue since the job's already run into quite a lot of money."

"But I thought you said the job would cost only ten dollars!" Alice protested.

"Yes, ma'am, that's true. I will only charge you ten dollars for my labor, but you must understand I need to be reimbursed for my sealer material. I can't just give you free materials."

"Of course not, young man," said the widow. "How much do I owe you?"

"I've used a hundred gallons of sealant, so to complete the job it will take three hundred gallons. I buy sealant for fifteen dollars a gallon, so the total bill will be forty-five hundred, plus the ten dollars." The widow, angry only at herself, wrote the handsome, polite workman a check. When recalling the incident for Don Wright, Burke said, "The woman was a real sucker."

Con men also rip off unwary customers on materials. Barns, houses, and fences are often painted with mixtures consisting of up to 80 percent gasoline and 20 percent paint. Not exactly fireproof!

On a beautiful spring morning in June, a man named Lawrence Williamson drove his pickup truck through an affluent suburb of Indianapolis. His son and teenage nephew were in the bed of the truck along with buckets of two-foot-tall tree saplings. The magnetic sign on the side of his truck read "Williamson Landscaping."

Larry approached Mr. Bell's home. "Hi! I'm Larry Williamson

with Williamson Landscaping, and these are my two sons. We've just finished planting some baby oak trees for your neighbors and we have a bunch left. I'm afraid they are going to die if we don't plant them quickly. If you're interested, I'll give you a bargain price."

Bell looked at the saplings and asked, "How much do you want for them?"

Larry said, "We'll sell them for fifteen dollars apiece. I usually sell them for fifty."

Bell turned to his wife. "How many should we take?"

She replied, "At that price, take twenty."

Bell wrote a check for $300 and Williamson reminded him to water and fertilize the trees faithfully for two weeks. Bell did as he was instructed, but soon the limbs withered and turned black. Bell contacted an Indianapolis tree surgeon for help.

"I don't know how to tell you this, but you've been swindled. If you dig up those saplings, you'll find that they don't have any roots. In fact, they're not saplings at all. They're probably just limbs," explained the surgeon.

Williamson Landscaping swindled at least ten Indianapolis-area families during a five-day period. The average score was $200 per family.

In Winterhaven, Florida, a couple of fast talkers convinced a blind man that his trees needed trimming badly. They said they'd do it for $50. When it came time to pay the con artists, the blind man was far too trusting. He had cashed his Social Security check that morning but had failed to sort his bills in order to know exactly how his $1, $5, $10, and $20 bills were placed in his wallet. He asked the con men to take out the $50 in five- and ten-dollar denominations. Unfortunately, the men took seven of his $20 bills.

As you can see, the con man will go to any extent to defraud a customer. Larry Williamson used two children, while two other con men deceived a handicapped man.

Gene was aware of travel trailer sales scams but he didn't know that the same people conned homeowners on driveway work. Henry Cooper told Gene that he could patch and seal his driveway for a good price. Gene hired Cooper to fix the driveway for $450. He paid Cooper $350 in advance and withheld $100 until the work was completed. Cooper did a terrible job. When Gene demanded that the work be done right, the middle-aged Cooper packed up his tools and drove away with the $350. The sealants used for such jobs are worthless mixtures of watered-down ingredients. About all the sealants do is change the color of the roof or driveway.

Before I started up ZZZZ Best, I used to use a watered-down sealant on carpets. In fact, on one occasion, when I was assisting another carpet cleaner, we ran out of the sealant, so I was told to use plain old water. We shamelessly charged our customer $100 for that service.

Sometimes we are approached by what seem to be legitimate professionals. Utility men, termite inspectors, bank agents, and so forth appear to have a good reason for entering your house. Posing as utility company inspectors, swindlers inform elderly residents that the utility company requires homes to be grounded and protected against lightning damage. They offer to do the work for $200 as a "favor." They proceed to nail two feet of lightning rod to the ridge of a roof, then wrap ten or twelve feet of aluminum cable around it. One end of another cable is stuck into the ground. The rest of that cable is nailed to the side of the house, and the other end is stuck under a roof shingle so that, from the ground, it appears that the two cables are connected under the roof. The entire device is worthless, and yet many people fell for this scam.

Two men claiming they represented Roberts Lightning Protection Company told a farmer in Marshall County, Indiana, that they had been hired to examine his lightning-rod system. While the farmer talked with one man, the other examined the farmer's system and then showed the victim wires that appeared to have been cut. "Lightning has already struck your system, and it has been destroyed," the farmer was informed. "To prevent your house from burning down in the next electrical storm, you'd better get it repaired."

The men offered to repair the system for $32.36, but when the job was completed, the farmer was presented with a bill for $323.60. Beware of changed bills. Fortunately, the farmer caught the "error" and reported the men to the police.

The day after Paul Burke pocketed $4,510 of Alice Carlson's retirement fund, he was already planning his next hoax. Using names, addresses, and phone numbers of elderly people he had met while patrolling neighborhoods, he came across Mrs. Smith.

He dialed her number and gave her the following spiel: "Mrs. Smith, my name is Detective Paul Burke. Do you have a savings account at the branch of the First National Bank? You do! I thought so. The president of the bank gave us your name and said you might be willing to help us in an investigation. One of the employees at your bank has been embezzling money out of people's accounts. We think we know who it is. Can you help? Go to the bank and withdraw all of your money. Take it home with you and I'll meet you there. We'll record the serial numbers on all the bills. Then you give the money to me, and I'll take it back to the bank and deposit it in your account. We can catch him with the marked bills."

Mrs. Smith enthusiastically agreed. She went to the bank and withdrew $10,000 from her savings account. Fortunately, on the way home she recalled a story she had heard on the news about con men who pose as police officers. She called the local police station. After she made her report, the police went home with her to wait for Burke. He never showed up.

In Dayton, Ohio, a seventy-six-year-old woman was swindled out of $500. The man identified himself as an employee of Dayton Power and Light Company. Guessing that she paid her bills in cash, he informed her that her last payment was made with counterfeit money. (If she would have said that she paid with a check, he would have apologized for the mixup.) Of course, the woman was shocked. "Gather up all your ten- and twenty-dollar bills and we will check them out for you," the man instructed. Holding the money in his hands, he appeared to dial a number, then read off the bills' serial numbers. He handed the phone to the woman. She spoke into the phone and when no response came, she turned to the man, only to find that he was gone.

Mr. Boyles was scammed in a home improvement swindle. During the scam, the con artist learned where the old man hid his life savings inside his mobile home. Several months later, three men knocked on Boyles's door and introduced themselves as representatives of the Social Security Administration. They said he was scheduled to receive an $80 increase in his monthly check, but they needed to verify the condition of his living quarters before they could approve the increase. After the men "inspected" the mobile home and left, Boyles discovered that his entire life savings of $70,000 was missing.

Are you crying yet? No matter how many stories I hear, it doesn't get any easier to listen. Here are some steps to take to prevent yourself from becoming a victim.

1. Don't think you're too smart for this to happen to you. Con men are extremely persuasive. Con men love when victims think they are too smart.

2. Don't open the door to strangers, ever. A stranger is someone you don't know. That includes utility workers, mail carriers, telephone workers, garbage collectors, social security reps, and even police officers. All these people can be talked to through the screen door. If you don't have a screen, I would suggest purchasing the new steel screen doors. A police officer can give you the name and number of his station for you to check over the phone.

3. Always get a written estimate. Make sure that the costs of labor and materials are fully disclosed.

4. Never pay cash. This allows you some time to cancel the check if there are any problems. Remember, the check can be cashed immediately, so I suggest allowing work to be done only on Sundays so that you have an extra day.

5. Purchase the materials yourself. Don't allow a traveling repairman to use his own materials. Most cons are perpetrated at the materials level. Overcharging for inferior materials is a common con.

6. Get ten referrals from any traveling handyman. I say ten because it is too easy to get a couple of people who have not yet discovered that they have been scammed. Get five current referrals and five at least a month old.

7. Check with your local police department regarding home improvement scams. Usually these types of scams happen in clusters. The police usually have reports of active scams.

8. Never pay any up-front costs. If money is needed for materials, purchase the materials yourself.

9. Beware of high-pressure sales. Understand that these people are calling you—you are not calling them. A pushy sales pitch is a dead giveaway for a swindler.

10. Did I mention not to open doors for strangers?

As Don Wright reports, in a nationwide study of consumer fraud, nine out of every ten victims of consumer fraud do not even bother to report it to the police. Fifty percent of the victims felt they had no right or duty to complain; 40 percent believed the authorities could not be effective or would not want to be bothered; 10 percent were confused about where to report such victimization.

In chapter 3, I introduced the con-artist clans called Travelers. Don Wright says America has more than 8,000 of these traveling crime families, who are primarily of Scottish, Irish, and English descent. These families are called Travelers because they travel throughout America from state to state and town to town. Travelers often meet up for parties so that they can brag about their latest scams. Police officers and Travelers themselves estimate average earnings of $200,000 per year per family, from a combination of truck work, shoplifting, home improvement, and home invasion scams.

Jimmy Burke, a Traveler, was a skilled shoplifter by age seven. At eleven years old, he earned $4,000 a week, shoplifting and paving. By fourteen, he lived and traveled on his own. By eighteen, he was earning nearly $300,000 a year. When he was thirty-two, he planned the biggest scam in Irish Traveler history: $3 million.

The 8,000 Traveler families make up more than 15,000 traveling cons. These families are born and raised to swindle and scam. Kids begin by shoplifting or selling worthless purses door to door for high prices. I interviewed Wanda Mary Normile, the sister of Jimmy Burke. She explained that growing up as a Traveler is a way of life. Stealing, lying, and cheating are the morals of a Traveler. *Not* to steal would be criminal.

Many of the Travelers' parties are meeting places for prospective couples. Each person has to prove himself or herself as a true Traveler. The men must be able to pull off a roofing and driveway job with ease, while the women must prove that they are skilled shoplifters. Modern-day Travelers are much like the Gypsies of old. Gypsies are still around and should not be confused with the select group of Travelers.

In January, English Traveler Tommy Young stopped at the residence of an eighty-five-year-old blind woman who was living on a disability pension. Young offered to clear her home's sewer pipes for $100. After he did the work and was paid, he looked at her house and said, "Lady, you need some roof work done."

She said, "Well, I can't afford that right now."

Young answered, "You can't afford not to do it. Your roof could collapse the next time it rains."

"Oh, my. What should I do?"

Young explained that he didn't do roofing, but he knew someone who could. One of his Traveler partners came over the next day, sprayed diluted paint on her roof for twenty minutes, and collected $500.

Travelers like to scam the same person twice. Often traveling with family members, Travelers will prey on the same victim with different scams. Whatever the need, there is a scam.

A trio of English Travelers, Jack Harris, Rick Harris, and Mike Hanrahan, were on the run from the police in Kansas and were believed to be camped in a park on the outskirts of Lafayette, Louisiana. They offered residents of southern Kansas City free termite inspections. They told the homeowners that termites were present in their homes. They offered to exterminate the termites for prices ranging from $280 to $550, and they provided five-year guarantees. One homeowner called the Kansas Consumer Protection Agency to examine his house. They found no evidence of termite damage. The Travelers escaped again, but not before they collected at least $1,180 in "extermination" fees.

Most stories end like the ones you've just read. Our last story shows how one man's due diligence enabled police officers to arrest one Traveler. When Robert McDowell answered his doorbell one Saturday in May, little did he know what was about to happen. George Stewart, who was about forty years old, said that he had just finished a local roofing job and had some leftover material. He offered to put some acrylic roof coating on McDowell's roof. Normally, Stewart charged $375, but he said he could do it today for $200. Stewart waved a Perma Rock brand acrylic roof coating brochure by McDowell's eyes to assure him of the quality.

McDowell said that he couldn't pay until Monday, but Stewart agreed to do the job anyway. After the job was done, the roof looked like it had been sealed. The men agreed to see each other again on Monday. McDowell was suspicious, because the sales pitch was a little too smooth. He called a neighbor, who was an experienced contractor, to take a look at the job. The neighbor took a hose and simply washed away the work that had been done by Stewart.

When Stewart came to collect his money, the police were waiting. Incredibly, he and his cronies had coated between 400 and 500 roofs in the Rio Grande Valley during a two-week period, swindling homeowners out of nearly $100,000!

Note that McDowell didn't pay the men anything up front. He also waited to pay the balance until the weekend was over. Then he sought the advice of an experienced contractor to check up on the work. By doing just these three things, he was able to protect not only himself but others as well. Although his due diligence wasn't perfect, it was enough.

So the next time a stranger comes to your door selling anything other than Girl Scout cookies, tell him or her you're not interested. If the solicitor insists on knowing why, explain that a former carpet cleaner turned fraud hit man warned you that if it sounds too good to be true, it's probably ZZZZ worst.

CHAPTER 12

The "L"
Long-Distance Calling

In 1976 the first prepaid phone cards were introduced in Europe. Since then such cards have been introduced in the United States. Marketing departments for telecommunications companies have been hard at work over the last few years promoting prepaid long-distance calling cards. As a result, the prepaid card market is expected to top $2 billion in sales by the turn of the century, according to *Telecard World* magazine.

Americans are always looking for ways to save money. Long-distance telephone calls can add up quickly, especially when calling loved ones. We hear about special long-distance rates from big companies such as MCI and Sprint, but what about all those other companies? Claiming to save the consumer more money, many small companies—legitimate and illegitimate—are sprouting up.

My radio show producer received a direct-mail piece offering incredible savings on long-distance phone calls. The prepaid long-distance phone card offered 10 percent and 25 percent discounts. In order to receive the 10 percent discount, the customer had to prepay for a year at a minimum of $10 a month. Every call after the initial $10 would receive the 10 percent discount. When my producer called the 800 number, it had already been disconnected. Remember, the "premise" is only as good or stable as the company behind it!

Phone cards are not the same as calling cards because they function in opposite ways. A prepaid telephone card is a debit card and represents phone time that has been paid for in advance. A person making a long-distance call with a calling card is actually using it like a credit card and thus is promising to pay the phone company at a later date, usually at the same time as their monthly statement.

Most phone cards sold in the United States are of the remote memory type, that is, the value of the card is not on the card itself but rather is stored on computer. These cards can be used with virtually any type of phone. There are also cards that have their value stored on a magnetic or optical band or in a silicon chip embedded in the card. These stored-value cards are inserted into specially designed public pay phones that keep track of the value of the card as it is used.

Phone cards have become popular because they are so easy to use. The user first dials an 800 number to access the phone company's network and enters a personal numeric code, usually referred to as a PIN, to access his or her account. Then the caller dials the number he or she wishes to call. If the user has a stored-value card, he or she simply inserts it into a specially designed public pay phone. Most cards, regardless of type, provide excellent voice prompts to guide the user through the process.

If your card runs out of value, after dialing your PIN you will usually hear a voice prompt informing you of the balance remaining in your account. If your account should be depleted before you have terminated your call, most services provide an audible warning. Most cards are rechargeable. Your card should have an 800 number for servicing and recharging accounts printed on the back.

The appeal of these cards is obvious. It is so much easier to remember a PIN number than carry around change. Business travelers in particular like the convenience of phone cards. Savings is the main reason for their popularity. Usually prepaid long-distance time is priced at a flat rate per minute. This allows for more calls during peak hours at further distances. The savings can be as much as 50 percent compared with the cost of the same call made with a phone company calling card.

Also, the liability of phone cards is much lower. Calling cards have no limit as to the number of calls a person can make. If a calling card is stolen, thousands of dollars can be charged to the card before the owner even realizes the card is missing. If you lose a prepaid phone card, the amount of your loss is limited to the value of the card.

Competition has made choosing the right company a difficult task. As more and more companies enter this lucrative market, the consumer may find it difficult to choose the right company. This provides the perfect setting for fraud. Con men are always ready to take advantage of a great opportunity to mock a legitimate company with a scam.

In February 1996 the *Discount Long Distance Digest* reported on the frauds and scams that plague the Internet. Like multilevel marketing (MLM), the Internet can be a quick and inexpensive way to advertise. Though the Internet is certainly not the only outlet that scam artists use to recruit victims, it is currently the cheapest way for them to find others willing to peddle their product.

Most phone card scams we have seen involve MLM. MLM is a viable way to market many different goods and services (see chapter 13), but a disproportional amount of telecard scams involve companies that use MLM to recruit agents. Many request hefty up-front fees to become a distributor. These up-front fees help keep these companies afloat long enough to sucker in even more distributors, until the company can no longer cover up the scam and is forced to close down.

Although not every phone card company that requires up-front fees is a fraud, there is enough abuse to justify due diligence by the consumer. Here are some tips from the *Discount Long Distance Digest* to help you evaluate whether a company is running a scam or a legitimate business:

1. Common sense. Does the deal make sense? If a company is selling prepaid calling cards for $.099 per minute, watch out. Since the average cost to a calling card company to process these calls is actually MORE than they are charging, it is highly unlikely that the company will be around to actually provide services to its customers and pay its agents. A good deal is one thing, but a ridiculous offer is another.

2. Proper licensing. Make sure that the company is properly licensed in each state it is doing business in. Many prepaid card companies do not obtain proper federal and state licensing. This is a huge red flag. If a company doesn't have accountability, stay away from it.

3. Taxes. Make sure that all taxes are included in the retail price of the card. Many card companies never bother to mention taxes. If the company cannot give you specific information on the tax situation in each state it sells in, it is likely that you are legally responsible for collecting taxes if you become a business operator. As a

consumer, make sure that taxes are not added to the bill in your monthly statement. This could come back to haunt those of you who invest in a long-distance card company. Imagine getting a knock on the door from your state tax collection agency, demanding that you pay taxes on all the cards you have sold in the last few years. Ever heard of tax evasion?

4. Come-ons. Don't be tempted by come-ons like "Get in on the ground level!" or "Limited time offer!" or "This market is exploding! Act now!" Chances are, if the company is so desperate that it has to use these types of slogans, then the operators are either inexperienced or have a get-rich-quick attitude. Many long-distance phone cards are sold in conjunction with MLM opportunities. Not only are the cards sold as a great way to save money on long-distance calling, but you can also capitalize on a business opportunity as well.

5. Longevity. Check to see how long the company has been in business. Try to avoid doing business with a company that has been operating less than a year, especially ones that use MLM. If a company has been in business for only a few weeks, it has not yet had sufficient time to test its product or credibility.

6. Membership. Is the company a member of the Telecommunications Resellers Association (TRA) or another respectable industry trade group? There is absolutely no reason why it should not belong to at least one of the industry's top trade groups. If it isn't a member, ask why not. Whatever the excuse, it is not a good sign. Shady operators tend to keep a low profile

among their peers in the telecom industry, so you won't find many scam artists belonging to organizations like TRA.

7. Check up. Inquire or check with different industry trade groups to see if the company is a member. Check with the local Better Business Bureau to see if any complaints are pending. Check with the state Public Utilities Commission or Public Service Commission. Check with the state attorney general's office to see if the company is under investigation. If the company is publicly held, ask for a copy of its annual report from the investor relations department, or check with a stockbroker for info on the company. Check the Internet by using keyword searches via a search engine such as Lycos. Agents may have been complaining about them via the Internet for weeks or even months. Check with the company's local Chamber of Commerce.

8. References. Ask the company for references from satisfied customers. They should be able to supply you with a short list of happy customers. If not, ask why (maybe they don't have any happy clients). Ask who provides their underlying carrier services. Then check with the carrier to see if the phone card company is a valued customer. They should have a network account agent assigned to them if they are doing a decent amount of volume. Ask for that person's name, and call him or her. Ask who the owners, or principals, of the company are. The agent should be happy to tell you who owns or runs the company. Check to see if the company has recently changed

management or ownership, and if so, why? Ask if the company is currently operating under Chapter 11 (bankruptcy). You might not find out that it is financially troubled unless you ask.

9. Expiration. Always be sure to check the expiration date. Some cards become invalid after a certain date, so you could wind up with a card that is worthless.

Even after taking the key steps of due diligence, sometimes the scam still looks good. Most people find out after they sign up that the company they are dealing with is suspect. There are a few ways to know that you have a bogus long-distance phone card:

- If you dial the 800 access number on the back of the card and it refers you to a 900 number, hang up. Many 900 numbers begin with 800 to give the impression that the call is toll-free. No phone card should have a 900 number on it.

- After talking a few minutes while using the card, if you are interrupted by a voice from the operator asking you to please deposit another 50 cents, then fraud is probably involved.

- If the card has local access numbers that come from out of the country, check it out.

- If the card has any information regarding the county library on it, take it to your local county library to check it out.

Unfortunately, people like Steve M. don't realize how much of a problem long-distance phone fraud is. Steve, like many of us, wasn't looking to change his long-distance phone carrier until he received a phone call. The salesman, claiming to be from Sprint, offered him the Sprint Worldwide plan. The special promotion would allow calls anywhere in the United States and Canada, at any time of the day, for a flat rate of 10 cents per minute, discounted to 5 cents per minute for the first four months. Calls to Costa Rica, where Steve had friends, would only be 55 cents per minute, again at any time of the day, discounted to 27.5 cents per minute for the first four months.

Because Sprint was a reputable company, Steve decided to accept the plan. After receiving the paperwork, he realized there was a processing fee and that the first four months were prepaid based on the average of his normal long-distance phone rate. Steve sent in the money for the processing fee as well as copies of his last four long-distance phone bills. When everything was added up, Steve had mailed in approximately $500.

Steve became a bit uneasy when his check had cleared and he had not yet received his card. When Steve called Sprint's customer service number, he was informed that the Worldwide plan had not been offered for several months, and that they had no records of any promotion that would give those kinds of rates that Steve was promised. When Steve gave the salesman's name, no such name was found in the company records, and the address that he had mailed the check to was a P.O. box. Steve M. never got his money back!

Where there is a will, there is a way! Never let your guard down, even if someone claims to represent a major company. Don't assume that the person on the phone or the information you receive in the mail is legitimate until you check it out. In Steve's case, had he immediately called to verify the special promotion, he would have saved $500.

For those of you skeptics who may be saying, "It will never happen to me," or "This is too much work to do for a silly phone card," remember this: Perpetrators seldom make their living off of one big scam. They succeed by our propensity to "let our guard down" when it comes to purchases that are under $1,000. They strive to steal $100 from 100 people as opposed to $10,000 from one person. In the big picture of fraud, it's the seemingly small and insignificant consumer issues—like prepaid long-distance phone cards—that count.

CHAPTER 13

The "M"
Multi-Level Marketing

All you have to do is look in the "Business Opportunity" section of your favorite newspaper or magazine and you will see the following questions: Are you interested in an exciting business opportunity? How would you like to make money while working only part-time? Would you like to work at home? Can I show you the business of the future? How would you like to run a business with no inventory? If you don't have much money, I have a business for you. Would you like to retire early?

Have you ever been approached by a family member or total stranger with one of these lines? Welcome to the wonderful world of multi-level marketing (MLM), also known as network marketing, where all your hopes and dreams can come true.

Companies such as Amway, Avon, Excel, Herbalife, Mary Kay, and Tupperware have opened the doors to hundreds of copycats, some legitimate and some that hide as pyramid schemes. In this chapter I address MLM companies that are not pyramid schemes. (For more information on pyramid schemes, see chapter 16.)

To differentiate the legitimate MLM companies from those that are merely well-disguised pyramid schemes, I suggest asking the following three questions:

1. How much are you required to pay to become a distributor?

2. Will the company buy back unsold inventory?

3. Are the company's products sold to consumers?

If the startup cost is substantial, be careful. The startup fee in multi-level companies is generally small. Usually you are paying only for a sales kit sold at company cost. These companies will make it easy and inexpensive for you to start selling.

Pyramid schemes, however, make nearly all of their profit on signing up new recruits. Therefore, the cost to become a distributor is usually high. Caution: Pyramids often disguise entry fees as part of the price that includes purchase of training, computer services, product inventory, and so forth. These purchases may not even be expensive or required, but there will be considerable pressure to take full advantage of the opportunity.

If you could be stuck with unsold inventory, beware! Legitimate companies that require inventory purchases will usually buy back unsold products if you decide to quit the business. Some state laws require buybacks for at least 90 percent of your original cost.

If the company's products cannot be sold to consumers or there is no product, stay away! This is a key element. Multi-level marketing, on the other hand, like other methods of retailing, depends on selling to consumers and establishing a market. This requires quality products, competitively priced. Pyramid schemes, on the other hand, are not concerned with sales to end users of the product. Profits are made on volume sales to new recruits, who buy the products not because they are useful or attractively priced, but because they must buy them to participate. Inventory purchase should never be more than you can realistically expect to sell.

Let's define some common MLM terms:

Sponsor. To sponsor another individual is to bring him into the business by persuading him or her to sign an application and become a distributor. Jack receives no money for sponsoring Jill but agrees to train, supply, and motivate her. In turn, Jack receives a bonus from the corporation based on Jill's sales volume as she develops her business.

Leg. Every new distributor whom Jack sponsors becomes a "leg" in his organization. When Jack sponsors Jill, she is only one of his legs, along with anyone else whom Jill might ultimately sponsor. The number of legs Jack has is the same as the number of people he has personally sponsored.

Personal group. A personal group consists of all the distributors Jack has sponsored, plus those whom they have sponsored, and so on, up to the first direct distributor. To say that Joe is in Jack's personal group doesn't mean that Jack is his boss. It simply means that Joe is somewhere in the "family tree."

Distributor. A distributor is one who is officially signed up to sell the company product.

MLM. Multi-level marketing is a system of selling in which you sign up other people to assist you, and they, in turn, recruit others to help them. A percentage of the recruits' earnings goes to the distributor who signed up the recruit, and to the person who signed up the distributor, to the person who signed up that person, and so on. Thus the term *multi* (many) *level* (distributors) *marketing* (earning percentage dollars). Not all MLM plans work exactly the same, but this is the general idea. Usually there is an emphasis on recruiting more distributors in order to increase income. Products sold is also a key to making more money.

Multi-level marketing plans in and of themselves, as long as they are not pyramid schemes, are totally legitimate businesses. Like most products or businesses, the company is only as good as the person who is selling it. This chapter is dedicated to the con men who camouflage their deception under the umbrella of MLM. The con is simple: empty promises.

We will look at the ten most common empty promises I have seen in the multi-level marketing industry. Again, these are not restricted to MLM plans exclusively, so please pay attention to the methodology of the con.

1. MLM is a great business opportunity. The implication is that *anyone can do it*. Not true. We're each built differently. Just because the company is great and many of its distributors have had success does not mean that it is a great opportunity for you. Many people do not have the skills to run their own business. Running a business takes a lot of organization and discipline. Without a grasp of those skills, it is impossible to run a successful operation. Unfortunately, not everyone is a born leader. Many skilled craftspeople have decided to start their own business after working for someone else for many years. They know "the business" but they don't know how to "run the business."

Consider the following example: Steve, a skilled automotive detailer, decided to take advantage of a great business opportunity. A new "no water" cleaning product had been developed for detailers and consumers through an MLM plan. He knew his craft, and living in sunny, yuppie California, he knew the business was out there. What he didn't realize was the capital he would need to get started. Advertising, letterhead, business cards, licensing, and having a minimum balance in a business bank account were only a few of the costs. Steve also didn't have any idea where to go for many of these things. All he had to worry about before was detailing. Now he had to run a business.

To many of the people whom distributors go after, the perception of running a business is exciting and new. They believe or are told that since so many other people have been successful in the industry, they will be also. In his book, *Promises to Keep*, Charles Conn writes that Amway, probably the most successful MLM in the world, has a 50 percent fallout rate, while Avon has 150 percent fallout. And these are two of the most ethical organizations!

2. Making money part time. Every time I hear an MLM pitch, one of the first benefits the salesperson brings up is that it is only part-time. Now let's think this out logically. Amway says that a decent presentation takes about one hour. I consider part-time to be about three hours a day, three or four days a week. Given those numbers, a part-time distributor would give nine to twelve presentations a week. The best salesman in the world closes on the average about 10 percent of his presentations. If a distributor was a great salesman, he would close about one deal a week. Most sign-up fees are around $100, so his commission would be around $10. Now this does not include any products ordered, but I think you get the idea. Part-time sales just won't cut it!

Michael, a bright young man, was at the post office one day. A man in his late twenties asked Michael if he would be interested in an exciting business opportunity in which he could work part-time. Michael, always looking for a way to get ahead, decided to meet the distributor the next evening in a coffee shop. To his dismay, he learned the distributor held a full-time job that lasted from 9 A.M. to 5 P.M. every weekday. After a full day of work, the distributor had to drive one hour to the meeting place. The presentation lasted two hours and the distributor sometimes drove home without closing the sale. The distributor got home at about 9 P.M. I guess his idea of working part-time is working half of a twenty-four-hour day!

3. Working at home. The idea of working at home appeals to most of us. People with families don't want to spend two to three hours a day commuting to and from work. This also appeals to many homemakers who have children and are home all day. I see a couple of fallacies involved in MLM being a true work-at-home business. Although a lot of money can be saved on office rental space, many of the other advantages do not apply. Usually people who work at home save money on clothes, lunch, and auto expenses. Distributors, however, always have to look sharp, meet at restaurants, and drive to wherever a potential recruit may be. Finally, working at home can have many outside distractions, including personal phone calls, visiting friends, household duties, and taking care of children if one has them. Stacey, who was in her late forties, decided to work part-time from her home selling cookware. Within the first month, she was away from home at least three times a week, making dinner at strangers' homes. Working part-time and from her home actually took too much time *away* from her home.

4. Expand your free time with the family. No business starting from the ground floor is going to produce free time immediately. I don't like this sales approach because it goes to the heart of people's emotions. Free time usually means family time. Who doesn't dream of spending more time with the family? Free time is a dream that very few Americans enjoy. It takes

most businesspeople a lifetime to figure out that running a business can be a twenty-four-hour-a-day job.

I've never met anyone in MLM who had more free time as a result. In fact, it's when I'm enjoying my free time at the mall on a weekend that someone approaches me to offer me the opportunity of a lifetime.

5. MLM is the business of the future. I know that MLMs are here to stay, and with the computer age and the World Wide Web, we will see an increase in these companies. What is the future of MLM? All I know is that nothing is guaranteed. Who are MLM plans for, the consumer or the seller? The law of supply and demand always dictates the success of a business. As soon as someone can sell it cheaper and faster, then business is lost.

A caller to my radio show asked about the future of MLM. In his hometown of Spokane, Washington, which has approximately 250,000 people, he figured that if he were to believe the plan he was presented by an MLM company, he would have to recruit 279,936 people. The plan was to have six groups of six recruits each, recruit six more recruits, and so on through four more levels. The distributor showed him how much money that would generate. On paper it looked like 36 circles. The caller properly multiplied $6 \times 6 \times 6 \times 6 \times 6 \times 6 \times 6 = 279,936$. This certainly would not be a part-time task! In my opinion, the biggest problem that all MLM companies will face is oversaturation. This prevents me from recommending it as a business opportunity. There just aren't enough recruits for all the distributors. Everyone wants job security, and the distributor knows that if he can present a business opportunity with an endless future, then he is selling job security. *Nobody* can promise the future.

6. No inventory. This changes in structure from company to company, but what is the intended perception of "no inventory"?

When Susan began selling a health food supplement, one of the benefits was that she was promised she would not have to carry any inventory. She found out immediately that that was not true. When she signed up, she received an information notebook with tons of information packets. As part of her sign-up fee, she also had products to sell along with the free samples. To promote her business, she had business cards and letterhead made up along with some fliers. The company explained that when an order came in, all she would have to do is order that amount of product from the company, and they would send it right out to her. In business, most people want their products yesterday. In order to avoid delays in servicing her customers, she had to order and pay for products ahead of time. She also needed stamps and envelopes to ship the products out. Soon her little one-bedroom apartment looked like a warehouse. She was constantly selling and ordering products but she never made any profits.

Whether it be samples, paperwork, or actual product, every business has some form of inventory. Stefanie, a twenty-three-year-old mom, began selling a mineral supplement part-time. Not only did she have bottles of product stacked up for people to come by and pick up, but she also had boxes of promotional tapes that she mailed out to potential customers. Like Susan, her house began to look like a warehouse.

7. Low investment. Have you ever heard the saying, "It takes money to make money"? No business ever gets started for nothing. Most people who are approached by MLM distributors don't have an extra $2,000 lying around. *Low* is a relative term.

When Stefanie began selling her product, the introductory cost was only $24.95. She was told that she could start her business for under $25. This was the breakdown of some of her early costs: business cards = $30; product = $200; promo tapes = $200;

labels = $75; postage and promo piece = $350; envelopes = $70. Her $24.95 investment now totaled about $950. This was the absolute bare minimum she needed to start out with. For Stefanie and her husband, it was all their savings.

I've seen too many people begin MLM without knowing the total start-up costs. A low figure like $24.95 is deceptive.

8. How would you like to retire early? With fallout rates starting at 50 percent for Amway and 150 percent for Avon, it doesn't seem as though too many people can retire early. Early retirement is not a reality for most people. Retirement takes many years of successful planning and hard work.

Amway's founders Richard M. Devos and Jay Van Andel have been reported as being worth anywhere from $250 million by *Forbes* to $300 to $400 million by *Fortune* magazine. Today Amway boasts approximately 1 million distributors worldwide. Devos and Andel can retire anytime they want, but those 1 million distributors truly cannot.

9. MLM is the fastest-growing industry. *Fastest-growing* doesn't mean *best,* nor is it an indication of stability. Many different businesses are using MLM as a means of promoting their product. Due to the cost of advertising, businesses have cashed in on the opportunity to build a sales force without investing in people. Today's business has to pay an employee a minimum wage, benefits, insurance, and Social Security, to name a few of the costs. MLM allows businesses the luxury of having a sales force without those extra costs.

One thing *fastest-growing* doesn't mean is guaranteed success. Guaranteed success is exactly what a distributor is trying to deceive you into believing. I see people starting businesses all the time based on a temporary trend. Many MLM products are based on trendy diet supplements. When Rubbermaid hit the stores, Tupperware distributors took a big hit. Factors such as these are out of your control. Remember, not all MLM companies have been in business for twenty-five years like Amway.

10. It doesn't hurt to listen. The idea behind this statement is that it is no big deal to take a few minutes to listen to a business opportunity that could change your life. The presentation will be easy and painless, right? If you don't mind high-pressure sales pitches, super-hyped rallies, and mental manipulation, then it's true—it doesn't hurt to listen. But it all sounds pretty painful to me.

The most common stereotype of MLM is: This isn't Amway, is it? Why are people so suspicious about Amway? "60 Minutes" did an investigative story on them and they passed. Charles Conn, while doing an exposé on Amway, was converted. Yet most people associate Amway with pushy hardball sales. Yet it is the smaller, upstart companies that you must watch out for. Many of these MLM companies host huge rallies to promote their programs. These rallies whip people into an emotional frenzy. Stories of people who go from rags to riches excite even the dead. It all sounds so good, and after all, these nice people wouldn't intentionally hurt me, would they? The hopes and dreams of thousands of people are destroyed when they fall victim to MLM schemes.

The deception that takes place in these "empty promises" is cruel and inhumane at best. They are as wolves in sheep's clothing. MLM distributors are very friendly, almost too friendly, and they portray themselves as a "friend helping a friend." The wolves will say anything they think you want to hear in order to get you to sign up.

I am also concerned about the companies' emphasis on

material possessions. Every person I met in prison was moti-
vated by material possessions. People often become obsessed
and put pictures of homes or cars on their refrigerator as a
motivator. Remember, wealth-driven appetites are insatiable! I
fear for those distributors who are driven only by material
possessions.

Here are five quick steps to follow to protect yourself from a
bad investment.

1. Take your time. Don't let anyone rush you. Beware of
"Get in on the ground floor."

2. Ask questions about the start-up costs, about the
average earnings of active distributors (not just the
top salespeople), about the company's buy-back policy, about the company officers.

3. Get written copies. Obtain as much company literature as you can.

4. Consult with others. Check to see if there is any
interest in the products you might be selling. Ask
family and friends if they have ever tried them.

5. Practice due diligence. Investigate and verify all information. Do not assume that official-looking documents are either accurate or complete. Always check
out their claims.

As I was writing this chapter, I received a phone call from an
elderly lady who had been totally defrauded by an MLM. Ema
invested in two different MLM plans, one called Platnum and the
other Profit Builders International. Both plans had two things in
common. First, they both sold insurance investments. Second,
they were both total frauds. Ema was one of Profit Builders

International's top producers in 1993. She had just earned a new Cadillac Northstar and business seemed to be booming.

In September 1993 Ema was one of the first investors in Platnum. Her experience to date with Profit Builders International had been very positive, so she decided to invest in another MLM. Platnum supposedly sold life insurance policies that would be picked up by facilitators after the plan was in effect for five years. By December 22, 1993, the attorney general had shut down Platnum. The insurance policies turned out to be fictitious. To make matters worse, in 1994 her commission checks from Profit Builders began to bounce. By April everything had collapsed. The insurance never existed.

After the dust had cleared, Ema was out a total of $2 million. It was too late when she found out that one of Profit Builders' founders was Robert Darnel, who had started up seven MLMs. Another player in Profit Builders was Terrance Cope, also known as Sam Friday, who was in an MLM called the Pinnacle Club.

Of all network marketing companies currently operating in the United States, one in particular stands out for its broad violations of law and ethics. The name of the company has changed several times. Currently it is called Nutrition for Life and operates out of Houston, Texas. It was formerly Consumer Express of Lake Charles, Louisiana, and later Nutrition Express (also of Houston, Texas). C. J. Caton wrote a practical handbook about the MLM industry. His case study was Nutrition Express. He revealed that Nutrition Express committed fraud in almost every conceivable area of network marketing.

This chapter is meant not to discourage you from starting your own business, but to help you make an intelligent decision. Companies such as Amway, Avon, Excel, Mary Kay, Tupperware, and Herbalife are legitimate companies, but they do not have the time to investigate each and every distributor to make sure that he or she is representing the company correctly. Consider all the evidence before you dedicate your time and resources. Whether you're dealing with an Amway distributor or a new MLM, listen for those ten empty promises. Your money and your livelihood are at stake.

CHAPTER 14

The "N"
900 Numbers

The newest business opportunity fraud involves 900-number lines, warns the Federal Trade Commission. Today tens of thousands of consumers may be investing in this fraudulent business. These 900 lines are used for sports, stocks, soaps, horoscopes, psychics, charities, and businesses alike. Although 900 numbers can be used correctly, swindlers have manipulated the phone lines into powerful weapons of destruction.

Simply put, 900 numbers are pay-per-call services for a variety of information. These services allow a large number of callers to reach a single telephone number at the same time. The calling party is charged a fee greater than the cost of transmitting the call. The fee can be either a per minute charge (like $2.95) or a flat fee charge per call (like $9). Fees for pay-per-call services are set by the company that provides the program, not by the telephone company.

The Federal Communications Commission (FCC) has set some basic rules by which pay-per-calls must operate. The FCC's pay-per-call rules require that:

1. All interstate pay-per-call services must be offered through telephone numbers beginning with a 900 area code prefix.

2. No telephone company may disconnect, or interrupt in any manner, local or long-distance telephone service for failure to pay interstate pay-per-call charges.

3. Local telephone companies must, where technically feasible, offer their subscribers the option of blocking access to 900 numbers. This blocking must be made available to both residents and businesses.

4. Telephone companies must provide, at no charge, to all interested persons: (1) a list of all 900 numbers carried and identification of the service provider's name, business address, and business telephone number; (2) a short description of the service provided over each 900 number; and (3) the total cost or cost per minute and any other fees applied to each 900-number call.

5. Companies that use 900 numbers must maintain a local or toll-free telephone number to answer questions and provide information on subscribers' rights and obligations with respect to use of pay-per-call services. This number must be included on any telephone bill containing pay-per-call charges.

6. Telephone companies must provide, to all telephone subscribers, an annual disclosure statement explaining all rights and obligations of both subscribers and telephone companies with the respect to the use and payment of pay-per-call services. A brief statement

must also be included on telephone bills containing pay-per-call charges.

7. Pay-per-call services cannot be offered to consumers through collect telephone calls.

Businesses are using 900 numbers in new and exciting legitimate ways. I am all for small businesses and entrepreneurism, just as long as the skin of the truth isn't stuffed with a lie. For example, "The Arsenio Hall Show" promoted a 900-number poll on Michael Jackson's appearance for AIDS-related charities in June 1992. Twenty thousand calls were received in three hours, and the charities received $10,000 from the venture. The *Los Angeles Times* raised $280,000 in advertising revenue in 1995 with its Choose to Cruise Sweepstakes promotion using a 900 number. When you consider that the price per minute to callers was 50 cents, that's a huge response! WTTV, a Chicago PBS station, runs its fund-raising campaign over a 900 number. The station estimated a net of $200,000 after costs in 1994.

As you can see, many reputable businesses use 900 numbers. But when consumers see big companies using 900 numbers, this tends to lower their defense against small companies who use them, too. Perceived value and credibility are the keys to any good advertising campaign. The con man knows that if he can replicate a legitimate business with his scam, he can deceive many people.

The FTC has launched Project Buylines, which targets the latest and hottest business opportunity fraud today: the chance to operate your own 900-number line, according to Jodie Bernstein, director of the FTC's Bureau of Consumer Protection. "We came across a huge number of ads for these scams as we did follow-up on Project Telesweep, the massive federal crackdown on display rack and vending machine business opportunity frauds that netted nearly 100 cases. We found far fewer ads for vending opportunities, but the number of ads for 900-number business opportunities is skyrocketing," Bernstein says.

The following is an example of a 900-number business opportunity advertisement:

Earn $1.00/min. with your own FREE #*

1-900-123-4567 ext. 890
$1.99/min. 5 min. max.
must be 18

*with purchase of operation manual
$39.95 + $3.00 shipping and handling

Here is an ad I found on the Internet:

Learn how you, too, can become a millionaire in this explosive new industry! Now you can learn how imaginative entrepreneurs are using numbers to sell information of all kinds over the telephone. From the mundane to the exotic, hundreds of real-life programs covering every possible application are profiled here. Exclusive knowledge available nowhere else! Money is made in the 900-number industry—but by whom? This comprehensive guide tells what programs have been tried, which are still around, and which failed. Learn from the experts exactly what elements make a successful 900-number information service. This book will spark your imagination, giving you the inspiration, the ideas, the insider's perspective and the know-how to

launch your own money-making 900-number information service. To order send $19.95.

Unlike vending-machine business opportunities, in which
the investor has to service, restock, and trouble-shoot as many
as 50 to 100 racks or machines, pay-per-call franchisees are
promised something easier. The pitch is that one need only
purchase the lines, advertise, and wait for the profits to roll in.
In March 1996, through Project Buylines, the FTC charged
seven companies with making blatantly false earnings claims
and failing to give investors federally required prepurchase
information that may have tipped off the investors to the fraud.
Why do so many people fall for this scam? The promise of high
profits for little work, and our propensity to believe that there
is a shortcut to financial success. The seven companies are:

* Genesis One Corp., which does business as Bureau
  One out of Los Angeles

* Innovative Telemedia, Inc., of Boca Raton, Florida

* Bureau 2000 International, Inc., and Malibu Media,
  Inc., which do business out of the same L.A. address

* Gold Leaf Publishing and Distributing Company,
  Inc., of Orlando, Florida

* Pioneer Communications of Nevada, Inc., based
  in Los Angeles

* JP Meyers Company, Inc., of Southampton,
  Pennsylvania

* Ad-Com International, Inc., of Valley Village,
  California

In the cases against Genesis One, Innovative Telemedia, and Gold Leaf Publishing, the FTC charged that the earnings claims were false, noting that few, if any, investors made the promised amounts. In an additional charge against Innovative Telemedia, according to the FTC the marketer failed to pay its investors the agreed-upon portion of revenues from calls to the 900-number lines.

Many of these 900-line business opportunities lure prospects because of the outrageous amounts of money that are supposedly available at no risk. Always beware of money-making opportunities that claim easy earnings. Nobody gets rich quick and easy!

In the Project Buylines cases, the defendants generally offered business ventures that consisted of pay-per-call information or entertainment programs that consumers accessed by calling 900 numbers. For a base price that varies from a few hundred to nearly $4,000, investors get a package that purportedly includes (1) one or more 900-number lines, (2) recordings of the programs and instructions consumers will hear when they call the lines, (3) prepared advertisements and/or assistance in preparing and placing ads, and (4) other technical support. The defendants all made claims that investors would make a great deal of money, citing earnings claims ranging from a few thousand to more than $200,000 a year.

In every case except the one against Innovative Telemedia, the FTC also alleges that the defendants violated the FCC's and FTC's franchise rule. This is a prepurchase disclosure rule designed to help consumers fully analyze a business opportunity and avoid fraud. The rule requires franchise sellers to give potential investors a basic disclosure document containing detailed information about the franchise, its senior officers, its financial history, and the names of current and prior franchisees. The defendants *failed to disclose all material facts.*

The FTC's franchise rule is, essentially, an antifraud rule. It provides consumers a road map for checking out businesses so that they can protect themselves against scams. Jodie Bernstein warns consumers to be wary of classified ads touting 900-number riches, especially when the marketers fail to give consumers detailed written information about the business.

As law enforcement catches up with these 900-number business scams, operators keep getting more creative. Some services will keep you on the line for an extended length of time before you are able to get all of the information you called for, driving up the cost of your call. Never call any 900 number that doesn't fully disclose the cost up front.

Some unscrupulous telemarketers have begun using toll-free 800 numbers to mask 900 numbers. When you dial an 800 number, listen carefully to the recorded information you hear. Voice mail allows con men to place a disclaimer of a call being transferred to a 900 line at the end of the voice-mail message. Many times consumers tune out everything on a voice-mail message except the information they are looking for. Listen to the complete message, especially when calling someone you are not familiar with.

One of the latest types of scams is phony billing or invoicing, in which 900 lines overcharge customers. On my national radio show, "Consumer Hotline," a woman called in regarding one such scam. Mrs. C. was quite alarmed when she received a bill for approximately $5,000 from a 900 phone line. All the calls had been made while she was at work, so she asked her son if he knew anything about it. Unfortunately, he admitted he had made calls to a 900 sex line number.

Mrs. C. thought she had call blocking on 900 numbers. She called the phone company and found out that the 900-line company was able to get around the blocking by using a phony

800 number. Since her son was underage and the phone line he had called was for adults only, Mrs. C. was outraged, not only at her son but also at the company. She analyzed the bill and noticed that she had also been overcharged $1,290. Wanting to clarify the situation, she called the billing company, but it didn't want to cooperate. She then turned to the Better Business Bureau. As is the case most of the time, this company had a long track record.

It's amazing that these companies not only overcharge on their invoices but also find ways around the blocking system. I am alarmed by the fact that children have such easy access to adult phone lines. These 900 companies also lure children with Santa Claus or video game lines. Sierra On-Line, a computer game company, sponsors a 900 line for clues to its games and claims that "it is one of the most consistent call-minute generators in the 900 industry."

Although it is legal for game companies to provide this service, it seems obvious to me that they are taking advantage of an opportunity to get kids to use phone lines without their parents' permission. Around Easter 1993, one eight-year-old boy called the Easter Bunny every day for a month while his mother was doing household duties. Fortunately, the 900 company in this case waived the hefty phone bill.

Unfortunately, most companies are not as honorable. There are some steps to take if this situation happens to you. You should first try to resolve your complaint with your local or long-distance telephone company or with the company that furnished the pay-per-call service. Your bill should include the name and telephone number of the long-distance company that transmitted the call, and that company must provide to you, free of charge, the name, address, and telephone number of the 900-line company.

If you are not able to resolve your problem with the telephone company or the 900-line company, you may file a complaint with the FCC's informal complaints and public inquiries branch. If it appears that the 900-line company violated one of the FCC's regulations, your case may be handled by the FCC. Be aware that not all complaints regarding pay-per-call services are handled by the FCC.

As reported by the National Consumer Law Center, MCI agreed to settle a major class-action lawsuit involving 900-number fraud. MCI had to pay for all 900-number telephone calls during the period from January 1, 1988, through November 1, 1994. MCI had provided 900 numbers in connection with programs offering sweepstakes, games of chance, awards, prizes, and gifts. The company also provided information on unclaimed funds, financial information services, credit cards, and catalog cards. As part of the settlement agreement, MCI has set aside a total of $43 million to distribute in refunds to eligible consumers.

Phone companies have to be the first to take responsibility for many of these scams. They shouldn't allow pay-per-call companies to bypass 900-number blocking. Phone companies should act as a corporate watchdog to help protect consumers. Now, with the MCI settlement, perhaps the message will get across. Ultimately, though, you, the consumer, have to take the responsibility to check out any 900-line business opportunity before investing, protect the accessibility of your phone to unauthorized people, and review your phone bill every month to check for 900 charges and overbilling.

CHAPTER 15

The "O"
Obtaining Patents

A growing number of fraudulent invention companies are offering patent services to unsuspecting inventors. The patent process can be confusing because of all the legal ramifications. As in all industries, there are a few individuals who are willing to compromise their integrity for money. Many anxious inventors, seeking to make it rich, are victimized by these individuals or companies who are ready and willing to take advantage of inventors who have worthless products. Although unethical patent practitioners are an extremely small percentage of the overall profession, fraud in the industry is increasing every day. According to the Better Business Bureau, fraudulent invention promotion companies are scamming approximately 25,000 unsuspecting inventors out of approximately $200 million annually. This chapter is dedicated to protecting entrepreneurs and the great inventions of tomorrow.

To understand how difficult it is to obtain a patent, let's look at one example of how one unethical invention company is still in operation. The investigative programs "20/20" and "48

Hours" reported on the case against American Inventors Corporation and its clone company, American Institute for Research and Development.

Attorney Rick Martin is leading the attack against American Inventors for its alleged bogus practices. The fraudulent company has made millions of dollars from victims' money. Martin has accumulated about a ten-foot-high stack of written victim statements, which he has forwarded to the Federal Trade Commission and the U.S. Department of Justice regarding the illegal activities of American Inventors. Martin is fighting an uphill battle against this multi-million-dollar company and its deep pockets.

How does an inventor go about marketing or manufacturing a new idea? How does he or she find reputable information on developing inventions? To understand the patent process, you should understand what a patent is.

In 1790 the first patent law was put into effect. The law as it stands now is a revision enacted on July 19, 1952. It is codified in Title 35, United States Code. The patent law was created to protect not only manufactured inventions but ideas as well. Until recently, utility patents were granted for a period of seventeen years, assuming that the required maintenance fees were paid. Under new legislation stemming from the General Agreement on Tariffs and Trade (GATT), utility and plant patents will expire twenty years from the date of filing. (We will talk about the difference between a utility and a plant patent later in the chapter.) This allows a company exclusive rights to their product for twenty years and prevents competitors, usually with more financial power, from stealing an idea and marketing a version of their own.

An example of how a patent can protect an invention is the case of *Oiness v. Walgreen*. Steven Younger and Rudolf Fiedelak, co-inventors of a small folding headrest called a Headchair, filed a patent application for the Headchair on October 11, 1984. The patent was issued on October 1, 1985, as U.S. Patent No. 4,544,203 ('203). Younger, Philip Oiness, and other investors formed the corporation Sun Global Enterprises, Inc. The inventors assigned the '203 patent to Sun Global. In March 1984 Sun Global began manufacturing the Headchair, and sales commenced three months later.

In mid-1985 Walgreen Co. began selling a folding headrest that virtually destroyed the market for Sun Global Headchairs. In June 1986 Oiness formed a new corporation, Sun Products Group, Inc., to sell the Headchair. Sun Products acquired the assets of the defunct Sun Global and thus acquired the '203 patent. Oiness and Sun Products then sued Walgreen Co. for infringement of the '203 patent. The district court held its first trial on the case in April 1991. The jury found that Walgreen Co. had willfully infringed the patent and awarded Oiness $300,000 in damages.

The patent law is intended to protect an inventor during the patent process as well as the seventeen to twenty years of protection time. An inventor who doesn't have the capital to market his or her product has the option of selling the idea to a company. This provides a manufacturer and inventor an opportunity to capitalize on a product together. An inventor can receive royalties for a product that was never even produced by the inventor himself.

I caution you to beware of companies that promise to evaluate, develop, patent, and market inventions. Many people have sought advice from invention promotion firms and received nothing in return. Some of these enterprising inventors take years to develop their product and only minutes to make a decision on how to market that product. Don't let your enthusiasm make you vulnerable to false promoters. Take the time to develop a marketing plan for your new creation.

Take notes as I identify how to differentiate between legitimate firms and those that seek to defraud. Remember, con men like to use the same techniques as legitimate companies do. Many times advertising methods and consultations seem the same.

Some invention promotion firms advertise through TV, radio, newspapers, and magazines. The ads target independent and first-time inventors because they are more naive about the process. The ads will often use a toll-free phone number to appear professional and legitimate. These phone lines really don't give any information on how to obtain a patent. All information leads back to the advertiser. Oftentimes, when you respond to the ad, you will get a salesperson who will ask for detailed information about your invention. The key is not to give away your idea over the phone. Never disclose your idea in its entirety until you have the patent!

The Inventors Awareness Group (IAG) is trying to prevent fraudulent promoters from advertising. The IAG has been contacting publishers and other media that have allowed advertising by these companies, asking them to stop. Many victims are spending their life savings on useless services and information while magazine, radio, TV, and newspaper companies are profiting from the false advertisements.

Watch out for "marketing evaluations" and "free consultations." Any honest company should provide a free consultation, which includes a general marketing evaluation. A fraudulent firm may try to charge several hundred dollars for vague and basic marketing statements. In contrast, a reputable company will provide a specific analysis of the product, consumer, and marketability. The report should be specific to your product and demographics.

Many phony invention firms will try to get an excited inventor to pay an up-front fee. They package this as an exclusive marketing and licensing fee for their services as an agent. They may charge $10,000 and require a percentage of any royalties the invention may earn. Any request for an up-front fee, except by a manufacturer who is making a prototype, is an automatic red flag. Unfortunately, people continue to be victimized by this all-too-familiar technique.

The following example shows how companies are taking advantage of unsuspecting prospects. As you will see, the companies are failing to disclose all material information regarding the patent process. Invention Submission Corporation (ISC) agreed to an out-of-court settlement with the Federal Trade Commission. The settlement required ISC to pay $1.2 million into a consumer fund for failing to truly evaluate ideas. Part of the settlement requires the company to inform inventors that the company does not evaluate ideas.

Part of the confusion in obtaining a patent depends on what type of invention one has. Most people don't know that there are three types of patents—utility patents, design patents, and plant patents. In his article *Patent Basics*, David Pressman describes the three:

1. Utility patents. A utility patent is the most common type of patent. It covers inventions that function in a unique manner to produce useful results. Examples of utility inventions are Velcro, new drugs, electronic circuits, software, manufacturing products, new bacteria, new animals, or anything else under the sun that can be made by humans.

2. Design patents. A design patent covers the unique, ornamental, or visible shape or design of an object. If

a lamp, a building, or a computer case has a truly unique shape, its design can be patented.

3. Plant patents. A plant patent covers asexually reproducible plants. Grafting is a perfect example of this process. Through cutting and combining fruits or buds from trees and flowers, a new kind of fruit tree or flowering plant can be produced.

Since most inventors are not aware of the three categories of patents, they would do well to seek the advice of outside counsel. Finding a company or lawyer who knows how to file the proper patent is very important. An improperly filed patent is worthless. American Inventors Group (AIG) received a complaint from an inventor in Muncie, Indiana. The inventor paid thousands of dollars to Invention Submission Corporation (ISC) based on fraudulent advice the salesman had given her. The salesman told her that ISC does not make any money on what she pays them; instead, ISC makes its money from manufacturers. If ISC does not make any money from the up-front fees paid by inventors, the company should provide an accounting of where all that money goes. The salesman also seemed to be practicing patent law when he recommended that she apply for a design patent in lieu of a utility patent. Furthermore, he stated that $3,000 of her fees would immediately be sent to the patent attorney to apply for a design patent. AIG never saw any records that proved that ISC paid any attorney $3,000. ISC boasted that it was the only invention promotion company following government guidelines—only because they repeatedly settled out of court. Thanks to the FTC and the AIG, Invention Submission Corporation has nothing to boast about any longer.

Another problem that often plagues new inventors is patent fees. If you don't use any patent attorneys or agents, and excluding the costs of drawings, typing, photocopying, time, and postage, the only fees you must pay are government fees. Most Patent Trademark Office (PTO) fees are as follows:

1. Utility patents. To file a provisional patent application, you'll have to pay:
   - a provisional patent application filing fee.
   - a utility patent application filing fee.
   - a utility patent application issue fee.

   To keep the patent in force for its full seventeen-year term, you must make three maintenance fee payments as follows:
   - Maintenance Fee I, payable 3.0 to 3.5 years after issuance.
   - Maintenance Fee II, payable 7.0 to 7.5 years after issuance.
   - Maintenance Fee III, payable 11.0 to 11.5 years after issuance.

2. Design patents. To file a design patent application, you must pay:
   - a design application filing fee.
   - a design patent application issue fee.

3. Plant patents. To file a plant patent application, you must pay:
   - a plant patent application filing fee.
   - a plant patent application issue fee.

The law does not require maintenance or provisional patent application fees for design or plant patents.

Here are a few steps from the FTC to help you protect your-self from phony invention promotion firms:

* Before you sign any contracts or agreements, make sure to ask, in writing, how much money it will take for the use of the company's services. Be sure to get the total cost. If you hear an answer like "It depends" or "We will have to see," consider that a red flag.

* Watch out for firms that refuse to disclose details regarding their qualifications and history. A reputable firm should have plenty of information to give you regarding their past successes or dealings with other inventors. A company should be able to provide at least three clients that can verify the company's credibility.

* Make sure your idea is patentable. Many unscrupu-lous firms will take up-front money knowing that the patent is already taken. Do a patent search at the library. Before you realize that you are infringing on someone else's patent, a phony firm may have drained you financially.

* Many companies try to gain your confidence by instructing you to describe your invention in writing, mail it to yourself, and keep the envelope sealed. This ploy is used to give the inventor a false sense of protection.

* Ask the invention promotion firm for a list of clients who made more money from their invention than they paid the firm. Again ask for at least three wit-nesses. Also, find out how many times the invention promotion company's patents are rejected.

* In reality, few inventions make it to the marketplace. Be cautious of overzealous firms that promise quick, high returns. No one can guarantee the success of an invention.

* Watch out for firms that claim to have special relationships with manufacturers. Be cautious of firms that promise they will find you a manufacturer. Again, ask for specific examples of their successful products.

* Avoid firms that point to their full-color brochures and advertising campaigns as proof of credibility. Be wary of slick ads on radio and TV and in national magazines. Many con men will divert the attention of customers away from the actual business by pointing to the so-called image of the company.

* Always investigate a firm before making any commitments. Check with your local attorney general's office, the Better Business Bureau, and the Federal Trade Commission.

* Before signing any agreements, read the contract in full. Never agree to terms that are not fully disclosed in the contract. Any verbal agreements need to be included in written form. If possible, have your agreement reviewed by an attorney.

* As in most frauds, beware of high-pressure sales tactics. Be patient. Don't be rushed into making any financial decision.

* Watch out if you can never directly reach the salesman by phone and must always leave a message. This may indicate the salesman is most likely working out

of his home. Not all businesses that are home-based are frauds—it only makes it difficult to track the salesman if anything goes wrong.

Most experts agree that only 2 to 3 percent of all inventions are ever successfully marketed. Since the majority of invention promotion companies that advertise nationally have a near-zero success rate, don't invest in them too quickly. The following steps can save you both time and money:

1. Call your local government agencies and private organizations before consulting with an independent invention promotion firm. You can call the U.S. Patent and Trademark Office at 703-5570-4636, the U.S. Small Business Administration at 1-800-827-5722, your local Small Business Development Center, the United Inventors Association of the United States of America, the National Congress of Inventor Organizations at 801-753-0888, and the Minnesota Inventors Congress at 507-637-2344.

2. Record your invention in a bound notebook or on a piece of paper. Describe in detail how your product works, especially its special features. Write a description of its key elements. Sometimes the key elements are the true invention. Make sure your recordings are signed and witnessed by colleagues or friends who are neither financially associated with you nor related to you.

3. Perform your own patent search by going to the library. Ask one of the clerks for assistance.

4. Consult with professionals and local business-people to see whether your invention is marketable.

Remember the law of supply and demand. If no one wants the product, then you have virtually nothing.

5. Consider filing your patent application on your own. Do your homework. Invention promotion firms are services, not necessities.

Obtaining a patent can be very time-consuming and confusing, but don't lose hope. Many simple yet great ideas have proven to be very lucrative. Think of Famous Amos, who patented his special type of cookie, or Mrs. Fields, who did the same thing with her recipe.

Sometimes company names, slogans, or phrases can be valuable and should be protected by registering as a trademark or copyright. I remember when Pat Riley, the former L.A. Lakers coach, registered the phrase "ThreePeat" in reference to NBA teams winning three championships in a row. It didn't mean much at the time until the Lakers won two consecutive NBA championships. The next year, millions of shirts were made with the phrase "ThreePeat" printed on them.

Another popular slogan comes from Anheuser-Busch, Inc. We all know the phrase "This Bud's for You." Well, a Cleveland florist sought to register that phrase for his fresh-cut flowers. Budweiser had been using that phrase for years and contested the application, saying it would be confusing to customers. Anheuser-Busch won the case of *Anheuser-Busch, Inc. v. The Florist Association of Greater Cleveland, Inc.*

In the case of *Litton Systems, Inc. v. Honeywell, Inc.*, Litton did not submit prior art to the Patent and Trademark Office for its new optical coating method. Later this oversight would cause a misunderstanding between Litton and Honeywell that was eventually resolved. The application designated two Litton employees, Dr. David T. Wei and Anthony W. Louderback, and was issued as patent '958 on March 6, 1979.

In 1981 Louderback left Litton to form his own optical coating company, Ojai Research, Inc. Louderback preserved his relationship with Litton by entering a licensing and exclusive consulting agreement with his former employer. The licensing agreement permitted Louderback to practice the '958 patent. Louderback's exclusive consulting contract lasted until February 25, 1983. Under this agreement, Litton owned any inventions, developments, and discoveries Louderback made on the licensed process. The agreement also forbade Louderback from disclosing the patented technology.

During the exclusive consulting agreement with Litton, Louderback made improvements and modifications to the Litton process. Under the terms of the consulting agreement, Litton owned these improvements. Louderback violated this agreement by withholding the improvements from their rightful owner, Litton. On August 31, 1993, after three and a half months of trial, the jury reached a verdict. The jury reported that Litton had proved claims of infringement based on the '958 patent. The jury awarded Litton $1.2 billion in damages.

Even though Litton had not fully developed the invention, it had the original idea and had patented it. I can't stress how important it is to properly protect your invention. Don't be pressured into making a quick decision. Trade the short-term pain for the long-term gain. All businesses are built over time. Con men love inventors who are looking to go through the system quickly. Don't become another victim.

CHAPTER 16

The "P"
Pyramid Schemes

The following is a letter I received in the mail at my home. The author is unknown—which is the first clue that it is a fraud!

Dear Friend,

Greetings! I am a retired attorney, and about two years ago one of my clients came to me with this letter. The letter he brought is basically the same as the one you have in your hands presently. He asked me to verify that its contents were legal. I advised him to make a few small changes in it and then it would be all right.

I was very curious to see how it would turn out and asked him to keep me informed as to the success he achieved. I thought it was a long shot, so I decided against participating. About two months later he called to tell me he had received over $800,000 in cash. I didn't believe him, so he asked me to try it and find out for myself. I thought about it a few days and decided I really didn't have anything to lose, so I asked for a copy. I followed the instructions exactly and mailed out 200 copies, and sure enough the money began to arrive! After three months the money stopped coming. I kept a precise record of my earnings and they totaled $968,493.00!!

I was earning a good living as a lawyer, but as anyone in the legal profession will tell you, there is much stress that comes with the job. I told myself that if things worked out I would retire from my practice and enjoy the things that I had been putting off for too many years. I decided to try the letter again, but this time sent 500. Well, three months later I totaled $2,344,178!! I could not believe my good fortune. I met with my client for lunch some weeks later. He explained to me that there are quite a few letters going around. What makes this one different was the fact that there are six names on the letter, not five like most of the others. This fact alone results in your name being on far more returns. The other factor stems from the help I gave my client in making sure that the whole deal was perfectly legal.

I would bet by now you're curious to know what little changes I told him to make. Well, if you sent a letter like this out, to be legal, you must actually sell something if you expect to receive something in return. So, when you send a dollar to each of the six people on the list you must include a slip of paper with "PLEASE PUT ME ON YOUR MAILING LIST." You must also include your name and mailing address. The item you receive for your dollar is the letter and the right to earn $$.

Follow the simple instructions exactly, and in less than three months you will receive over $800,000.00!!

1. Immediately send $1.00 to each of the six people listed on the next page. Wrap the dollar bill in a note

saying "Please Put Me on Your Mailing List."

2. Remove the #1 name from the list and move the rest of the names up one position. Then place your name in the #6 spot. This is best done by typing a new list and taping it over the old one.

3. When you have completed the above instructions, take these pages to make 200 copies. The more you send out, the better the results.

4. Order 200 or more names from a mailing list company. Ask them to send you a mailing list of "Opportunity Seekers."

5. While waiting for your mailing list to arrive, place your copies in envelopes. Stamp and seal them. Do not put your return address on the envelopes! This will only peak [sic] the curiosity of the viewer.

6. When your mailing list arrives, place a label on each of your envelopes and drop them in the mailbox. Within 90 days you will receive $800,000.00 in cash!!

7. Keep a copy of the letter so you can use it a second time. Mail it out again in about six months, but mail it to the addresses you received a dollar from. It will work again, only better!!

This is a service and is 100% legal.

Frauds and scams are not always as obvious as the above example. Thousands of Americans have lost millions of dollars participating in pyramid schemes. Many of the victims knew they were gambling (although they didn't know the odds were rigged against them). Many others, however, thought they were trying to start up a small business of their own. These people were fooled by pyramid schemes disguised as legitimate business opportunities.

Simple pyramid schemes are similar to chain letters like the one above. The more elaborate pyramid schemes, though, are like wolves in sheep's clothing, hiding their true nature in order to fool potential investors and evade law enforcement.

What is a pyramid scheme? Pyramid schemes are illegal scams in which large numbers of people at the bottom of the pyramid pay money to a few people at the top. Each new participant pays for the chance to advance to the top and profit off payments from others who join later. In each case, the idea or goal is to push yourself up from the bottom by replacing yourself with a friend or loved one. The problem that often accompanies these schemes is that the people involved begin to view friends and relatives as "future participants." That's because you are programmed to believe that the opportunity will work for everyone. *FIGURE 9* shows a diagram of a typical pyramid.

To join, you might have to pay anywhere from a small investment to thousands of dollars. In the example in *FIGURE 9*, $1,000 buys a position in one of the eight boxes on the bottom level. Each thousand goes to the person at the top of the pyramid, the promoter. If all eight boxes on the chart fill up with participants, the promoter will collect $8,000 in addition to the $6,000 he received earlier from those who joined above you, and you and the others on the bottom level will each be $1,000 poorer. When the promoter has been paid off, his box is removed and the second level becomes the top, or payoff, level. Only then do the two people on the second level begin to profit. To pay off these two, sixteen empty boxes (people) are added at the bottom, and the search for new participants continues.

Each time a level rises to the top, a new level must be added to the bottom, each one twice as large as the one before. If enough new participants join, you and the other fifteen players who began with you may make it to the top. However, in order for you

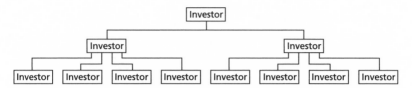

FIGURE 9. Diagram of a typical pyramid scheme. As the bottom grows proportion-
ately larger, more money flows to the very few at or near the top.

to collect your payoffs, 168 people would have to be recruited, and half of them will lose $1,000 each, at least temporarily.

Of course, the pyramid may collapse long before you reach the top. In order for everyone in a pyramid scheme to profit, there would have to be a never-ending supply of new partici-pants. In reality, however, the supply of participants is limited, and each new level of participants has less chance of recruiting others and a greater chance of losing money.

Mr. Owens, a nineteen-year Simi Valley, California police veteran, was charged in Ventura County (his place of residence) for his participation in an illegal pyramid scheme. Along with Mr. Owens, two other officers were convicted, two others resigned, and a fifth was fired.

LAPD Commander Tim McBride, a spokesman for the department, said, "Some people don't think their way through it before they get involved—both civilians and officers," adding that pyramid schemes are illegal.

Darryl Mouner, an attorney representing Owens, could not explain why officers get involved in such schemes. "Apparently they didn't know better. They are no different from anybody else," he said.

James Ellison, senior deputy district attorney in Ventura County, said, "The leaders of the schemes claim they are legal, based on the word *endless* in the law. The penal code section outlaws endless chains, so they say, 'We're going to put an end-ing date on ours, therefore it is not an endless chain.'"

Ellison noted that that claim is bogus and the scheme still violates the law. "The end date doesn't make any difference, since the whole scheme is dependent on getting new members in order to redistribute money."

There is no product sold in these schemes, which are vari-ously dubbed "Friends Helping Friends" or "Money Tree Gift Exchange." "They are based strictly on the exchange of cash," Ellison adds.

The penalty for this felony crime is a maximum of three years if convicted.

Diane Marchant, an attorney who represents police officers, issued a warning to law enforcement agencies: "The bottom line is, if you are in one of these, get out."

As good as these opportunities sound, the reality is that they are illegal. *"Ignorance is no excuse for breaking the law."*

Let's analyze this letter using the three characteristics of fraud. First, *Drawing big conclusions from little evidence:*

1. "I am a retired attorney." The implication here is that he has performed "due diligence" regarding the legal-ity of this letter. What proof does he provide? As a lawyer, he would be listed by the state. He would also have a law degree. And yet he never even provides us with his name.

2. $800,000 cash earnings in two months. A huge income for two months and very little work. Where is the supporting documentation? Bank receipts? Even if he could substantiate his claim, that does not prove the scheme is legal.

3. $968,493 cash earnings in three months. If he keeps such good records, why not show them? Again, no proof of this income. In the case of ZZZZ Best, many investors at the top of the Ponzi scheme made money not knowing it was dirty money.

4. $2,344,178 cash earnings in three months. Again, big numbers with no proof.

5. "This is a service and is 100% legal." If he is a lawyer, is this his specialty? What kind of a lawyer is he? How do I know he knows what the law is? Police officers are going to jail for schemes just like this one. Should we trust him simply because he gives us a title but no name?

6. Why doesn't the lawyer provide a list of other people who have participated and found success? NO PROOF!

7. The false notion that you can get something for nothing: $800,000 without working!

Next, *Failure to disclose key material facts:*

1. Is this really a legal means of earning an income? Check with the Better Business Bureau. What are your tax liabilities? How much do you pay in taxes if you earn $800,000?

2. What is your original investment? The cost of envelopes, mailing lists, labels, postage, copies, and so forth all comes out of your pocket.

3. Does everyone make money? Most people lose money.

4. Will you be put on any other mailing lists? You can bet on it!

5. Who is behind this?

6. What percentage of the people involved actually participate? Do 800,000 people actually join? What is the fallout rate?

Finally, *Diversion:*

1. "Dear Friend." The letter begins with a personal greeting.

2. "I am a retired attorney." This implies that he knows the law and you can believe the following information.

3. The ends justify the means. Because it has worked, it must be OK for you to try.

4. "There is much stress that comes with the job." Every job has stress. It's a part of life.

5. "I would retire from my practice." This is an appeal to everyone's desire to be financially independent enough to stop working.

6. "And enjoy the things that I had been putting off." A classical appeal to your emotions rather than your logic. Con men want you to feel, not think. How many people do you know personally who have benefited from something like this?

7. $800,000 in cash. Your greed wants that money, thus diverting you from what you know to be true.

8. What do you have to lose? Forget what everyone else

says, forget what the law really says, everyone else is
doing it.

9. The names. I left out the six names that were in this
letter. These names give the appearance that people
all over the country are doing it, and you can, too.

10. The numbers. I purposely omitted the letter's example of how the system works in dollar figures. I know
that printing those numbers would entice even some
of the readers of this book. The numbers are huge,
and they look good. Greed for financial gain with
little effort is the largest motivator in these schemes.

Why do so many people fall into this trap? Three reasons:
greed, gullibility, and desperation. A young couple came to me
asking about a potential business opportunity. Their combined
credit card debt, which was about $30,000, was starting to con-
sume them. Eager and desperate, they fell prey to a pyramid
scheme that claimed to pay off $16,000 for a $1,000 investment.
They were also encouraged to use their credit cards to get the
$1,000. Wanting to retire their debt quickly, they entered into
two pyramids. Their debt increased to $32,000, and the inter-
est on the $2,000 cash advance was growing daily. After two
frustrating months, they had not been able to recruit anyone
under them. The pool of people had quickly dried up.

I can't emphasize this point enough: "You don't work, you
don't eat." The tragedy of welfare is that America has learned
that you can get money for doing nothing. Karl Marx stated
that democracy would never work because once the people
realized that they could vote themselves money (welfare), the
system would crash. The old work ethic, which was based on

good, hard, honest work and patience, has been replaced by the "I want it now for nothing" mentality.

Some pyramid promoters try to make their schemes look like multi-level marketing methods. Multi-level marketing is often a lawful and legitimate business method that uses a network of independent distributors to sell consumer products (see chapter 13). To look like a multi-level marketing company, a pyramid scheme takes on a line of products and claims to be in the business of selling them to consumers. However, little or no effort is made to actually market the products. Instead, money is made in typical pyramid fashion, by recruiting. New distributors are pushed to purchase large and costly amounts of inventory when they sign up.

Here is a checklist to follow when a suspicious pyramid opportunity comes your way:

1. Get the name, phone number, and address of the person you are doing business with.

2. Get a list of random referrals from the person you are doing business with.

3. Investigate the referrals, the business, and the person you are doing business with.

4. Take your time.

5. Consult others before making a decision.

6. Remember, there is no such thing as getting rich quickly and easily.

Remember, pyramid schemes are purposely disguised to hide their true nature. These opportunities are designed to fool potential investors. No one is immune—even law enforcement officers.

CHAPTER 17

The "Q"
Quackery

Did you know that Michael Gladych has uncovered a number of flaws in Newton's law of gravity? Or that a group of scientists in Arizona have discovered a new way to send prayers to heaven for $9.95? How about Amanda Fielding, who claims she knows how to increase consciousness and awareness by drilling holes in your head? These are just a few examples of what we will refer to as "quackery."

For the purposes of this book, a quack is an untrained person who practices medicine fraudulently. A quack is also someone who pretends to have knowledge or skills in a particular field. Quacks use anecdotes and testimonials instead of facts and science. Simply defined, a quack is someone who takes an unproven remedy and sells it. A quack is an outright impostor and a fake! Consider the following examples.

Jim Richard Brinkley was a brazen medical quack who was the world's foremost practitioner of "goat-gland science." Brinkley also hosted a radio program called "Doctor Brinkley's Medical Question Box." He was born in 1885 and attended the dubious Eclectic Medical University of Kansas City.

Brinkley theorized that by transplanting the sexual glands of the ever-lustful goat into the male scrotum, he could renew manly vigor and restore sex drive. "So far as I know," he once explained, "I was the first man that ever did this operation of taking the goat testicle and putting it in the man's testicle."

Brinkley convinced a farmer to hand over $750 to be a guinea pig. A year after that first transplant, by pure random chance, the farmer's wife gave birth to a baby, named Billy.

In the late 1930s Brinkley's luck caught up with him. After dodging medical boards and the law, the courts finally ruled against him, labeling him a fraud. By the time he died, more than 16,000 men bore the scars of his goat-gland operation, and thousands of others had been swindled in his second scam, colored water masquerading as medicine. Like most con men, Brinkley made a living off of gullible and desperate people. Hiding behind a medical degree, he committed fraud for fame and fortune while his victims suffered the consequences.

Unfortunately, Dr. Brinkley isn't the only or the last quack to victimize society. Quackery is a $25-billion-a-year business in America alone. Like I always say, follow the "money trail" and you'll find the fraud. Open up any newspaper or magazine and you're sure to find the latest, greatest cure for anything from obesity to AIDS. Medical quackery promises the world, and sometimes, as in the case of Dr. Brinkley, it even seems to work, but is it true medicine?

Doctors who spend at least eight years in higher education are still fighting the traveling medicine man. Oh, sure, the wagon and tonics are gone, but the methods remain the same. The methods promise an alternative to medical treatment, usually at a lower price. Instead of scientific proof, however, the modern-day medicine man uses actors, athletes, and a variety of people to endorse his products. Even with full-color packaging, effective salesmanship, and modern-day marketing, it's ironic how the new pitch-man uses the same techniques as the old-fashioned medicine man. Quacks advertise in the best newspapers, magazines, and radio and television shows to spread their latest findings. Whether or not the advertisements are true is the real question.

According to an article in *Alternative Medicine Digest*, Annie Potts, from the former hit television show "Designing Women," says that alternative medicine helped her get pregnant. Potts, who had given birth fifteen years earlier, wanted another child, but at age forty she thought she would no longer be able to conceive. She consulted a physician who prescribed a fertility drug called Clomid. Potts had a negative reaction to the drug, so she turned to Chinese medicine. Even though Chinese medicine is not fully accepted by the medical community, at age forty-three Potts gave birth to a child with the aid of Chinese herbs and a man named Dr. Chiang.

Testimonials like this one are powerful but are not an exact science. How many women never get pregnant? It would have been nice if the article had included some scientific statistics to help support the Chinese methods. Would Potts have had a baby without the Chinese medicine? I'm no doctor, but I know that you never judge the sum of the whole by its parts. In other words, just because it worked for Annie Potts doesn't mean that it works for everyone.

I saw an ad hawking shark cartilage as a cure for bone conditions. The ad never mentions any corroborating scientific or medical proof from outside unbiased medical agencies. It does say that 170 million doses have been tested—but on what or whom, we do not know. It also claims that "thousands" already know about shark cartilage. We don't know if this is truly a modern-day medical miracle or another way for a quack to make a quick buck.

Perpetual opportunist and entrepreneur Jerry Rubin was always trying to make a quick buck, whether it was from throwing cocktail parties that he charged admission to or marketing a nutritional company. In 1992, Rubin was claiming to be pulling down $60,000 a month selling the so-called nutritional beverage called Wow. Most people would call it coffee laced with vitamins.

Unfortunately, as long as coffee and vitamins are legal, such practices are okay. Quackery, like fraud, is not a legal conclusion. Remember, quackery can be as simple as someone taking an unproven remedy and selling it.

Another infamous quack was Henry Gaylord Wilshire, a real estate developer-slash-quack. You might recognize Wilshire's name as one of the main streets that runs through Los Angeles. The Wilshire Horse Collar, which was about a foot in diameter and covered with leather, supposedly generated a electromagnetic field that Wilshire claimed would cure just about anything—for $65. By the time the Better Business Bureau had finished with Wilshire, he had turned Los Angeles into the national epicenter of medical charlatans.

Dr. William Jarvis, a professor of preventive medicine at Loma Linda University and founder of the National Council Against Health Fraud, has devoted his life to fighting quackery. Dr. Jarvis states, "Anytime you have affluent elderly, you will have real problems with quackery, because the people have too much time on their hands. They're bored, and they have nothing to do but think about their ultimate death."

Many of the ads I see in magazines are directed toward the elderly. In fact, advertisers are using more and more healthy-looking elderly people in their marketing campaigns. I am always amused when I see an ad that reads, "Feel young again!" At age thirty I already feel the effects of aging. I know that I will never feel twenty again. How can a sixty-year-old man expect to feel thirty?

On his Web site, Dr. Jarvis mentions a story about Dr. William Kellogg, the inventor of Kellogg's Corn Flakes. Kellogg believed that vegetarianism and enemas could cure anything. He also tried to make up his own religion. Considering some of his more outlandish ideas, I'm glad he stuck to corn flakes!

Whether it's pills or gadgets, it seems as though many of these so-called quacks enjoy some level of success. How do we account for all the testimonials? Dr. Jarvis explains it this way: Some patients really aren't sick to start with, although they have no way of knowing it; and others experience the placebo effect, a well-known phenomenon in which patients claim to be cured or feel better after knowingly receiving a sugar pill instead of real medicine. Because chronic illness consists of peaks and valleys rather than a steady downward curve, many chronically ill people appear to be cured or on the mend when they are actually in one of their peaks. This accounts for the high volume of testimonials that quacks use. A smart quack runs hundreds of "tests" until he finds enough testimonials to peddle his product.

The problem is that these quacks don't have to measure up against any objective truth. Medicine is based on hard science, whereas quackery is based on testimonials. Men like Dr. Jarvis want proof! Most new therapies are unproven by scientific standards. Dr. Jarvis fears that unproven treatment is dangerous. In the infamous Laetrile controversy, a cancer treatment that supposedly came from the pit of an apricot, the treatment was eventually disproved. How many people went on to suffer pain, even die, because false medical treatments were used instead of scientific methods?

While everyone was trying to find a cure for cancer, a new disease erupted in the eighties. Former cancer quacks are now taking their crackpot theories into the world of AIDS. One alleged cure for AIDS involved standing in front of a mirror while thinking positive thoughts, and another prescribed a combination of goat's milk, Ovaltine, and hang-gliding. All it takes is one AIDS patient to go into remission, and everyone will be drinking goat's milk.

Although some quackery may cause death, even Dr. Jarvis admits that most quackery is nothing more than an old-fashioned medicine man scheme. Most people stand to lose their money before they lose their life. Quackery is something that we might not be able to get rid of, but we can be made more aware of the many schemes in circulation today.

In the tradition of David Letterman's Top Ten List, Dr. Jarvis has his own Down-and-Dirty List of the Top Quack Remedies:

1. Remedy: Anti-oxidants.
   Claim: These vitamins neutralize free radicals, the negatively charged particles that run around in the system like bullets, knocking holes in cellular membranes.
   Dr. Jarvis: It works if you eat food that contains anti-oxidants. But, according to some studies, taking anti-oxidants in pill form may actually create the problems they're supposed to solve.

2. Remedy: Herbal supplements such as alfalfa for arthritis or pau d'arco for cancer.
   Claim: Nature's medicine for nature's child.
   Dr. Jarvis: Some of these products are grown in the Orient with fertilizers that contain heavy metals. They're sent to this country marked NOT FOR HUMAN USE.

3. Remedy: Homeopathic medications such as Cardio Fortifier and Sunsource Cold Relief.
Claim: An infinitesimal amount of a drug—its "spirit-like essence"—is enough to kick-start the healing process.
Dr. Jarvis: If a company says its products are homeopathic, the FDA says it doesn't have to prove that it works.

4. Remedy: The kombucha mushroom.
Claim: A treatment for AIDS.
Dr. Jarvis: It isn't a mushroom, it's a colony of bacteria. One of the things sometimes found growing with it is a fungus that produces aflatoxin-B, one of the most potent dietary carcinogens known to humanity.

5. Remedy: Chelation therapy.
Claim: Cleans out clogged veins; inexpensive alternative for bypass surgery.
Dr. Jarvis: Inappropriate for vascular diseases; presents high risk for kidney failure.

6. Remedy: Healing magnets.
Claim: Said to reduce pain and improve circulation.
Dr. Jarvis: There's no evidence that magnets do anything that they are claimed to.

7. Remedy: The healing touch.
Claim: By gesturing mystically, practitioners can smooth the ruffled energy field of the patient.
Dr. Jarvis: This is also called medieval witchcraft.

The reason all these dubious products and methods are used is a result of a lack of trust in the medical community and a lack of understanding of how to evaluate what is read, heard, and seen. What are some of the steps you can take to help you differentiate between medical fact and quackery fraud? Although I am not a doctor, I would suggest the following five steps:

1. Time. Time is the vindicator of all truth. Try to stay away from new and unproven products. The test of time always proves whether or not a product is worth using. Seek advice from medical experts who have proven themselves over time.

2. Substance. Always seek substance over experience. In medicine testimonials, especially those regarding relief from pain, it is difficult to objectively prove how much pain one can tolerate.

3. Patience. Everyone gets sick or feels pain from time to time. Depending on how old you are or what kind of medical condition you are in, the healing process varies for different ailments. A lifetime of eating fast food isn't going to be reversed by two weeks of taking pills.

4. Validate. Always confirm claims with outside sources. I have found that the best way to verify a claim is to seek the opinion of those who have no economic gain at stake.

5. A/B/F. Talk to the attorney general, Better Business Bureau, and Federal Trade Commission to see whether there are any formal complaints against a company's products.

Don't be fooled. Quacks go after anyone using any method to sell their magic cures. In *Quacks of Old London,* Robert Tucker wrote about one of the most successful quacks of the eighteenth century, Joanna Stephens. Before 1736, Stephens lived comfortably, scamming nobility with her cure for "The Stone," as kidney and gallbladder stones were commonly referred to in those days. As her rich clientele began to dwindle and die off because of death, she devised a new plan. Two years later, Stephens ran an advertisement in *Gentlemen's Magazine* offering to make her cure public—for 5,000 pounds!

The public went into a frenzy trying to raise the money, while members of the British nobility tried to outcontribute one another in hopes of winning the public's grateful appreciation. When the sum total reached only 1,356 pounds, Stephens spoke before Parliament and a committee of the most respected medical minds of the day, which isn't saying much. She humbly requested the rest of the money—for the benefit of the public, of course. Parliament, hoodwinked by her supposed philanthropy, decided to pay the remainder of the money to Stephens.

In return for the 5,000 pounds, Stephens made her cure for "The Stone" public by publishing it in the *London Gazette.* Everyone anxiously awaited her miracle remedy. Unfortunately, her frightening cure consisted of "a Powder, a Decoction, and Pills." The powder consisted of calcined eggshells and snails. The decoction was made by boiling several herbs together with soap and "swine's cresses burnt to blackness and honey." The pills also used snails along with wild carrot seeds, burdock seeds, and honey. The powder, mixed with cider or other liquor, was to be ingested three times daily, followed by a half pint of the decoction. If the decoction "disagreed," the pills could be substituted.

Did Stephens's cure work? No! That is, unless you kept score based on the death count. If a quack doesn't kill someone, then he or she is considered a success.

It is no secret that the U.S. medical system is in a state of terrible disarray. Although conventional medicine excels in the management of medical emergencies, certain bacterial infections, trauma care, and many complex surgical techniques, it is still looking for answers in the areas of disease prevention and the management of new illnesses that seem to be cropping up at a steady pace. As people seek quick, easy, and inexpensive answers, quacks are fast to respond. Most quackery remedies are limited in the damage they can cause you physically, but financially the figure is still at $25 billion a year! The only cure I can think of is to check things out before the purchase is made!

CHAPTER 18

The "R"
Real Estate

While surfing the Net, I came across an article about a group of people who had bought condos in the Highlands, a luxury condominium complex on New York's Long Island. The buyers were now in financial limbo. A developer, John McNamara, had pleaded guilty to a multi-million-dollar swindle of General Motors, which included real estate fraud. McNamara was basically working a massive pyramid scheme. He borrowed money from General Motors to buy, convert, and export GM vans that did not exist. It is a classic pyramid scheme—robbing from Peter to pay Paul. Instead of vans, McNamara used the GM money to invest in real estate, a gold mine, commodity trading, and oil businesses. To pay off his creditors, the federal government was auctioning most of McNamara's vast real estate holdings, including the Highlands condominiums. These condo owners are as much the victims as his creditors, since the development remains unfinished and they cannot sell or refinance their homes.

In this chapter we look at some common real estate scams ranging from phony land sales, timeshares, and unowned properties to empty promises. They serve as an example of how far a con artist will go to commit fraud.

Although buying land may seem like a safe investment, it can be very speculative and risky. Many properties that were bought more than twenty years ago are not worth their original price today. Due to property taxes, association dues, and undeveloped land, owners are actually losing money. One such case occurred in the infamous Antelope Valley, California, where hundreds of hard-working Latinos were scammed.

According to John M. Glionna, a *Los Angeles Times* staff writer, the L.A. district attorney's office now alleges, in seven felony charges, that millionaire developer Marshall Redman defrauded several people in a land deal. Several of the real estate firms Redman controlled sold land to Latino families from blue-collar neighborhoods. The prospect of owning a home seemed like a dream come true because owning a home was finally affordable to these families.

Redman was accused of selling 2,500 undeveloped properties in Kern, Los Angeles, and San Bernardino counties at prices ranging from $19,900 to $39,900. "Few buyers got what they paid for," according to a six-month *Los Angeles Times* review.

The buyers received no title insurance and no title search and were sold land that was zoned exclusively for business or industry. Prosecutors claim that Redman sold land he didn't own; in one case, the land was in the middle of a freeway. In another scam, Redman sold the same lot to several investors. Furthermore, Redman made promises of water and sewer hook-ups as well as telephone service and electricity, which were never provided. Now, about 250 families live in the harsh high-desert weather conditions of hot days and cold nights. This appalling scheme took a decade to uncover.

Land scams like Redman's continue to happen on a daily basis. The Federal Trade Commission provides the following tips, as described in the Interstate Land Sales Full Disclosure Act, to help consumers in purchasing real estate:

The Hard Sell. Be wary of sellers who offer land primarily as a great investment opportunity. Any investment has risk, so be cautious. They may show you slick brochures and videos that show beaches, lakes, tourist attractions, shopping malls, schools, and hospitals. Some sellers spin a tale of paradise, show you model homes, and all but guarantee in writing that the land's value will increase rapidly. When you hear promises like "prices will rise," be on your guard.

The Full Disclosure Act. Remember that you have rights as a land buyer. To help protect consumers against land sales scams, the Interstate Land Sales Full Disclosure Act was passed in 1968. This act generally applies to developers selling or leasing, through interstate commerce, 100 or more unimproved lots. Under the act, developers must register their subdivisions with the Department of Housing and Urban Development (HUD). They must also give consumers a summary of that registration in a disclosure statement, called a Property Report, before a contract or agreement is signed. The report contains information about the property, such as distances to nearby communities over paved or unpaved roads; present and proposed utility services and charges; and soil and foundation conditions that could cause construction or septic-tank problems. Read the report carefully. It is meant to provide basic information about the property without salesmen embellishments.

The Shopping Process. Whether you are looking for a residential, rental, or vacation spot, know what you are buying before committing yourself to making a down payment and years of monthly payments you might regret later. (I provide a buyer's checklist later in this chapter.) Shop for your property. Take the time to look around and compare, just like you would when you shop for clothes.

Cancellation Rights. Ask about your cancellation rights before you sign a contract. If the lot is subject to the Full Disclosure Act, the contract should specify a "cooling-off" period of seven days (or longer if allowed by the state law). This is also known as the buyer's remorse clause. During this time, you may cancel the contract for any reason by contacting the developer, preferably in writing. Also, if the contract does not state that you will receive a warranty deed within 180 days after signing the contract, you may have up to two years to cancel. If the land is not covered by the Full Disclosure Act, check the cancellation clause in the contract. In some contracts the buyer has only three days to cancel the transaction.

Always keep with your contract any promotional materials or newspaper articles about the development in which you are buying. In the event of fraud, this will provide proof of any misrepresentations that were made prior to your purchase.

Complaint Handling. This pertains to certain amenities that may not have been built as promised, such as swimming pools and tennis courts. If any misrepresentation exists, complain immediately, in writing, to the seller. If that does not solve the problem, write to your local or state consumer protection office.

Why do consumers need to take such precautions? Isn't the contract and fact that you are dealing with a licensed real estate agent enough due diligence? Unfortunately, scam artists have no limits, as we will see in the following case involving Rodney Swanson.

Former real estate salesman Rodney Swanson, age forty-seven, faces a maximum term of twelve years in state prison and about $8 million in fines when he is sentenced. "He sold promissory notes and partial interests in commercial and residential properties to investors, but in some cases he did not own the property he was selling," explains Deputy District Attorney Anthony Colannino. The Sierra Madre man was convicted of sixty-two counts of securities fraud, money laundering, and grand theft stemming from a real estate investment scam that bilked nearly eighty people out of $10 million. Sadly, the victims were longtime family friends and members of his Burbank church. Those friends each invested anywhere from $10,000 to $775,000, according to Colannino. As tragic as the loss of money was, that did not compare to the web of deception Swanson wove around family and friends. One of the victims was Swanson's high school history teacher and track coach. As you can imagine, these people were devastated.

Stories about con men stealing from family and friends are becoming far too familiar. It seems as though trust is becoming a lost character trait.

When I appeared on "The Maury Povich Show," one of my fellow guests was a dear lady named Terry W. As her home was about to go into foreclosure, a seemingly nice, empathetic man had offered to help her. His plan would enable Terry to get her home back and not lose it to the bank. All she had to do was trust him.

His plan was to have her sign over the property to a third party of his choice, who would then sell the property back to Terry. This process would allow Terry to repurchase her home with a new interest rate on her mortgage. The process, although a bit confusing to Terry, seemed as though it might work, so she took a leap of faith. I need not tell you what happened next. Not only did she lose her home, but she never recovered the money she gave to the con man for "fees and payments."

Con men prey on people like Terry who are in desperate situations. All too often we think a con man will be a long-haired, tough-looking, nose-ringed psycho with tattoos all over his body. In reality, most scams are perpetrated by friendly, slick-talking, sharp-dressing, white-collar criminals.

Financial pressure, poor location, or impatience can result in a rushed decision. Bob Joyal, a buying agent, suggests the following eleven steps to take when buying a home:

1. Hire a buyer's agent. Never sign a buyer broker agreement which requires up-front fees. Get a referral for a buying agent near you rather than responding to an advertisement.

2. Get deeply involved in the process. Don't rely solely on the buying agent. You are making the largest investment of your life. Read the contract in full!

3. Get loan approval. Many times mortgage scams happen because buyers have failed to get prior loan approval before falling in love with their dream home. Get loan approval at the beginning of your shopping process so that you know the loan will not be a last-minute problem. You don't want to waste your time looking for something you can't afford.

4. Get a list of homes in your neighborhood of interest. Do your homework. Find out how much the homes have been selling for in that neighborhood for the past eight months.

5. Pick neighborhoods with good schools and low crime rates. Neighborhoods never go from bad to good. Schools and crime are really two of the most important things to look for when buying a home.

6. Talk to the neighbors. Make sure you can live with your neighbors. Don't guess what the neighbors are like. Knock on doors and meet them.

7. Drive by the neighborhood at 5:00 P.M. Find out what traffic is like during rush hour. Check how much activity the neighborhood gets.

8. Don't buy a newly built home. Although new homes are very clean, they don't save money. New homes may also have additional taxes, especially those in planned communities.

9. Look for homes with good curb appeal and open floor plans. Remember, first impressions are important here. The first thing you see from the street is the front of the house. For resale purposes, or to have a home that will increase in value, it must look good from the street. Floor plans of three bedrooms and 1.75 baths are generally the best.

10. Look for homes that are centrally located. Make sure your potential home is near a safe shopping area, schools, and freeways.

11. Stay away from high-traffic areas. Homes located on busy streets and intersections as well as single-story homes surrounded by two-story homes are not good investments.

Above all, avoid being rushed into a decision. Clifford Keller of Bakersfield, California, made a living out of scamming people who were under a lot of pressure. According to the *Los Angeles Times,* Keller pleaded guilty to grand theft and forgery in 1988 but disappeared before his sentencing date. Before Keller's capture, he was one of two men involved in a $2 million mortgage scheme. Keller tricked more than fifty Southern California investors into buying nonexistent second mortgages. Investors purchased second trust deeds, which turned out to be fake, from the now-defunct Old Ranch Management and Investment, Inc., of La Palma, California. Authorities found Keller at his daughter's home and placed him under arrest. Unfortunately, it does not look like the investors will be getting their money back.

Home buyers and investors are targets for a variety of rip-offs and scams. One popular investment fraud has to do with timeshares. A vacation timeshare gives you the right to use a vacation home for a limited, preplanned period over a number of years. American consumers own about 1.5 million time-shares. One survey, taken from the Internet, estimates that about 870,000 of these timeshares currently are available for resale. You could get taken in by a timeshare resale scam.

Questionable salespeople are likely to tell you that the market for resales of timeshares is "hot" and that their company has a high success rate in reselling these units. They may claim they have extensive lists of sales agents and potential buyers. These lists may consist of people who have never heard of the company or have no interest in buying a time-share. For an advance "listing" fee, often around $300 to $500, these salespeople promise to sell your timeshare for a price equal to or greater than the amount you originally paid. To entice you, they may offer a money-back guarantee or a

$1,000 government bond if they cannot sell your timeshare within a year.

The market for timeshare resales is poor because there is no secondary market. In fact, a survey found that only 3.3 percent of owners reported reselling their timeshares during the last twenty years. Also, the market for resales may vary considerably, depending on the location of the unit and the season of the year. It may be unlikely that the company can resell the timeshare at all. Those whose timeshares are not resold after a year may find that either their fee is not returned or they are presented with a bond worth as little as $60 or $70, according to the FTC. Beware of any timeshare that is sold as anything other than a vacation spot.

Real estate fraud isn't limited to purchases only. Rental listing companies have also defrauded consumers. In a continuing crackdown on consumer fraud, four people were charged with eighteen counts of grand theft and a series of other business code violations in connection with two companies they operated, Global Management in Sherman Oaks and Quality Rentals in Burbank. Over nine months these rental listing companies cheated customers by lying about their services and refund policies. The companies lured customers by offering exclusive lists of properties, promising rent reductions and lower move-in fees, and offering to refund the customer's $150 deposit if nothing suitable was found within ninety days.

Customers of Quality Rentals and Global Management told investigators that most of the properties on the lists were already rented, were in poor condition, or did not have the promised amenities. Some properties were renting for higher amounts than advertised, as well.

When customers complained about the allegedly poor service, they were denied their promised refunds. Deputy City Attorney

Mark Lambert said, "State law requires rental services to refund all but $25 to customers who do not find suitable rentals."

Unfortunately, authorities state that such operators typically shut down when they learn they are under investigation and relocate somewhere else under new business names.

No matter what the angle, fraudulent real estate scams are being perpetrated in every conceivable way. Protect yourself by being prepared before you start shopping for real estate. Remember, trust is something earned, not given.

CHAPTER 19

The "S"
Stock Fraud

It is a scandal that goes largely unreported. Its victims include executives, office workers, retirees, police officers, homemakers, plumbers, engineers, policemen, and virtually every other occupation you could imagine. Victims range from those with Ph.Ds to those possessing only a high school education, and they live in big cities and small towns in every state. Thousands of Americans fall victim to fraud and abuse perpetrated each year by stockbrokers and brokerages selling stock options.

When Jim Morgan, a retired truck driver, placed the $100,000 profit he received from the sale of his Southern California home of over thirty-five years with a national Wall Street brokerage, he thought his instructions were direct and very explicit. Jim demanded full safety of principal, conservative investments, and absolute, total liquidity.

Jim and his wife Mary (not their real names) were approaching seventy and had both experienced serious medical problems in addition to providing ongoing financial assistance to an adult son who had been experiencing business difficulties. They had never seen $100,000 at one time in their lives. Jim, who'd worked for the same company in a union job for thirty-eight years, did not have retirement savings, just a small pension.

Just two years later, Jim and Mary discovered that their money—all $100,000 of it—had been placed in a high-risk, long-term, nonliquid aircraft-leasing limited partnership. In addition, the partnership's value had fallen by over 40 percent over those two years. Jim was heartsick. "I trusted the big, national brokerage firm to give me what I asked them for: safety and security. After all, that is what they advertised and I was stupid enough to believe them. These guys never told me the truth . . . and made a lot of commissions to boot," he said in an article in *Personal Investing News.*

Jim is not alone. More than 8,000 securities fraud arbitration claims are filed in the United States every year. That's more than twenty-two new cases a day, representing real people and families, investors who have been "burned" and abused by stockbrokers and firms. Both a financial and emotional price are paid by the victims. I experienced firsthand just how much pain a victim of stock fraud endures. When ZZZZ Best fell apart, the horror stories began to roll in by phone, fax, and letter. Investment portfolios were destroyed, college funds were depleted, and loans went unpaid, all because I took shortcuts in business. The only way any good can come out of such a catastrophe is if I help others avoid falling victim to a similar scam. This chapter is dedicated to doing just that!

The problem of investor abuse is much larger than the 8,000 new case filings each year. It is estimated that for every case filed, at least nine others are not filed because of lack of knowledge and information.

In this chapter I focus on penny stocks. Although there are many forms of securities fraud, penny stocks seem to have a high rate of abuse. Penny stock scams are now the number one fraud and abuse threat facing small investors in the United States. A September 1989 report by the North American Securities Administrators Association (NASAA) to the U.S. House Telecommunications and Finance Subcommittee estimates that Americans lose at least $2 billion—I didn't say *million*—each year as a result of schemes involving penny stocks. NASAA found that the penny stock industry is increasingly dominated by utterly worthless or highly dubious securities offerings that are systematically manipulated by repeat offenders of state and federal securities laws and other felons, some of whom have been identified as having ties to organized crime. I knew many of these people personally during the ZZZZ Best days or met them in prison.

The names of one or more individuals with a background of violations of securities laws, felony indictments, convictions, or reported ties to organized crime were found in more than four out of five of the major penny stock enforcement cases examined in the NASAA report to Congress. The Better Business Bureau reported that two individuals with organized crime backgrounds have been involved in some way with at least forty (11 percent) of the 360 "blank check" blind pool offerings registered by the SEC since 1985. Two people are now in prison in Paris for their part in a global penny stock scheme involving a U.S. stock fraud that may have reached $1 billion. The promoter in question has been identified as being involved in organized crime, particularly with the Genovese crime family in New York.

Even in the best penny stock, investors are believed to lose all or some of their investment 70 percent of the time. The presence of fraud pushes up that figure to 90 percent. Abusive promoters of these low-priced securities rely on high-pressure telemarketing techniques to lure in hundreds of thousands of new, unsophisticated investors, a majority of whom are first-timers to the market.

Jim L. (one of his many aliases) had a full-time day job, but with assets that consisted only of a phone, patience, and an easy way of talking, he managed to parlay a nighttime sideline into an ill-gotten fortune. The routine went like this. Jim would phone someone—let's say Mrs. Smith—and quickly assure her that, no, he didn't want her to invest a single cent. "Never invest with someone you don't know," he preached. But he said he would like to demonstrate his firm's "research skill" for free by sharing with her the forecast that a particular penny stock was about to experience a significant price increase. Sure enough, the price soon went up.

His second phone call wasn't to solicit an investment, either. Jim simply wanted to share with Mrs. Smith a prediction that the price of another penny stock was about to go down. "Our forecasts will help you decide whether ours is the kind of firm you might someday want to invest with," he added. As predicted, the price of the penny stock subsequently went down.

By the time Mrs. Smith received the third call, she was a believer. She not only wanted to invest, but insisted on it—with a big enough investment to make up for the opportunities she had already "missed out on."

What Mrs. Smith had no way of knowing was that Jim had begun with a calling list of 200 persons. In the first call, he told 100 people that the price would go up, and the other 100 were told it would go down. When it went up, he made a second call to the 100 who had been given the "correct" forecast. Of these, 50 were told the next price move would be up and 50 were told it would be down.

Once the predicted price decline occurred, Jim had a list of 50 persons eager to invest, including Mrs. Smith. After all, how could they go wrong with someone so obviously infallible in forecasting prices? But go wrong they did, the moment they decided to send Jim a half million dollars from their collective savings accounts.

What are penny stocks? There is no set, accepted definition of penny stock. Some people define it as stock priced under one dollar, some under five dollars. Some people include only those securities traded in the National Quotation Bureau, which is commonly referred to as the "pink sheets," while others include the entire over-the-counter, or OTC, market. (By the way, ZZZZ Best started out on the pink sheets in January of 1986 at 5 cents a share and was quickly manipulated to a price of over $4 per share.) The Securities Division considers a stock to be a penny stock if it trades at or under $5 per share and trades in either the pink sheets or on NASDAQ.

A true penny stock will have less than $4 million in net tangible assets and will not have a significant operating history. In other words, if a company has real assets, such as equipment and inventory, and is engaged in a real business, such as manufacturing, then the Securities Division does not consider the stock to be a penny stock even though the shares are low-priced.

Abuse of penny stocks is not new and dates back at least to the 1940s and 1950s, a period when worthless shares in uranium mine stocks were bought and sold over the counter of a Salt Lake City coffee shop. However, it is only in the last decade that broker dealers specializing in penny stocks have grown from a handful of small firms. Penny stocks have evolved from a primarily regional phenomenon with active penny markets in Denver, Utah, and Spokane, to a problem of truly national proportions. The number of firms specializing in penny stocks a half decade ago was fifty-five in fewer than six states. Today, an estimated 325 penny stock firms have set up main offices in twenty-nine states, employing several thousand brokers.

How does the market work in theory? Historically, the OTC stock market has acted as the birthplace and cradle for many new and expanding companies. It is in this marketplace that many of these companies raise the capital needed to commence or build on existing operations. The process of distributing ownership certificates (stock) is called an initial public offering (IPO), or a new issue.

Trades in exchange-listed stocks are facilitated by a stockbroker who seeks the best available price in an auction system, with the transaction taking place on the floor of the New York Stock Exchange (NYSE) or another national or regional stock exchange.

Be aware of the fact that most penny stock companies have no reporting requirements with the SEC. That is, they do not have to submit quarterly 10 Qs or comply with the auditing standards that are set by the SEC. Basically, this means that they are accountable to no one. This was a big advantage for me while perpetrating the ZZZZ Best fraud. Today, penny stock brokers do whatever they can to hide from the SEC, including recommending stocks listed on the Vancouver Exchange. Why do that when America is flooded with investment opportunity? Because the reporting requirements of the Vancouver Exchange are not nearly as demanding as those of companies under the scrutiny of the SEC.

OTC trades are carried out within, or between, the trading departments of brokerage firms. These brokerages, or a single brokerage firm as often is the case in penny stocks, are called market makers when they carry an inventory of the stock and quote the prices at which they are willing to buy and sell securities. The difference between the "bid" (the price at which a customer may sell a security) and the "asked" (the price at which a customer may buy a security) is known as the "spread." For instance, if a penny stock is bid at 1½ ($1.50) and asked at 2 ($2), then the spread is 50 cents, or 33 percent of the bid price. This latter amount is the minimum that an investor would have to recoup in order to break even on an investment in the stock. In most securities transactions, your broker acts as your agent, arranging a transaction directly between you and a third party. You pay the broker a commission for arranging that trade.

Penny stocks are susceptible to price manipulation. A common and easy manipulation is for a broker to gather a large holding of a penny stock at a very low price. Through the use of high-pressure sales techniques, the sales force of the broker hypes the stock and stirs up demand, which seemingly justifies the continual rise in prices given by the broker. The price continues to rise until there are no more investors who will buy, and then the bottom falls out and the price plummets. Sometimes the broker will buy back the securities at the fallen prices to recapture the stockpile for a future revival of the stock; more often investors are simply left holding the worthless stock.

A June 1984 survey by NASAA and the Council of Better Business Bureaus revealed these penny stock problems:

- In Colorado, the 1982 collapse of the Denver penny stock market resulted in thousands of Coloradans losing hundreds of millions of dollars.

- One penny stock company's prospectus revealed it "has engaged in no business whatsoever and has no operating history." It disclosed also that it "would not start business until the offering was completed and could provide the investor with no information whatsoever as to our intentions."

* The president of one computer firm was revealed to be
  a fifteen-year-old high school freshman. The vice president was sixteen; his father had been convicted on two
  counts of perjury in connection with an earlier SEC
  investigation.

How are so many individual investors being burned? Paul
Young, one of the nation's leading investment fraud experts,
provides the following four reasons why so many individual
investors are being defrauded:

1. Suitability. This is by far the most common abuse
   committed by brokers and firms: selling people
   investment products for which they are not suitable
   in light of their individual circumstances, needs and
   goals, or objectives. Basically, this means that if you
   don't know anything about the business you are
   investing in, you have no objective standard to compare the broker's warrants and representations about
   the company's performance with an outside source.

2. Misrepresentation. The second most common issue
   found in securities scams is outright lying or failing
   to tell the truth.

3. Commission and churning. Brokers simply sell higher-
   commission products to investors because the commission is higher for the broker. "Churning" is when a
   broker or firm repeatedly buys and sells in an account
   to generate more commissions.

4. Miscellaneous abuses. Unauthorized trading, failure
   to follow instructions, breach of fiduciary duty, and
   others.

When Mary, a recent retiree, specified "no high-risk investments," she got hit with a grand slam. She invested her life savings, but it wasn't until months later that she discovered her $600,000 investment was lost. First, the broker had set her up with a high-risk stock that she wasn't suitable for. By doing this, he obviously misrepresented the services that his firm was providing for her. The stock he invested in had a very high commission rate for the broker, and he kept buying and selling repeatedly. He failed to follow her instructions by performing unauthorized trading. The abuse was so flagrant in this case that Mary was able to go through arbitration and eventually recover her money.

Arthur Levitt, chairman of the U.S. Securities and Exchange Commission, spoke to students at Florida Atlantic University in Boca Raton regarding tips on finding a good stockbroker:

- Ask your friends and business associates for the names of brokers they have used with success.

- Interview prospective brokers and firms. Don't be tempted to go with the first one you interview.

- Check out the broker and the firm. How long have they been in business? What is his or her education and prior experience?

- The branch manager also should be interviewed. Ask the same questions posed to the broker.

- References are important. Ask the broker for the names of twelve current clients. Call each one and ask questions.

- Broker product knowledge is critical. Does the broker want to sell you a certain type of investment or propose, in writing, a comprehensive strategy?

* Commissions count. You are entitled to know, before you buy, the fees and commissions you will be paying. Ask!

* Monthly statements are sometimes difficult for customers to read because they do not detail commissions. Go over your statement each month.

* Take responsibility for your money. Get involved in all phases of your investments. Never grant discretionary authority. Keep informed.

Be sure to practice due diligence when it comes to investing your money with other people. Make sure that they have your best interest at heart. Swindlers tend to copy reputable firms by using the same methods in identifying individuals who may have an interest in stocks. The telephone, mail, advertisements, referrals, and image are the top five ways brokers go after new victims. Don't rely on these alone. Use the tips above.

So-called boiler-room operations remain the best way for swindlers to defraud investors. A telemarketer can make 100 to 200 calls a day from anywhere. Stephen Michaels has owned and operated some of the biggest boiler rooms on both the East and West coasts. Stephen, a frequent guest on our nationally syndicated radio program, now assists law enforcement on the federal, state, and local levels. In fact, on the local level he now works closely with LAPD Officer Ron Gould, who heads up the Gray Squad, a senior citizens' crime prevention outreach program. He says, "It was easy to cheat someone who you didn't have to look at face-to-face." Michaels also admits that he could very easily sell the "sizzle and not the steak" over the phone. Newspapers and magazines offer attractive investment opportunities all the time. Since very little is done to check on the companies advertising, this becomes an easy way for firms to promote their worthless penny stocks.

An old scheme, which looks alot like a Ponzi scheme, involves paying fast profits to initial investors and asking them to refer you to others. Then you get the initial investor to reinvest, plus a second investor from the referral.

Some firms go first-class to entice you, showing you plush offices, decorating, desks, and brokers in suits. This is to give the image of success similar to that of a major brokerage firm. Penny stock firms love to do this because they do not have the name recognition of a Merrill Lynch.

A young schoolteacher from the Los Angeles area received a direct-mail piece advertising information on penny stocks. She recognized the name from a recent magazine she had read a few months earlier. Wanting to invest for the future and not knowing much about the industry, she decided to call the 800 number. The man on the phone was very polite and seemed to be interested in helping her make a good decision. He invited her to their regional office, which was in downtown Los Angeles. The sixtieth floor was totally dedicated to the firm, with a receptionist and waiting room immediately outside the elevator door.

A broker in a suit came out and escorted her around the facility. The whole experience took her breath away. She couldn't believe how professional this company was. She felt very comfortable investing until sixty days later, when she discovered that nearly all of her $125,000 inheritance was gone. Fortunately, she later received an arbitration award for $140,000.

There is the old saying, "Don't believe anything you hear and only half of what you see." As an investor in today's stock market, you have to take the extra step. Watch for the following warning signs to alert you to a possible penny stock fraud:

1. High-pressure sales techniques. Investing in legitimate

stocks is long-term. A little company is not going to skyrocket in a couple of weeks. The con man doesn't want you to wait a day so you can discuss the opportunity with some family and friends. Always seek counsel from someone who is nonbiased.

2. Expectation of quick, high profits. Historically, penny stocks usually don't move quickly. Anytime you hear buzz words like *quick* and *high,* be cautious.

3. Low risk or no risk. It's unbelievable how blatant some people can get. Every investment has risk. If you hear "no risk," run!

4. Blind pools and blank checks. Never give blank checks or invest without being told exactly how your money will be spent. It just isn't a good idea to hand over too much control.

5. Unauthorized transactions. In some cases, an unauthorized trade is simply a mistake, but you should complain immediately, both verbally and in writing, to your broker, your broker's manager, and the Securities Division. Make sure your broker always checks with you before making an investment.

6. Mismarked trade confirmations or new account cards. Be wary if your trade confirmation is marked "unsolicited" if your broker did, in fact, solicit the trade. While it may be a simple mistake, unscrupulous penny stock brokers often mark the confirmation as unsolicited to avoid the registration laws and the "fair, just, and equitable" standard. Watch for misstatements about your net worth, income, and account objectives as well. Investing in penny stocks

is speculative business and involves a high degree of risk. Often brokers will enhance the new account card to make it seem that you are suitable for a penny stock investment when you are not.

Not all penny stocks are scams. Despite all the problems and the millions of dollars involved with them, there are legitimate companies whose securities trade in the pink sheets at very low prices. Struggling young companies just starting out are perfect examples. Investing in a young company early can eventually, in years, pay off nicely.

To choose the right company, you must know something about the business in which the company engages. Like I said earlier, you must be able to evaluate the feasibility of the company's business plan and the company's ability to compete in its market. Be patient. You may have to wait for years for the company to experience the necessary growth needed for a good payoff. (Of course, a little bit of luck wouldn't hurt.)

If you do decide to gamble with penny stocks, the Better Business Bureau has a few tips before investing:

- Determine how much you can afford to lose. Don't gamble any of the money you need for regular expenses or future plans.

- Get it in writing—and read it. Don't rely on the talk of a penny stock salesperson.

- Hang up on abusive, high-pressure telephone salesmen. Remember, penny stock salespeople will sometimes go to great lengths to get a sale.

- Try to get independent verification of the "bid" and "ask" prices that are quoted. Ask the broker for the names of at least two other firms trading in the stock.

* Beware of claims of advance knowledge about pending announcements that will drive up the price of the
stock. The SEC calls that insider trading. When it
comes to penny stock, almost all such claims are
phony. Insider trading is against the law. No legitimate brokerage firm is going to encourage you to
invest on the basis of "secret" or "not yet announced"
information.

* Don't be impressed that the brokerage firm owns a big
chunk of the stock. A penny stock salesperson may
attempt to woo a prospective customer by pointing out
that his or her brokerage firm holds a major portion of
the outstanding float of a stock. Keep in mind that the
firm may have paid little or nothing for the stock.

* Exercise caution when it comes to profit predictions
and special analysis. If the broker indicates that his
firm is recommending the stock, ask to see a copy of
the related research report. Established brokerage
firms have research departments that publish detailed
analyses on the pros and cons of individual stocks.

* Check out the brokerage firm and the stockbroker.
Call your state securities agencies for a report on their
track record of disciplinary infractions.

Use common sense. The chances of a penny stock becoming the next Apple Computer or Standard Oil are slim to none.
Don't be pressured into any investment. And, above all, don't
invest in carpet cleaning companies run by eighteen-year-old
kids with big egos!

CHAPTER 20

The "T"
Telemarketing

"I can't believe I fell for it," Janet D. says now. She thought she knew what a fraud was. But when she received an official-looking sweepstakes postcard telling her she could win $1 million in return for her $20 "registration fee," she decided to respond. Later a man called, asking for her credit card number to certify she was a "cardholder." A few weeks later she received a box of vitamins she'd never ordered and a $200 charge to her credit card. When she called to complain, the company's phone had been disconnected.

In December of last year, federal agents arrested more than 400 people in locations across the United States on charges of fraudulent telemarketing. The number of arrests is most significant because they highlight a substantial change in law enforcement's ability to investigate and prosecute fraud conducted over the telephone.

Fraudulent telemarketing commonly refers to any fraud scheme that uses the telephone as a means of making contact with prospective victims. The term includes everything from

phony investment deals, which frequently solicit tens of thousands of dollars or more from victims, to charity requests, which
may seek only $20 or $30 per victim. According to *Criminal Law
News,* experts estimate that American consumers lose $40 billion
per year to a wide range of telemarketing schemes.

There are four common subsets of telemarketing:

1. **Premium Promotion.** Premium promotion is when
an award or bonus is given with purchase of the company's product. Commissioned telemarketers mislead
each victim into believing that he or she has won a
valuable prize and must make a "token" purchase of
the company's product in order to be eligible to receive
the award. Such sales are fraudulent, regardless of
whether the victim receives the product and the
bonus, because the sale was induced by a promise that
never materialized.

2. **One in Five Promotion.** In this scenario, victims are
told that they will receive one of five listed awards,
typically cars and cash, and are led to believe that
they have an equal chance of receiving any of these
awards. Instead, virtually all victims receive a "gimme
prize," cheap merchandise such as costume jewelry or
a worthless travel certificate.

3. **Sweepstakes Promotion.** Victims are led to believe
that they have won or are highly likely to win a
sweepstakes drawing. In "Say No to Drugs" promotions, victims are led to believe that the money
solicited will be used to help save children from
drugs and alcohol.

4. **Recovery Schemes.** This involves contacting people who had lost money to telemarketers on prior occasions and soliciting additional money as a fee for helping the victim recover money lost to other telemarketers.

Unfortunately, telemarketers prey on our elderly, just as door-to-door solicitors do (see chapter 11). In Los Angeles, programs like the Grey Squad have been developed to prevent the elderly from being defrauded. Ron Gould, who heads the Grey Squad, says, "Telemarketers and law enforcement alike recognize the vulnerability of the more trusting, forgetful, and lonely elderly."

Scam artists sell "dummy lists" of their victims to telemarketing companies nationwide. I must have "idiot" written in front of my name because I get more junk mail and telemarketers than anyone I know.

Julia Craig reports in the *Criminal Law News* that there are numerous federal and state laws that regulate the business of telemarketing, touching on everything from the hours during which calls can be made to the use of phony phone names. In 1994 Congress amended the mail fraud statute, Title 18, United States Code, Section 1341. Under federal law, a telemarketer commits fraud if he or she intentionally misleads or deceives another person in order to get money from that person, and if interstate telephone calls or mailers are used as part of the scheme. Craig writes that false statements include half-truths and statements designed to deceive. Some telemarketers believe that they are protected from prosecution if they grant refunds to anyone who complains to them. However, under federal law, a refund does not "cure" the fraud.

In the 1980s, law enforcement found it difficult to locate telemarketers because victims were too embarrassed to report their losses. Telemarketers would also use phony salespeople names so owners would claim that they had no idea their salespeople were lying and that the telemarketer in question had already quit.

Since 1993 the FBI has increased undercover investigation with Operation Disconnect. Over 200 arrests and convictions resulted from the FBI's work. Many of the telemarketers arrested had been tape-recorded. Senior Sentinel was a code name for one of the missions under Operation Disconnect. Senior Sentinel obtained tape recordings of telemarketers by using one of fraudulent telemarketing's more nefarious hallmarks, the repeated victimization of vulnerable individuals. As noted above, once a person sends money to a telemarketer, it is inevitable that the person's name and phone number will be passed on to other telemarketers in other companies, who will proceed to capitalize on the vulnerability demonstrated in the first sale. FBI agents got permission to transfer former victims' phone lines to a telephone answered and recorded by law enforcement.

Craig reports that federal sentencing guidelines enable prosecutors to seek in excess of ten years for convicted telemarketers. The length of the sentence depends primarily on two factors: the amount of loss generated by the scheme and the type of scheme. The defendant's past criminal history can also be a factor.

When Laura A. of Maryland got a call from a charity asking her to donate $50 to "help find a cure for childhood leukemia," she was told that "almost all" of her contribution would go directly to research. Only after her check was cashed did she find out from a magazine article that that same charity forwarded only $5 of each $50 donation to research and kept the rest for "overhead" and "promotion."

The Alliance Against Fraud in Telemarketing, along with the FTC, put together a brochure called *Swindlers Are Calling*. The following are eight things you should know about telemarketing fraud:

1. Most telephone sales calls are made by legitimate businesses offering legitimate products or services. Wherever honest firms search for new customers, so do swindlers. Phone fraud is a multi-billion-dollar business that involves selling everything from bad or nonexistent investments to the peddling of misrepresented products and services. Everyone who has a phone is a prospect; whether you become a victim is largely up to you. [In fact, one of the few legitimate things I did while I owned ZZZZ Best was telemarket for business. Mom and I started calling for clients from our garage in the beginning, and we worked our way up to 300 telemarketers before I resigned.]

2. There is no way to determine positively whether a sales call is on the up and up simply by talking with someone on the phone. No matter what questions you ask or how many you ask, skilled swindlers have ready answers. That's why you should always check out the organization before you actually buy or invest. Legitimate callers have nothing to hide.

3. Phone swindlers are likely to know more about you than you know about them. Depending on where they got your name in the first place, they may know your age and income, health and hobbies, occupation and marital status, education, the home you live in, what magazines you read, and whether you've bought over the phone in the past.

4. Fraudulent sales callers have one thing in common: They are skilled liars and experts at verbal camouflage. Their success depends on it. Many are coached to "say whatever it takes" by operators of the boiler rooms, where they work at rows of phone desks, making hundreds of repetitious calls hour after hour. The first words uttered by most victims of phone fraud are "The caller sounded so believable. . . . "

5. Perpetrators of phone fraud are extremely good at sounding as though they represent legitimate businesses. They offer investments, sell subscriptions, provide products for homes and offices, promote travel and vacation plans, describe employment opportunities, solicit donations, and so on. Never assume you'll know a phone scam when you hear one. Even if you've read about the kinds of schemes most commonly practiced, innovative swindlers constantly devise new ones.

6. The motto of phone swindlers is "Just give us a few good 'mooches,'" one of the terms they use to describe their victims. Notwithstanding that most victims are otherwise intelligent and prudent people, even boiler-room operators express astonishment at how many people "seem to keep their checkbooks by the telephone." Sadly, some families part with savings they worked years to accumulate on the basis of little more than a fifteen-minute phone conversation. That's less time than they'd spend considering the purchase of a major household appliance!

7. The person who "initiates" the phone call may be you. It's not uncommon for phone crooks to use direct

mailings and advertise in reputable publications to encourage prospects to make the initial contact. It's another way swindlers imitate the perfectly acceptable marketing practices of legitimate businesses. Just because you have written or phoned for additional information about an investment, product, or service doesn't mean you should be any less cautious about buying from someone you don't know.

8. Victims of phone fraud seldom get their money back, or, at best, they get no more than a few cents on the dollar. Despite efforts of law enforcement and regulatory agencies to provide what help they can to victims, swindlers generally do the same thing other people do when they get money: They spend it!

"The magazine ad said I could get a loan approved over the phone," says Thomas N. of Michigan. He thought his money worries were over when he saw the ad promising low-rate loans. When he called, the agent asked for his checking account number so the company could withdraw $250 for its "service fee." But Thomas never received a loan, and when he called his state's attorney general's office to complain, he found out that the company was being sued by dozens of other customers for fraud.

Telemarketers come in many shapes and sizes. Capitalizing on growing environmental awareness, some businesses are selling so-called water purification or filtration systems. Callers use scare tactics to convince you that your tap water is filled with impurities or cancer-causing substances. You may end up paying $300 to $500 for a device that is worth less than $50.

Another common promotion is the so-called free or low-cost vacations, which come with extra charges, hidden restrictions, and hard-to-meet conditions. You might be required to join a travel club first. Then comes the bad news. A vacation-for-two may include only airfare for one. You could be charged extra for "peak season" reservations. As a result, your vacation ends up costing two to three times what you would have paid had you made your own arrangements.

Some health-conscious consumers fall prey to telemarketers selling vitamins. As with many other scams, the sales pitch may include the incentive of a prize to get you to pay as much as $600 for a six-month supply of vitamins that are worth as little as $40.

How can we tell when these seemingly legitimate businesses are really overpriced rip-offs? From *Swindlers Are Calling*, here are nine tip-offs that a caller could be a crook:

1. High-pressure sales tactics. The call may not begin that way, but if the swindler senses you're not going to be an easy sale, he or she may shift to the hard sell. Most legitimate businesses respect an individual's right to be "not interested." High-pressure sales tactics take a variety of forms, but the common denominator is usually a stubborn reluctance to accept no as an answer.

2. Insistence on an immediate decision. If it's an investment, the caller may say something like, "The market is starting to move even as we talk." For a product or service, the urgency pitch may be that "there are only a few left" or "the offer is about to expire." The bottom line is that swindlers insist that you should or must make your decision right now! And they always give a reason.

3. The offer sounds too good to be true. The oldest advice around and still the best: An offer that sounds

too good to be true probably is. Swindlers know this, so they make three or four statements that really are true. Then, when they spring the big lie about what they're selling, you'll be more likely to believe it.

4. A request for your credit card number for any purpose other than to make a purchase. A swindler may ask you for your credit card number or, in the most brash cases, several credit card numbers for identification or verification that you have won something. Don't give your number out. If you do, always check your monthly statements for unauthorized charges.

5. An offer to send someone to your home or office to pick up the money or some other method such as overnight mail to get your funds more quickly. This is likely to be part of their "urgency" pitch. It could be an effort to avoid mail fraud charges by bypassing postal authorities or simply a way of getting your money before you change your mind.

6. A statement that something is "free," followed by a requirement that you pay for something. Although honest firms may promote free phone offers to attract customers, the difference with swindlers is that you generally have to pay to get whatever it is that's "free."

7. An investment that's "without risk." Except for obligations of the U.S. government, all investments have some degree of risk. If there were any such thing as a risk-free investment with big profits assured, the caller certainly wouldn't have to look through the phone book to find investors!

8. Unwillingness to provide written information or references such as a bank or names of satisfied customers in your area that you can contact. Swindlers generally have a long list of reasons: "There isn't time for that" or "It's a brand-new offer and printed material isn't available yet" or "Customer references would violate someone's privacy." Even with references, be cautious. Some swindlers pay off a few customers to serve as references.

9. A suggestion that you should make a purchase or investment on the basis of "trust." Trust is an admirable trait, but it shouldn't be dispensed indiscriminately, and certainly not to unknown persons calling on the phone and asking that you send money. Even so, "trust me" is a pitch that swindlers sometimes employ when all else fails.

Remember, the people who call you offering these "great deals" are very, very good at lying. In fact, you might call them professional liars. On the phone they can be anything you want them to be and more. Many elderly persons fall prey to telemarketers simply because nobody friendly has called in days. Telemarketers can make their company sound so reliable and irresistibly attractive that anyone could fall for their scams. People who fall for telemarketing scams are not stupid, only naive. Don't allow yourself to become a victim. Follow these "Ten Ways to Avoid Becoming a Victim," as provided by the Alliance Against Fraud in Telemarketing:

1. Don't allow yourself to be pushed into a hurried decision. No matter what you're told to the contrary, the reality is that at least 99 percent of everything

that's a good deal today will still be a good deal a week from now! The other 1 percent isn't worth the risk of finding out!

2. Always request written information, by mail, about the product, service, investment, or charity and about the organization that's offering it. For legitimate firms this shouldn't be a problem.

3. Don't make any investment or purchase you don't fully understand. The beauty of the American economy is the diversity of investment vehicles and other products available. Unless you fully understand what you'd be buying or investing in, you can be badly burned. Swindlers intentionally seek out individuals who don't know what they're doing.

4. Ask what state or federal agencies the firm is regulated by and/or is required to be registered with. If you get an answer, ask for a phone number or address that you can use to contact the agency, and verify the answer yourself. If the firm is not accountable to any regulation, you may want to increase your level of caution accordingly.

5. Check out the company or organization. Never, ever assume the company is legitimate. Swindlers want to assume that most people never follow through. Look at it this way: Most victims of fraud contact a regulatory agency *after* they've lost their money; it's far better to make the contact and obtain whatever information is available *while you still have your money.*

6. If an investment or major purchase is involved, request that information also be sent to your accountant, financial adviser, banker, or attorney for an evaluation and opinion. Swindlers don't want you to seek a second opinion. Their reluctance or evasiveness could be your tip-off.

7. Ask what recourse you would have if you make a purchase and aren't satisfied. If there's a guarantee or refund provision, it's best to get it in writing and be satisfied that the business will stand behind its guarantee before you make a final financial commitment.

8. Beware of testimonials that you may have no way of checking out. They may involve nothing more than someone being paid a fee to speak well of a product or service.

9. Don't provide personal financial information over the phone unless you are absolutely certain the caller has a bona fide need to know. That goes especially for your credit card and bank account numbers.

10. If necessary, hang up. If you're simply not interested, if you become subject to high-pressure sales tactics, if you can't obtain the information you want or get evasive answers, or if you hear your own better judgment whispering that you may be making a serious mistake, just say good-bye.

Consumers Research, Inc., obtained the following script during one of its roundups by officers of the Arizona and California Corporations Commissions. This is a typical script telemarketers use in trying to make one of their bogus deals:

(Client's name), let me ask you something. Providing everything I've told you checks out and the opportunity is as good as I've told you it is, this is something you want to do, isn't it?

(Pause for response) So basically, if you like the program, you and I have a deal, right?

(Going for the close) Mr. (Client's name), what you're saying to me is that the only thing standing in the way of doing business today is the paperwork, right?

(If Yes) Great! So to recap and make sure I understand, you could sit down and write a check in the amount of $— today to participate in this once-in-a-lifetime opportunity without any problem, right?

(If No) I appreciate that. What dollar amount could you handle right now?

(Get amount and go for the close) So once again, what you are saying is that when you get this information and everything checks out just like I have told you, I will have myself a new client, right?

The scammer also may try to pressure you with references to the amount of work he's going to have to do on your behalf to get things started. Note how the script tries to play on your honesty, counting on you to hold yourself to the commitments the scammer is soliciting:

(Client), what I've got to do when we get off the telephone is set the records up properly. It is well in excess of two hours of paperwork and computer work.

(Client), I'm not happy with doing the work, but I'm absolutely delighted because I've got to believe the more money you make and the faster you make the money, the more and faster you'll be participating in new filings, am I right?

So, (Client), on the basis we've discussed, I'm sure you can see the kind of money we're talking about. So that I can do my part here, will there be any problem setting up the pick-up for (day) and (time)? Can I depend on that?

You see, (Client), I was brought up to believe that in today's day and age, the only thing that two people have between themselves is their own personal word.

Remember, manipulation is the key to the telemarketer's technique. Ask yourself: Why is this person trying so hard to change my mind or get me to agree to something I know so little about?

Another script seized by the Arizona Corporation Commission had these notes:

(Use five senses at least twice! Sight-Sound-Touch-Smell-Taste!)

SIGHT: Can you see where this will save you money? It's looking better all the time, isn't it?

SOUND: How does this sound to you? I think you can hear opportunity knocking, can't you?

TOUCH: Is this starting to feel better to you? That has a nice touch to it, doesn't it?

SMELL: Does it smell sweet enough for you yet? The aroma of success sure is sweet, isn't it?

TASTE: Would you like to have a taste of victory? And here's the icing on the cake.

By the time the International Gold Bullion Exchange collapsed in 1983, 25,000 customers had lost an estimated $300 million. Investors purchased precious metals, getting a discount price in exchange for agreeing to a delayed delivery program. Small checks were mailed monthly to assure customers that their investment was earning money. Some insistent individuals received their gold and silver, but, for most, delivery never came.

As P. T. Barnum noted, "There's a sucker born every minute." If you take the time to follow these steps with telemarketers, I'm confident that you will not be one of those suckers.

CHAPTER 21

The "U"
U.S. Postal Service Fraud

The U.S. Postal Service is the world's largest postal system. Every day millions of parcels are mailed throughout not only the United States but also the world. With that large of an enterprise, there's bound to be an abundance of fraud. Mail fraud, as you will see, takes many forms and victims. The criminals of mail fraud are well-respected members of their communities. They can be managers of Little League teams, belong to the PTA, and outwardly appear to be upstanding citizens. But as is the case with most white-collar crime, the perpetrator is often the person whom you would least expect.

The postal system provides a perfect shield for criminals. Mailbox centers are used as hubs for scam artists. A criminal can do business under the address of a mailbox center. Many centers even provide the box renter with a suite number as opposed to a P.O. box number, making it seem as though he is a reputable business operating at an accessible address. (Don't get me wrong, not all businesses that operate out of a postal center are scams.)

How bad is the problem of postal fraud? Martin Biegelman, who has been a postal inspector for eighteen years, provided the following information. In 1995 criminal investigations by postal inspectors resulted in the following:

» Mail fraud investigations resulted in 1,538 arrests.

» Investigations of mail bombs and explosive devices placed in mail receptacles resulted in 119 arrests.

» Interdictions of controlled substances in the mail resulted in 1,887 arrests.

» Interdictions of obscenity and child pornography in the mail resulted in 142 arrests.

» Mail theft by nonemployees and contractors led to 4,565 arrests.

» Mail theft or mistreatment of mail by employees resulted in 607 arrests and the removal of 1,116 individuals from Postal Service employment; 1,491 employees were also disciplined.

» A total of 297 employees were disciplined for miscellaneous crimes, including sabotage of equipment and theft of postal property. Of these, 59 employees were arrested and 179 were removed from Postal Service employment.

» The investigation of miscellaneous external crimes, which may include counterfeit and contraband postage, money order offenses, and vandalism, resulted in 536 arrests by the Postal Inspectors.

U.S. postal fraud can relate to any business that uses the mail to perpetrate a scam, such as phony business directories, Yellow Pages schemes, false billing scams, coupon fraud, rebate fraud, bribery, and bankruptcy fraud. For reasons of space, I focus on some of the hottest postal frauds.

Let's begin by looking at the current problem of unordered merchandise. A company sends you a gift in the mail—a ballpoint pen, a key chain, a tie. But you didn't order it. What do you do? Many people feel guilty about accepting an item they never paid for, so they make an effort to pay for it even though they did not want it. Don't feel guilty. Beware of any charges that company may try to give you. You are under no legal obligation to pay for an item you receive in the mail that you did not order.

Consumers may legally receive only two types of merchandise through the mail without prior consent: (1) free samples that are clearly and conspicuously marked FREE SAMPLES, and (2) merchandise mailed by a charitable organization that is soliciting optional contributions. In both of these cases, you are under no obligation to pay for the merchandise. In all other situations, it is illegal to send merchandise to someone unless that person has previously ordered or requested it.

These rules are codified in Title 39, United States Code, Section 3009. (I should know. I was convicted of seventeen counts of mail fraud.) That section of the Postal Reorganization Act of 1970 incorporates these protections for American consumers and makes the mailing of unordered merchandise unfair methods of competition and unfair trade practices under the law.

Remember, if you receive something you did not order, you can always mark the unopened package "Return to Sender." Never pay for a package that you did not order!

Another popular scam that the U.S. Postal Inspection Service warns us about is work-at-home scams. How often have you seen an advertisement that reads, "Assemble our products at home. Earn $200 per week"? Advertised opportunities to earn money by doing work in your home are frequently nothing more than fraudulent schemes and, at best, rarely result in any meaningful earnings.

Con artists like to target people who need extra money with work-at-home schemes. Victims usually include homemakers with children or people without jobs. Most of these ads usually promise "quick and easy money" with little investment and little effort. Some promotions stress that "no experience is necessary." The common characteristic in these schemes is up-front monies for information. Usually these scams require you to purchase something before you are able to start work.

A hot new work-at-home scheme is envelope stuffing. Most of these scams require up-front money for instructions on how to make money stuffing envelopes. When you pay the fee, you are typically sent a letter that says, "Run an ad like this ad and make money." The instructions tell you to place an ad just like the one you responded to. Keep in mind that modern technology has almost eliminated the need for legitimate envelope stuffing.

Other work-at-home schemes really don't offer work in the home but instead sell ideas for setting up home businesses. Other schemes require you to raise animals. There are even some that require you to produce items, such as sewing baby booties or aprons, making Christmas wreaths or toys, or fabricating other specialty products. You are not told that you are the one who must sell the items in order to make a profit. Basically, the promoters of these schemes make their money by selling you ideas or materials.

Economic pressure often forces people into falling for these mail scams. Stay away from any business opportunity that requires a fee for information about that business. They're not selling you a product or supplies, just information. What a rip!

The U.S. Postal Inspection Service also warns us about missing persons fraud. The missing persons scam is one of the more heartless crimes that is perpetrated. It preys on those who have lost loved ones and are desperate for their return.

The postal inspectors once investigated a promoter who was running a "recovery bureau." The bureau, which advertised through the mail, attempted to collect $20,000 on the basis of fraudulent claims that it knew the whereabouts of a California man's missing former wife and children. The Californian traveled to Michigan based on the promoter's promise that he could find and reclaim his family in that state. The man became suspicious when the contact he was told to visit in Michigan demanded a $20,000 payment before he would provide any information about the missing family. When the postal inspectors investigated, they found that his ex-wife and children had never been in Michigan and that the recovery bureau was a fraud.

The Postal Inspection Service warns families who have lost loved ones never to send money until the family or family member is delivered. Be cautious when information is made available at a price. Law enforcement should always be involved in a missing persons case.

The next common scam as reported by the U.S. Postal Inspection Service is postal job scams. You might have noticed an ad that says, "The U.S. Postal Service is hiring for full-time and part-time employment. Hourly salaries start at $25 an hour. For employment call 1-800-123-4567."

Postal inspectors warn that if you see this ad in your local newspaper, you are probably going to be very disappointed—and out about $30. In most instances, these companies require a pro-cessing fee, usually around $30. Frequently, the con artists pro-moting this "service" offer to provide you with training that they say will help you pass a required Postal Service pre-employment examination. Of course, this training is expensive because it demands the purchasing of books, study guides, and other train-ing materials. Some con men will even promise job placement in Postal Service jobs.

Another old yet reccurring scam is the six-cent or short-paid postage fraud. The U.S. Postal Inspection Service states that since about 1988, unscrupulous people have promoted a fraudulent scheme to sell "secret" information claiming it is legal to send a first-class letter for only two cents, three cents, or six cents. Usually the secret information is sold for $5 to $20. In return, what the victim gets is a copy of an out-of-date fed-eral law that was eliminated by the Postal Reorganization Act of 1970 (Title 39 of the U.S. Code).

Don't be conned into believing that while most of the country is paying 32 cents for a stamp, you could be paying just a few cents. There is no secret about paying for postage. In July of 1971, the Post Office Department became the United States Postal Service. The power to determine postal rates was given to the U.S. Postal Service. Postal rates are no longer established by direct legislative enactment but instead through administrative action by the Postal Service Board of Governors and the independent Postal Rate Commission. Also, section 3 of the act provides that postage rates, as well as classes of mail and fees for postal services, prescribed before the effective date of the new law, were to remain in effect until they were changed in accordance with the new administrative rate-making procedures outlined by the act. The next time you receive a letter selling you information about the two-cent, three-cent, or six-cent stamp, report your findings to the post office.

Finally, the U.S. Postal Inspection Service reminds us about foreign lotteries by mail. Say you hear the state lotto jingle on the radio. The announcer says the jackpot has been raised to $50 million. You've got a sudden case of lotto fever. Next thing you know, there's a brochure in your mail urging you to participate in some foreign country's lotto—maybe one in Australia or Canada—via convenient mail-order purchase of lottery tickets or a share in a pool of tickets. You start thinking that getting into a new game might improve your luck, and you ask yourself, "Why not do it?" The U.S. Postal Inspection Service can give you the answer: Don't do it. Why? Two reasons:

1. *It's illegal.* A federal statute prohibits mailing payments to purchase any ticket, share, or chance in a foreign lottery.

2. *It's impractical.* Unlike playing in your state's lottery, you cannot be certain that you will obtain the play you paid for.

Most foreign lottery solicitations sent to addresses in the United States do not come from foreign government agencies or licensees. Instead, they come from bootleggers who seek huge fees from those who wish to play. The activities are neither controlled nor monitored by the government. In other words, there is no accountability. Bootleggers can counterfeit confirmation letters and even tickets, and they are all totally worthless.

Congress has enacted limited exemptions in the prohibition of sending lottery material through the mail. However, no exemption has been made that would allow foreign lottery opportunities to use the U.S. mail to operate, promote, or enter one of its lotteries. First-time offenders convicted of knowingly violating the postal anti-lottery statute face penalties of up to a $1,000 fine and two years in prison. Persons who fall for such lottery scams are usually not prosecuted, just embarrassed that they fell for the old foreign sweepstakes scam!

The last example of U.S. postal fraud I will examine is insurance fraud. Remember, any use of the mail in an illegal scheme constitutes mail fraud. David Greenberg and Robert Hantz were the subjects of the book *The Super Cops*, which was later made into a movie. The television series "Starsky and Hutch" was also based on their exploits. In the mid-1970s Greenberg left the police force and was elected a New York state assemblyman. The next time Greenberg's name was in the papers was in the late 1970s, when he was convicted and sent to prison for insurance fraud.

Greenberg was a suspect in a series of false insurance claims filed by his company, Video USA, a franchiser of video rental stores headquartered in Brooklyn. The claims filed by Video USA involved robberies, burglaries, fires, and water damage. The insurance companies were Chubb, Kemper, Cigna, and Atlantic Mutual.

By 1989 the Inspection Service investigation resulted in the indictment of David Greenberg. The charges were insurance-related mail fraud. In April 1990 Greenberg and several others were convicted. The motive, as always, was to make a quick buck.

The law tries to protect consumers by making it illegal for any person or business to use the mail system for illegal or fraudulent activities. If you are ever scammed and part of the scam includes anything that has been mailed, you have a case. Many times the only legitimate part of the scam is what is being mailed. This does not protect the con artist from being convicted by the U.S. Postal Inspection Service.

Here are some helpful reminders on how to protect yourself from mail fraud:

1. Don't open mail that is not yours or merchandise you didn't order.

2. Don't pay for anything that you didn't order.

3. Don't go into business with anyone without meeting the person and visiting his or her facility, especially when dealing with work-at-home schemes.

4. Watch out for "too good to be true" offers that are really money-making scams.

5. Never pay up-front fees. If you must, use your credit card.

6. Don't ever respond to U.S. postal job opportunities through any source other than the U.S. Postal Service.

7. Use common sense! Two-cent, three-cent, or six-cent offers are blatant frauds.

8. Remember, it is illegal to become involved in foreign lotteries, chain letters, and pyramid schemes.

Beware of your mailbox! Every day con men are using it as a shield between you and proper due diligence. Even though the U.S. Postal Service works diligently to protect us, we as consumers must be alert. Frauds range from misleading coupons to $20,000 missing persons scams. Our only hope to stop them is through education. After reading this chapter, you are now equipped with the knowledge to protect yourself. All you have to do is use it!

CHAPTER 22

The "V"
Valet Parking

It was a cool February day as I drove my 1989 Nissan Sentra (also known as the Dentmobile) over the canyon from the San Fernando Valley to Beverly Hills. I had been asked to lunch by a doctor friend who has an office off Wilshire Boulevard. As is the case with most of the buildings in Beverly Hills, parking is underground. I pulled my car up to the smiling attendant (I later found out why he was smiling), handed him my keys, left the car running, got a claim ticket, and made my way up to the second floor.

The doctor and I took our time eating lunch. We both forgot about the pressures of working and simply enjoyed each other's company. It was 2 P.M. when I finally got off the elevator and handed my ticket to another smiling parking attendant who was sitting in a thick, glass-enclosed office. After examining my ticket and doing a few calculations, he told me I owed him $18.75.

"You're crazy!" I screamed, trying to remember that I was still on parole and that beating up some parking attendant would definitely send me back to prison.

"That's the price, my friend," he said as he pointed to a sign that read: $2.75 PER TWENTY MINUTES, MAXIMUM $18.75. "I don't set the rules, I just enforce them," he added.

"And I just won't comply with them," I replied. "My car isn't even worth $18.75!" When I told him that I wanted my ticket back so that I could get my doctor friend to validate it, he said that none of the offices validated parking.

Realizing that I had no other option, I reluctantly paid the attendant. He had one of those "I always get my way" looks on his face that only added insult to injury. It wasn't that I believed that *he* was actually keeping the money, because the building is owned by a large corporation, but he did get some kind of evil pleasure out of telling me (and probably others) how much they owed for parking. The irony of this story is that I also had to tip the guy who finally brought me my car!

I don't know about you, but I've just about had it with the price of parking my car. Having made such a bold statement, I would guard myself and say that for those who live in the Midwest or rural areas, you probably can't relate to such a frustration. But for many of us who live in Los Angeles, New York, Chicago, and even Atlanta, parking, and the tip that is almost always expected by a valet, has quickly become a major expense for the consumer. In fact, it is so bad in New York that many people simply don't own cars anymore.

I am of the opinion that this whole parking and valet business, along with its tipping, is ridiculous (I think I'm venting a little here so just bear with me—therapists say that such an exercise is actually helpful). With gas and car insurance prices on the rise, the last thing I need is to factor in an additional $500 a year for parking. I understand that in New York $500 would be a good price for one month.

In an outstanding article in the *Los Angeles Times* on the

subject, Marnell Jameson puts the problem into perspective: "Quick. You pull into a nice hotel. The porter takes three bags from your car to the front desk. Do you tip? If so, how much? Then the bellman takes your bags from the desk to your room. Tip? How much? While you're settling in, a bellman delivers a bottle of chilled champagne, 'compliments of the management.' Tip for a gift? As you leave for dinner, the garage attendant brings up your car. You noticed a sign near the registration desk that said overnight parking was $5 a day. Does that cover car retrieval, or do you tip for that? Oh, by the way, you only had three singles driving in."

Jameson later adds, "And that's just for a hotel. What about tips for beauticians, valets, food delivery drivers, frozen yogurt scoopers—who all have an implied hand out?"

If you don't think the valet parking problem affects you, I want an honest answer to the following question. Maybe you haven't had the experience I had at that Beverly Hills office building, but what about the last time you went out for dinner at a nice restaurant? Did they offer free valet parking? Let's say, for the sake of argument, that they did. Was it really free? Of course not. Even though the attendant gets paid a wage by the restaurant, he makes the *real* money from tips. That's why it bothers me when I see signs at many restaurants that say VALET PARKING $2.00. I've got to pay the $2.00 plus a tip.

I know what you're probably thinking. Not all parking attendants are bad and they're entitled to make a living. I agree. But the problem as I see it is the exploitation of a convenience-oriented society. Although it cannot be labeled a fraud or even a violation of a consumer's rights, building and restaurant owners are literally exploiting our laziness.

Valet parking is now offered not only at restaurants but also at selected shopping malls, markets, and even hospitals.

According to the *Los Angeles Times,* national surveys show that the average customer will tolerate a walk of 200 to 500 feet from car to destination. In a day and age when Federal Express and faxes are too slow, our hurry-up society has made the decision that our time is too valuable to spend an extra ninety seconds parking our cars. The cost? A multi-million-dollar industry that in the 1950s would have never gotten off the ground.

I have two objections to this industry. I'll spend the majority of the time on the first and will conclude with the second. The first is at the level of the office building owners who have made it a financial disincentive for tenants to provide validated parking for their customers by increasing the cost dramatically. Like all changes, the shift from free parking to $18.75 was very subtle. It has happened in my lifetime.

As a kid growing up, if I went to the dentist, doctor, or bank with my parents, there was never a charge for parking. Buildings had a ticket validation process in which you drove up and took a ticket, the little gate sprung open, and in you went. The parking attendant never had an attitude when you presented a validated ticket (like they do now for those few buildings that still offer free parking). And, as far as I know, attendants were content with the wage the building paid them.

But then it happened. Although I haven't been able to track down the first building owner who decided that the parking market could bear the expense, I have a feeling it all began at some corporate board meeting. Please allow me a little poetic license as I attempt to re-create what probably happened:

Seven men sat in the smoke-filled room in their usual semi-circle. "Bill, how can we generate more revenue to pay for these increasing property taxes and maintenance fees?" asked the treasurer of the company.

"I don't know," Bill replied. "Maybe we can increase the rent?"

"Won't work. We've already done that three times in five years," answered Alex, who constructed the building and now sat on the board.

"I've got it," said John, the company's chief financial officer. "Why don't we raise the price of parking?"

"What do you mean?" Bill asked, leaning forward and staring intently at John.

"Well, right now we provide validation stamps and stickers for tenants for almost nothing. Let's raise the prices, add another attendant, and say we are going to 'beef up security.' Then we'll tell the tenants that if they can't afford to purchase their monthly validation, they can simply allow their clients and patients to pay for it themselves. It will bring in at least another $100,000 a year."

The men exchanged glances, and a few of them even grinned. "If people complain, we just tell them that we are looking out for the safety of their vehicle and that's the cost of doing business," concluded John.

"That's a great idea," Bill said. "All in favor . . ." Everyone raised their hands.

OK, so I have an overactive imagination. But I'm willing to bet that the change occurred because of economic pressure. Instead of absorbing the cost of higher taxes and upkeep, the owners have passed on the cost to the consumer. Although in other chapters of this book I have provided advice directly from the Better Business Bureau or the Federal Trade Commission, I can offer no such wisdom here. It is perfectly legal to charge for parking in this country. In fact, some of the biggest parking fees you will ever pay are incurred when you go to a federal or state court! I've been there a few times. No, this problem isn't going to disappear. It'll probably get even worse.

The only advice I can leave you with corresponds to my second objection to the industry—namely, don't call laziness convenience. What I mean is, when you drive up to a mall or even a restaurant, *and you have the choice between valet parking or do-it-yourself-parking,* choose the latter, not the former. If you're like me and you've chosen valet parking in the past and tried to justify it by calling it convenient, be honest. You're lazy, and as a result you are willing to pay between $2 and $10 just to make life a little easier.

If you are one of those fortunate few who can afford this expense, my hat is off to you. But as for me, I'm going to pass up that valet every time. Why? Because it hits at a deeper problem. It is my opinion that our society has trouble differentiating between *needs* and *wants.* I had Mike Haga, an economist, on my radio show, and he gave a startling fact about how much our country has in outstanding, unsecured credit card debt. He said that the figure is over $1 trillion. And when I asked him how that figure got that high, he responded by saying we live in a culture that has blurred the lines between *needs* and *wants.*

We really didn't *need* that new stereo system or entertainment center—we just *wanted* it. And the reason we charged it is because we could not afford it. This is the pervading problem in our culture today. And since wealth-driven appetites are insatiable (there are never enough toys to satisfy the human heart), we just keep going deeper and deeper in debt.

So the next time you pull into a shopping mall and are rushed for time, and the temptation to use the valet arises, ask yourself if this is a need or a want. Then do what I do. Smile and wave to the attendant, just to see if you get a reaction. Remember, they're going to do it to you. I think prison has made me a little cynical—but you get the point.

CHAPTER 23

The "W"
Weight-Loss Scams

JoAnna Lund is a true modern-day success story. She's a fifty-one-year-old diet queen from DeWitt, Iowa (population 4,500), who, after a twenty-eight-year struggle, finally won her battle against fat. She lost an astonishing 130 pounds while creating Healthy Exchanges, Inc., a business that made her a nationally known spokesperson for healthy eating and led to her winning an Entrepreneur of the Year Award for 1993 and 1994. She has been featured in *Forbes*, on CNN, and on other national programs, and she was elected to represent Iowa at President Clinton's White House Council on Small Business last June—all because she quit dieting and started living healthfully.

JoAnna had tried virtually every diet program, pill, and product ever invented, lost over 1,000 total pounds—and promptly gained back 1,150 total pounds. By her forty-sixth birthday, she was at her heaviest, 300 pounds. She stopped believing that any diet could work for her.

She was right. Diets did not work for her. And they don't work for most people. Many companies promise the world but cause only further grief. A short-term diet is superficial by definition because it is temporary and almost always yields temporary results.

JoAnna discovered how to exchange those fat-, calorie-, and cholesterol-laden foods that were killing her for foods that are as healthy as they are good to eat and easy to prepare. Plus, she needed a program that she and her family could live with for the rest of their lives.

Unfortunately, simply cutting calories doesn't work for long. Surveys indicate that many dieters—more than 80 percent of women and 75 percent of men—eat fewer calories in their efforts to shed a few pounds. Simple calorie reduction doesn't guarantee successful results. A combination of eating fewer calories, exercise, and nutritional food intake is more valuable than lower caloric intake.

Being obese has serious health consequences, and losing weight can help reduce those risks. Some experts suggest that losing even 30 percent of excess weight can significantly decrease some obesity-related consequences. If you want to lose weight permanently, scientific evidence suggests it is important to make lifelong changes in how you eat and exercise. The Council on Scientific Affairs of the American Medical Association says that only through gradual long-term changes like these can you effectively lose weight and keep it off. JoAnna's story is no different from that of most people with a weight problem. There are so many programs to choose from, and most overweight people have tried them all. Many programs don't focus on lifelong changes like JoAnna's, and the result is a lifelong battle of losing and regaining weight.

Are you looking for a way to lose weight quickly and easily? Dieting is close to a national pastime. An estimated 50 million Americans will go on diets this year, and while some will succeed in taking off weight, experts suggest that very few—perhaps 5 percent—will manage to keep the weight off in the long run, yet they will spend millions of dollars trying. You may be tempted to try one of the widely advertised weight-loss programs that use a liquid diet, require special diet regimens, or claim to have a medically qualified staff.

But before you pay for any weight-loss program, take note: Although many diet programs may help you lose weight, there is little published evidence that most people *maintain that weight loss for any significant time.*

Be skeptical of approaches that promise easy, quick, or permanent weight loss. Such success is too often short-lived.

Webster defines *diet* in this way: food and drink regularly consumed. This definition gives us no indication as to how much food and drink one should consume. A controlled diet is really what most people are referring to when they use the term *diet.*

Dieting in the United States is big business. A multi-billion-dollar industry caters to approximately 34 million overweight American adults, millions of whom are dieting at any given time. Meanwhile, every year about 8 million Americans enroll in some kind of structured weight-loss program involving liquid diets, special diet regiments, or medical or other supervision. Yet weight-loss experts caution against fad diets, which rarely have a permanent effect.

Most dieters know that to lose a pound of weight, you need to reduce caloric intake or increase caloric demand by 3,500 calories. To help dieters do this, many professional weight-control programs offer special dietary and exercise plans as well as psychological support. Many such programs are independently operated though local hospitals, clinics, and physician-specialists.

One widely advertised program is very low calorie diet (VLCD). VLCD programs generally use 400- to 800-calorie-a-day liquid diet formulas as part of a twelve- to sixteen-week supplemented fast. They are often called semi-starvation diets. Available only through physicians in their offices or through hospital-based programs, VLCD programs require careful medical screening and constant medical supervision.

Most VLCD programs are targeted at people who are severely obese, that is, those who are at least 30 percent or more above their ideal body weight. Some VLCD programs now also accept individuals who are 20 percent or more above their ideal body weight. Typical weight loss may be around three pounds per week for women and five pounds per week for men. VLCD programs cost about $2,000 to $3,000 for the complete program, but some expenses may be reimbursed through health insurance.

Another widely advertised program is offered by diet clinics. Many of these programs are 1,000- to 1,500-calorie-a-day diets, where weight loss averages one to two pounds a week. You usually follow a carefully controlled menu plan. In some cases, you may be required to purchase specially packaged meals only from the company. This is not reimbursable through health insurance. The cost for these programs varies considerably from $250 to $1,000 or more. Be wary of initial low-price offers that may not include all costs.

Deceptive advertising is the biggest problem with diet programs. The advertisements usually make false claims and provide unsatisfactory products for overpriced services. The Diet Workshop, Inc., a franchiser of weight-loss plans and products, and the owner of its company-operated territories have agreed to settle Federal Trade Commission charges that they engaged in deceptive advertising by making unsubstantiated weight-loss maintenance claims and by implying without substantiation that the consumer testimonials they used represented the typical experience of dieters on the programs. The proposed settlement would prohibit the two respondents from misrepresenting the results of any weight-loss program they offer, require them to provide scientific data to back up any claims they make about weight loss and maintenance, and mandate that they make certain disclosures in connection with maintenance and other claims.

Moreover, the proposed settlement sets out standards for the type of evidence that would be required to support various maintenance claims. For example, claims about maintaining long-term loss would have to be based on evidence of consumers followed for at least two years. Furthermore, any ad claims the respondents make about maintaining weight loss would have to include the statement: "For many dieters, weight loss is temporary." Weight-loss maintenance claims in all but short broadcast ads would have to be accompanied by disclosures regarding the actual experience of Diet Workshop customers. Short broadcast ads would have to direct consumers to check with the company's local centers for detailed maintenance statistics. The proposed settlement also would bar the misleading use of testimonials and would require any testimonial to be accompanied by a disclosure that the result is not guaranteed.

The advertising for Diet Workshop programs (and many others like them that have yet to be prosecuted) included claims such as: "Join the millions who have learned how to become thin for life using Diet Workshop's nutritionally balanced weight-loss programs. Lose up to 20 lbs. in 6 weeks!" One statement read, "In 1982, I lost 32 pounds, and I am still thin today. You can be thin, too! You are assured that your QUICK LOSS is permanent loss."

The FTC alleged that through the use of such claims, Diet Workshop represented that most customers would reach their weight-loss goals and maintain their weight loss long-term or permanently. In fact, according to the FTC, Diet Workshop had no substantiation to support those claims or claims that consumers could reach their weight-loss goals in a specified period of time. In addition, according to the complaint, testimonials that appeared to reflect the typical or ordinary experience of people in the program were misleading. In some instances, client weight loss had vastly exceeded their goals—indicating that these people may not have been consuming all the food prescribed by their diet instructions. Because it supposedly monitors its program participants, Diet Workshop should have disclosed to their clients that failure to consume all the food prescribed could result in health complications.

There is no quick fix or easy answer to losing weight. Advertising that suggests that there is misleads consumers. Watch out for ads that don't mention the cost of the program. I saw one company's ad in a local coupon magazine which offered the first week free with purchase of its six-week special. The six-week program is a prepaid program with an additional registration fee. If the program is so good, why is it prepaid? Why can't customers pay weekly? What is a registration fee? Or, more important, how much is a registration fee? You're not getting anything for free with this ad.

I feel for those of you who have responded to these ads only to find out that all the diet center really cares about is money. Most programs are prepaid and most are expensive.

The Better Business Bureau constantly comes across companies like Bio Life of Aspen, a.k.a. 6 Day Bio Diet, Bio Diet, Six Day Bio Diet, and Aspen Spa. The BBB rated this company as having an unsatisfactory business performance record. In addition to misleading advertising claims and customer dissatisfaction with product results, complaints allege difficulty in obtaining refunds. Specifically, after consumers are asked to return any unused portion of the product in order to be eligible for a refund, the company asks for proof that the product was shipped; if no evidence of mailing was retained by the customer, the company refuses the refund.

There are so many diet pills and products that I cannot even begin to list them all. Companies that do not guarantee their products with full refunds are to be questioned. Some dieters peg their hopes on pills and capsules that promise to "burn," "block," "flush," or otherwise eliminate fat from their system. Certain pills may help control appetite, but they can also have serious side effects. Amphetamines, for instance, are highly addictive.

The Food and Drug Administration (FDA) has banned 111 ingredients once found in over-the-counter diet products. Substances such as alcohol, caffeine, dextrose, and guar gum have never proven to be effective in weight loss.

Beware of the following products that are touted as weight-loss wonders:

1. Diet patches, worn on the skin, have not been proven to be safe or effective. The FDA has seized millions of these products from manufacturers and promoters.

2. Fat blockers purport to physically absorb fat and mechanically interfere with the fat a person eats.

3. Starch blockers promise to block or impede starch digestion. Not only is the claim unproven, but users have complained of nausea, vomiting, diarrhea, and stomach pains.

4. Magnet diet pills allegedly flush fat out of the body. The FTC has brought legal action against several marketers of these pills.

5. Glucomannan is advertised as the "Weight Loss Secret That's Been in the Orient for Over 500 Years." There is little evidence supporting this plant root's effectiveness as a weight-loss product.

6. Bulk producers or fillers, such as fiber-based products, may absorb liquid and swell in the stomach, thereby reducing hunger. Some fillers, such as guar gum, can even be harmful, causing obstructions in the intestines, stomach, or esophagus. The FDA has taken legal action against several promoters of products containing guar gum.

7. Spirulina, a species of blue-green algae, has not been proven effective for losing weight.

8. Products containing Ma Jung. Ma Jung is really ephedrine. I almost went back to prison for using a product containing Ma Jung because it shows up as crystal methamphetamine in a urine test (just like the ones they give pilots and police officers). Knowing that a diet product can give a false positive is information that should be disclosed up front.

Whenever considering a diet program, the BBB advises checking with your doctor first. The experience of dieters and physicians indicates that there is no product that can be guaranteed to produce any weight loss.

How can you tell the sizzle from the steak when it comes to claims about weight-loss programs and products? The FTC suggests a healthy portion of skepticism. Here are some claims made by advertisers in recent years and the facts:

Claim: "Lose weight while you sleep."

Fact: Losing weight requires making significant changes affecting what kind of food—and how much—you eat. Claims for diet products and programs that promise weight loss without sacrifice or effort are bogus.

Claim: "Lose weight and keep it off for good."

Fact: Again, weight-loss maintenance requires permanent changes in your lifestyle. Be skeptical about products that claim you will keep off any weight permanently or for a long time. These claims may appeal to our laziness (especially mine!), but that doesn't make them true.

Claim: "John Doe lost 84 pounds in six weeks."

Fact: Someone else's claim of weight-loss success may have little or no relevance to your own chances of success. Don't be misled by a selected sampling.

Claim: "Lose all the weight you can for just $99."

Fact: There may be hidden costs. For example, some programs do not publicize the fact that you must buy prepackaged meals from them at costs that exceed program fees. Before you sign up for any weight-loss program, ask for all the costs. Get them in writing.

Claim: "Lose 20 pounds in just three weeks."

Fact: As a rule, the faster you lose weight, the faster you gain it back. In addition, fast weight loss may harm your health. Unless you have a medical reason, don't look for programs that promise quick weight loss.

Claim: "Scientific breakthrough . . . medical miracle."

Fact: To lose weight, you have to reduce your intake of calories and increase your physical activity. Ignore extravagant claims.

It is important for consumers to be wary of claims that sound too good to be true. When it comes to weight-loss schemes, consumers should be particularly skeptical of claims containing words and phrases like *easy, effortless, guaranteed, miraculous, magical, breakthrough, new discovery, mysterious, exotic, secret, exclusive,* and *ancient.*

Losing weight is not easy, but it doesn't have to be complicated. Focus on making slow and modest changes. A daily, disciplined regimen of a well-balanced, healthy diet and regular exercise is the key to maintaining a sensible dieting program.

Some guidelines for losing weight are:

1. Always consult a physician or qualified health professional.

2. Have accountability through family, friends, or a nonprofit support group.

3. Eat smaller portions of food.

4. Eat more fruits and vegetables for snacks instead of sweets.

5. Exercise regularly.

6. Have a plan and be realistic.

7. Limit portions of dairy products like cheese, butter, and whole milk; red meat; cakes and pastries.

8. Remember, there is no magic formula.

In 1991, about 8,500 commercial diet centers were in operation across the country, many of them owned by a half dozen or so well-known national companies. Before you join such a company, check out its history. Find out how many of its clients have been able to keep the weight off for a long period of time. Also check with your local Better Business Bureau, the FTC, and the FDA.

The FDA no longer regulates diet products before the products hit the shelves. The deregulation of the industry has caused an influx of fraud in this country. Just because you see a product on the shelf doesn't mean that it has been thoroughly checked out.

By the way, as I got out of the shower this morning I realized that it's time for me to start taking some of my own advice. I think it has something to do with being over thirty. The metabolism isn't what it used to be. Ah, to be young again!

CHAPTER 24

The "X"
Xerox Copies

The Information Age has proved to be an excellent time of prosperity for the con artist. Fakes and forgeries are increasingly infiltrating our society. With the advent of color copy machines, scanners, and color laser printers, con men can easily devise their schemes from their own homes. In the past, when people thought of copies, they thought of Xerox. We have come a long way in a short amount of time from the old Xerox copy days. Today's con artist always seems to be one step ahead. With a person's signature still representing a legal contract, the con man can use false documents and signatures to perpetrate his or her crime.

While running ZZZZ Best, I used many methods of photocopying to commit my crime. I am writing this book not to glorify what I did or to teach others to do the same, but to inform the consumer as to what extent a con man will go to to commit fraud. Remember, the con man already knows the scam; it's the consumer who needs the education.

In 1983 I abused my friendship with Tom Padgett by falsifying two insurance drafts. This led to Tom's resignation. Tom left Allstate Insurance for another insurance company called Travelers Insurance. To continue my phony restoration business, I needed confirmation from an insurance company. ZZZZ Best, aside from cleaning carpets, claimed to have an enormous restoration business. A restoration job is when the carpeting is taken out of an office building because of water damage, stains, or any other type of damage. Instead of cleaning the carpet inside the office building, the carpet is removed, cleaned and dried offsite, and then stretched out and placed back into the building.

I was looking for a verification letter supporting my $250,000 restoration job. I called Tom to see if he could give me some company stationery from Travelers Insurance. An insurance claim would verify the job. Instead of copying the letterhead, I used the real letterhead and forged the document myself. With today's technology, I could have made up my own phony letterhead without getting one from Tom. If I could have done it back then, I would have.

I decided to place my phony restoration jobs under a fraudulent business name. I opened a small, one-man office across town, had letterhead printed, and made it the official headquarters of Interstate Appraisal Services, an independent adjusting company owned and operated by Tom Padgett.

It is amazing to think that a con man would go to the extent of opening up a false business just to shield another fraudulent company. That is exactly what I did at ZZZZ Best, and it is exactly what other con men are doing today.

The art of fakery and forgery is not new. Unfortunately, con men are only getting better and harder to detect. In 1920 Albert S. Osborn wrote the first book on forgery detection. In his book he says, "The tools remain the same as they were in Shakespeare's time: the Brain and the Eye."

Renee C. Martin, a forensic document examiner, has been encountering forgeries for over forty-five years. Martin reports that a woman purchased a used car for $5,500. She put down $750 and requested that the dealer provide her with a loan for the remainder. On signing the loan papers for $4,750, she made sure that all the proper blanks were filled. No copy of the bill of sale was provided. She was told that the loan would have to be processed and the papers would be mailed to her.

When the payment book arrived with the copy of the transaction, she thought no more about it other than noting the amount of the monthly payment. About a year later, she wanted to make a lump-sum payment for the remainder of the loan and retrieved the contract to determine what she owed. Imagine her horror when she saw that the loan was for $15,000. When she reached the dealer on the telephone, all she got was double-talk.

They did manage to tell her, however, in no uncertain terms, that unless she honored the full amount of the contract, she would be sued. She gave her attorney the contract she had received in the mail. The signature on the contract looked odd. When asked whether she had actually signed this contract, she said she could not be sure. Her attorney contacted Renee Martin. When Martin received the original document, he asked for samples of her signature from canceled checks written at about the same date as the contract and compared them under a stereoscopic microscope. He found her signature had been forged. The woman successfully prosecuted the car dealer.

It is hard to imagine that a car dealership would perpetrate such a fraud, but it happens and every consumer should be made aware of it. Forging signatures is on the rise, as is creating false documents. Never sign your name to a contract without getting a copy and reading the whole contract, even if you have to take it home! No reputable company should oppose such a request.

Remember, a big company with a nice office and fine stationery might have a con man working the books. White-collar crime means just that—a person in a suit with a tie and a white-collared shirt. He will rip you off just as fast as any other con.

On my national radio show, "Consumer Hotline," one of my guests explained how a man who owned a printing company and a con man went into business together. The con man would take checks that he received from his business dealings and give them to his printing partner.

The printer would use his shop to reproduce thousands of fake checks. He could duplicate almost any check with the equipment he had in his warehouse. Fortunately, both the con man and the printer were caught—but not before they hit certain customers for over $100,000.

To prevent this from happening to you, always check through your canceled checks at the end of the month. If you notice any changes to the checks you wrote or that there are checks you didn't write, immediately report it to your local bank branch. Business owners should be especially aware of authorized written checks since they deal with larger amounts. Guard your checkbooks, keep good records, and occasionally call your bank for your balance.

There is no limit to a con. Renee C. Martin also had a case that dealt with a false contract from someone who had recently died. A woman called Martin about her problem. She was recently widowed and bogged down with her deceased husband's affairs. At the funeral, she was presented with an IOU for $10,000 with what appeared to be her husband's signature. She maintained that her husband would never have borrowed that amount without consulting her and denied payment. Additionally, there was something decidedly unusual about the signature. The estate was sued for $10,000 on the strength of the note. Martin examined the original note along with several canceled checks written by the decedent. It is not unusual after an individual dies that a signed contract or other official-looking document outlining huge debts or ownership of valuable property appears. Sometimes the signatures are valid.

Martin had experience in viewing hundreds of contracts, especially many attempts at extortion in one form or another. In this instance, the perpetrator had earlier had the husband sign a blank piece of paper. One ploy to get a signature is by asking someone to spell their name. Martin was able to prove that the signature, although it was indeed the husband's, was not intended to go with the IOU.

In this case the perpetrator had access to a legitimate signature, which was the foundation of his truth, and was able to create a phony document in hopes that only the signature would be examined. Fortunately for the widow, she had Martin to unmask the truth.

Like your credit card and your checkbook, guard your signature. Today's technology makes it too easy for the con man to use your signature as a binding contract. Try to create a distinctive signature that is yours. Experts say that the scribble that many doctors use is the easiest to forge. Try to have a clear, textbook signature. Believe it or not, a clear signature is harder for a forger to copy.

Keep a record of all your loans whether you are the borrower or the lender. Your records of loans should be disclosed to someone like your spouse. Accountability can be a great protector from fraudulent schemes. Have someone who can substantiate and corroborate your normal business practices.

Since I was never accountable to anyone at ZZZZ Best, I became my worst enemy. Whenever I needed phony financial statements or tax returns, I could call up Mark Morze and he could give me what I wanted—for a price, of course. Mark prepared all my doctored financials. When audits came, it would take Mark a few weeks to create phony bank statements and documents. To verify restoration projects, Mark used the Interstate Appraisal Services letterhead provided by Tom Padgett. It was amazing what Mark could do with Liquid Paper and a copier.

Never trust copies, especially when dealing with ex–carpet cleaners (just kidding). Don't rely only on the integrity of the people you are doing business with. Demand that you receive original and signed copies. If an auditor, banker, or lawyer had demanded original documents, I never would have made it to Wall Street.

It is estimated that the amount of counterfeit checks written annually against corporate accounts now totals about $1 billion, BankAmerica stated in "Checkmating Corporate Check Fraud," one in a series of white papers on key issues of interest to corporate treasury managers. Less than 15 percent of all monies from check fraud loss is recovered. Be careful who you take checks from! Color copiers, laser printers, scanners, and desktop publishing systems can produce professional-quality fraudulent checks at the touch of a button.

A 1992 U.S. District Court decision illustrates how the law governing bank deposits and collections can be interpreted today. In this particular case, a forger negotiated thirteen checks for a total of $650,000, drawn on the account of a company that routinely issued about 20,000 checks a month. The corporation subsequently obtained reimbursement for the bad checks from its insurance company, which in turn sued the paying bank to recover its loss. The paying bank usually ends up absorbing the loss for fraudulent checks. In this case, however, the court ruled in favor of the paying bank on the grounds that a bank following acceptable commercial standards should not be held liable in cases where the forgeries were of high quality. The forger successfully scammed the insurance company. Don't rely on your bank picking up the tab if it received fake checks written against your account that look exactly like your real ones.

To prevent fake-check fraud, many form companies are making security checks. Such checks incorporate ghosting, bleed-through numbers, and chrome metallic foil-stamping safety features. Ghosting features the word *safe* invisibly ghosted into the background which can be seen by marking with a highlighter pen or holding the document toward or away from light at an angle. Special ink dyes are used in the numbering process that cause the numbers to bleed through the paper so they are semilegible on the back side of the document. Chrome metallic foil-stamping involves a machine process that image-enhances your form and changes to a black image when color photocopied.

Fraud protection paper is even being introduced as a safeguard for your documents. The following are some of its special security features:

- Full chemical reactivity immediately signals fraudulent use by eighteen different substances. Indelible stains are produced when an alteration attempt is made.

- Invisible, covert fluorescent fibers, embedded in the sheet, allow for instant authentication of documents under UV lighting.

- Visible, overt fibers are randomly distributed across the front and back of the sheet and are immediately apparent yet impossible to successfully reproduce.

* A Fourdrinier original watermark, pressed into the paper during manufacture, is readily visible for instant authentication yet cannot be reproduced.

* Micro-printing enables a word or words to be printed so small that they appear as a line to the naked eye.

* Optically dead base sheet composition ensures the application of inks that are invisible to the naked eye but instantly apparent under UV lighting.

Ironically, many of these fraud prevention steps were created by Frank Abingate, who wrote the book *Catch Me If You Can*. He was a master at creating fraudulent checks, but he is now using his genius to prevent crimes against banks by inventing security features such as the ones mentioned above to help catch the crooks before they victimize the consumer or the bank. I admire Frank's work and only wish other former felons would do as much as he has done to help society.

Technology has forced us to take severe precautions. Think about how many official documents can be affected by such technology. Birth certificates, Social Security cards, and driver's licenses, which you use to verify your existence, can now be forged. Not so long ago, it was just a photocopy machine and Liquid Paper.

In early July 1996 in Orange County, California, the vintage Xerox copy scam was perpetrated. As reported by a local radio station, the suspect had copied five $1 bills and put them into the change machines of coin-operated laundries. He was successfully able to retrieve change for the copies and as of yet has not been caught. Don't be so caught up in the high-grade scam that you miss the simple copy machine scam.

Renee C. Martin reports, "Jeremy's fascinating case was that of a dentist who was being sued for not telling his patient that his gums were deteriorating. Finding himself in pain a year later, he went to another dentist, who had to pull out all his teeth. He immediately sued his former dentist for negligence. His attorneys sent copies of the first dentist's chart to Jeremy's counselor. These were forwarded to a nonbiased dental expert witness. The dentist's office records were included. In preparation for trial, discovery procedures were instituted that requested all copies of all documents relating to the case be again forwarded to the plaintiff's (suer's) attorney.

"When Jeremy's attorney contacted Martin, Martin looked at the photocopies and, as usual, requested the original documents. Much is lost in the photocopying process that only the original can provide. In comparing the photocopies against the originals, Martin found that the original dental chart did not match the photocopy that had been sent at the start of the suit. Jeremy's first dentist, realizing he had made a mistake, had changed the chart. Jeremy won his case!"

Let me anchor this problem of photocopies and forgery with an example that may one day affect you. An elderly woman checked into a New York hospital on May 1, 1992, for a series of operations. On that date, she signed a consent form. She signed additional forms on May 3, 4, 5, and 10. Each signature was weaker than the last.

Shortly after she had died, and while her $150,000 estate was being settled, a nephew arrived with a typewritten letter with the woman's signature. The document, which was dated well after the woman had compiled her will in 1987, stated that the young man would receive $75,000 as his inheritance. An alert attorney noticed that the signature on the document didn't resemble her earlier signature, written before her health deteriorated. The estate was saved because the attorney and the document examiner were able to compare signatures.

I'm amazed at how many people fill out paperwork without reading the entire document or fill out paperwork incompletely. Whenever you fill out paperwork, never leave a blank. If you don't have an answer, fill the space with an X. Once your signature is on the original document, make sure that you have a copy. If you leave both the original and the copy, an alert swindler can write his or her own ticket.

Renee C. Martin himself was scammed because he didn't follow his own advice. He once tripped on the sidewalk and scraped up his knee pretty badly. Martin was in a hurry when the nurse asked him to sign some papers. He refused to sign the papers because he had left too many blank spaces. The nurse would not allow him to leave without signing, so he signed the papers and rushed off. Sure enough, when he received the bill, it totaled $295 for service and treatment he never received. Knowing that they had his signature and the original documents, he didn't even try to fight it. This just goes to show you that even the experts get fooled.

While at ZZZZ Best I created more than 20,000 phony documents using only Liquid Paper, scissors, glue, and a photocopy machine. Imagine what a creative con man could do today!

CHAPTER 25

The "Y"
Yellow Page and
Other Phony Invoicing

This chapter is dedicated to the thousands of small business owners across the country who are overcoming the odds and prospering in a competitive economy. Although I cannot provide you with advice on how to succeed in business (remember, my company failed), I can tell you what "not" to do, and that includes steering clear of fraudulent yellow page invoicing.

Have you ever received an invoice for a yellow pages advertisement that you never placed? If you haven't yet received one of these latest invoice scams, you soon might! These scams target businesses both large and small. The con man hopes that the true details of the invoice will be lost in the paper chase. Many companies simply overlook the false invoice, thus allowing the con man to continue scamming others.

I must emphasize that this is not a scam perpetrated by the phone companies. The offenders belong to independent yellow page companies and even phony invoicing companies.

The familiar "walking fingers" logo and the name Yellow

Pages are not protected by any federal trademark registration or copyright. Therefore, you may be led to believe that anyone who uses the logo and the name Yellow Pages is legitimate. There is no connection between publishers of alternative yellow page directories and those of the well-known Yellow Pages.

Many times these fraudulent solicitations are made to look like legitimate invoices. Often the company will send a sample ad or listing of your company along with a bill. This ad or listing is just a spec or sample of what your ad could or would look like if you advertised in their "yellow pages." Solicitations that appear to be invoices are required to say on the solicitation itself that it is not a bill. However, many do not conform to these legal requirements. Whatever the case, perpetrators rely on the fact that the bill is often paid without due diligence. Many times the recipient pays the bill without reading through the statement, which may even include the words, "This is not a bill."

Although most legitimate yellow page or directory advertisements are billed along with the monthly phone bill, many people are conned into paying extra for their ads or listings. Companies such as Pacific Bell and GTE have yellow pages that advertisers can sign up for. They are then billed through their monthly phone service. However, companies such as the Donnelly Directory, which are independently owned (not by GTE, Pacific Bell, or any other phone company), solicit advertisers and bill them separately from the monthly phone service.

The con is made easy because everyone has access to a yellow page directory. Legitimate yellow page directories provide con men with their leads (names and phone numbers of businesses). With the names and numbers of businesses, the con man can get valuable information such as when the next publication is coming out and how their billing statements are scheduled. Now that he has the dates in which billing will occur, he knows how far in advance he can bill the company. The con artist simply copies the company's ad onto a phony invoice, mails it out, and waits for the checks to roll in. Owners, believing they are renewing their current yellow page directory ad, actually unwittingly sign up with bogus companies. The U.S. Postal Service reports that phony invoice scam artists succeed in collecting a significant percentage of all the bills they mail.

Let's look at the case of Fritz B. Fritz noticed that his invoice was a little higher than the last one, but he didn't pay much attention to it at first. Then Fritz noticed that the bill increased by four times the amount. Realizing that something was bizarre, he went back and checked his original agreements and paperwork. Things became very confusing, and he thought maybe it was his fault for not being able to reproduce facts that made sense. The truth was that Fritz was being scammed by phony invoices. Because he waited so long, he has had a lot of difficulty tracking down the exact source of the problem. Fritz is still trying to solve his case!

Unfortunately, Fritz is not alone. Many people are being conned into either paying for services they didn't order or paying double for current services. Although law enforcement officials are unable to place an actual dollar figure on the amount swindled each year, the fact that this type of con artist mails thousands of phony invoices and solicitations on a regular basis indicates that annual losses to businesses may run into billions of dollars. Companies that have poor bookkeeping or employees who are not attentive are especially susceptible to these scams. The con must rely on poor or unorganized business skills in order to work.

Most phony invoice scams actually begin with a phone call. The call helps the perpetrator to obtain names of key people within the organization. He needs to know who and what department is responsible for handling the invoicing. As usual, these con men are remarkably smooth on the phone and can get past any gatekeepers, whether they are receptionists, secretaries, or managers.

The next step is the invoice. Crafted to look exactly like a real invoice, the amount of the bill is usually small enough to go undetected. The con man has experience in knowing exactly how much he can get away with. Remember, he isn't looking for one huge payoff. He's looking for thousands of little payoffs. Some phony invoices even use scare tactics like "Past Due" to pressure companies into paying quickly without carefully examining the bill.

My radio show producer received a promotional piece for a yellow page ad. The advertisement included a clip of what his ad would look like. The notice looked official. It included proper information on his company and a billing statement that looked very legitimate. A postage-paid return envelope was even enclosed. He didn't remember ordering an ad or even talking to anyone about placing one, so he began to read the entire promotional piece.

He first noticed that it was set up not only like a billing statement but also like a contract. The contract was for a year without cancellation. He read further. In fine print he noticed the words "This is a solicitation and not a bill," without the quotation marks, of course. Not wanting to be tricked into placing an ad, he ripped it up and threw it away!

Most of the fraudulent yellow page firms do publish some kind of directory. The quality, circulation, and saturation of these companies are usually far inferior to what the buyer is expecting. Many times skilled con men will use copier machines to make duplications of actual yellow page ads with "Renewal" placed on the copy of the ad.

If you ever receive an invoice for a yellow page listing, be sure to read through it carefully. Never assume! U.S. Postal Service regulations state that the following disclaimer must be on the bill, invoice, or statement: THIS IS A SOLICITATION FOR THE ORDER OF GOODS OR SERVICES, OR BOTH, AND NOT A BILL, INVOICE, OR STATEMENT OF ACCOUNT DUE. YOU ARE UNDER NO OBLIGATION TO MAKE ANY PAYMENTS ON ACCOUNT OF THIS OFFER UNLESS YOU ACCEPT THIS OFFER, or THIS IS NOT A BILL. THIS IS A SOLICITATION. YOU ARE UNDER NO OBLIGATION TO PAY UNLESS YOU ACCEPT THIS OFFER. One of these disclaimers must be conspicuously printed on the face of the solicitation in at least 30-point type.

Print colors must be reproducible on copying machines and cannot be obscured by folding or other means. If the solicitation is more than one page, the disclaimer must appear on each page, and if it is perforated, the required language must appear on each section that could be construed as a bill. Regulations prohibit any language that modifies or qualifies the disclaimer, such as "legal notice required by law."

Often these phony invoicing schemes pose as debt collection agencies. One such scheme was exposed in Idaho. Attorney General Alan G. Lance announced that his Consumer Protection Unit had reached an agreement with Collection Procurements Acquisitions, Inc. (CPA), a California collections agency. CPA was forced to cease all attempts to collect charges consumers did not make. The company also agreed to fully credit every affected Idahoan's account and not report this debt to any credit reporting agency. The total amount of money CPA was attempting to collect was $2,534.92. The debts were for fraudulent 900 pay-per-call services that were charged to Idaho consumers in 1995.

Fraudulent yellow page invoicing companies, also in Idaho, also try to collect for services not rendered. On May 10, 1995, after a lengthy investigation, the Attorney General's Consumer Protection Unit entered into an assurance of voluntary compliance with Long Distance Billing Company (LDBC). LDBC was a collection agency for North Star Communications and was forced to cease collection attempts because the phone charges were the result of a fraudulent invoicing scam. To make matters worse, Norstar, formerly North Star Communications, sold these accounts to yet another collection agency in attempts to collect those illegal debts. Fortunately, they were caught.

No matter how big the company is or what it is selling, as a business owner be aware of the tactics used in phony invoicing. The Federal Trade Commission and the U.S. Postal Service suggest that consumers and business owners follow these tips:

1. Never place an order over the telephone unless there is no doubt that the firm you are dealing with is reputable. Get the organization's name, address, and phone number, as well as its representative's full name and position.

2. If a significant amount of money is involved, ask for business and local bank references and check them out. Find out how long the firm has operated out of its present location. If possible, visit the company or firm. You can also check with the Better Business Bureau for a reliability report.

3. Investigate the company and its product before responding.

4. Ask for a copy of a previous directory edition. Make sure the publication exists. Verify the circulation figures and whether its circulation suits your needs.

5. Check your records to confirm claims of previous business dealings.

6. Ask the publisher for written information about its directories. Ask for distribution figures, the method of distribution, and the directory's life span.

7. Establish effective internal controls for the payment of invoices.

8. Ask if the directories are available for free. If there is a fee, ask what the cost is.

9. Insist that employees fill out prenumbered purchase orders for every order placed.

10. Channel the bills through one department. This will eliminate any billing confusion.

11. Check all invoices against purchase orders and against goods or services received. Make certain that order numbers correspond with the invoices.

12. Verify all invoices with the person who gave written or verbal authorization.

13. Clear all invoices with the appropriate executives.

14. If the invoicing company claims to have a tape recording of the order, insist on hearing it.

15. Call your local Yellow Pages publisher to learn if it is associated with the company soliciting your business.

16. Check with consumer protection officials in your state and in the state where the company is located to learn if they have received any complaints about the

publisher. Keep in mind that suspect companies often shut down before complaints are registered or before local authorities have a chance to act.

Any type of bill or statement that is unsolicited or is for a product or service you did not receive is a phony invoice scam. Julio Carballo received a statement in the mail from Outstanding Young Men. The literature stated what an honor it was to be chosen as one of the nation's top young men. If Julio was elected into the society, he would be one of a select few who would receive a certificate and have his name published in a beautiful hardcover book.

A week later Julio received an invoice for one copy of the book. The cost was over $70 per book, and a minimum of one book had to be purchased in order to be inducted into the Outstanding Young Men Society. Angry at the fact that the whole deal was merely a con for buying a book, Julio stopped the interviewing process.

If you receive a phony invoice or a solicitation disguised as an invoice, the U.S. Postal Service suggests using the following procedure to report the matter to the Postal Service and your local Better Business Bureau:

1. On the envelope in which the phony invoice or solicitation arrived, note the date received and sign your name. Be sure all the solicitation material is returned to the envelope in which it was received.

2. Prepare a notarized affidavit like the sample below:
   To: Chief Postal Inspector
   Attn: Fraud Section
       United States Postal Service
       Washington, D.C. 20260

I, _____, being duly sworn, depose and say:

A. I am _____ (position)
   of _____ (company) located at
   _____ (address and zip code).

B. On or about _____ our firm received through the
   United States mail a solicitation from
   _____ (name and address) which resembles a bill, invoice, or statement of account.

C. I have dated and signed the solicitation material
   and enclosed it herewith.

D. Our firm has never done business with
   _____ (name) and we have not
   requested a listing or authorized the insertion of
   our advertisement in the publication referred to in
   the solicitation.

E. It is my opinion that the subject solicitation represents an attempt to elicit a remittance from my
   firm by means of deception.

   _____ (your signature)

   Subscribed and sworn to before me this _____ day of
   _____. My commission expires _____.

3. Send the solicitation material and the original affidavit to the Chief Postal Inspector, U.S. Postal
   Service. Keep a copy for your records, and send a
   copy to your local Better Business Bureau.

Don't allow yourself to be sold if you don't want to buy. The epitome of high-pressure sales is being pushed into buying something you never intended to buy. Invoice scams happen because people don't know that they can say no. If more people take the time to report fraud and abuse, we will be able to take a bite out of that $400-billion-a-year problem of fraud.

CHAPTER 26

The "Z"
ZZZZ Best

Not long ago, while I was speaking to a major accounting firm on the subject of fraud prevention, I asked the participants what they believed was the biggest problem in the area of consumer fraud—ignorance or apathy? A man sitting in the back row raised his hand and said, "I don't know, and I don't care!"

Throughout this book I have tried to give you a reason to care. If the figure of $400 billion a year in consumer losses didn't grab your attention, perhaps the horror stories in the previous chapters did. But for some, change will occur only if disaster strikes—and by then, of course, it's too late.

People truly believe that it will never happen to them. To shatter this myth, I am going to provide three examples from the ZZZZ Best case of victims who, like many of you, never thought they would be vulnerable to fraud. They fall into the following three neat categories:

1. The "I'm Too Smart to Get Conned" person
2. The "Greedy" person
3. The "Friend of the Perpetrator"

Before I begin, I think I should state explicitly that I am by no means adding insult to the victims' injury. I am also not shifting the blame for my crimes from me to my victims. What I am trying to do is help the consumer learn from the mistakes made by the victims of the ZZZZ Best fraud. Out of respect, I will use fictitious names, but rest assured that the people and the circumstances surrounding their losses are quite real.

I will call the "I'm Too Smart" man Dean. Dean is a lawyer who graduated first in his class. He has been successful most of his life, starting out with a big firm before striking out on his own. The income earned from his practice has made it possible for him to make outside investments.

When I first asked Dean to invest in ZZZZ Best, he never expected fraud. He saw me as a younger version of himself, hard-working and determined. Although he knew nothing about the carpet cleaning industry, the promise of a 100 percent return on his investment in just six months captured his interest. Still, he wanted to be cautious. "Why don't you borrow the money from a bank at 8 percent?" he asked me.

"Banks won't lend me money because I'm too young," I replied. "That's why I have to bring in outside investors." He accepted my answer, asked for some documentation, and said he'd let me know in a week if he was interested after he "checked things out."

For perpetrators of fraud, these are the three words that cause the greatest amount of anxiety: *check things out.* It is during this time that the investor performs due diligence. In the case of Dean, I expected him to consult with his associates in the law profession or with someone in the carpet cleaning industry to corroborate my offer with some outside source. Much to my surprise, Dean felt that he was too smart for that. He convinced himself that he knew enough about business to make this decision on his own. And that was fine with me. There is an old saying that goes: "Any lawyer who represents himself has a fool for a client." By not seeking an objective opinion about the investment, Dean became an easy target for fraud.

When it was all over, he was one of the biggest victims of the ZZZZ Best fraud. What's the practical application for today's investor? I don't care how much you know about business or how many odds you have overcome to be a success; it is impossible to make an intelligent investment decision about an industry you know nothing about. Swallow your pride, and before you throw large dollar amounts into any investment, seek outside, objective counsel.

I've lost count of how many times people have told me how they lost money in the stock market or some business venture. And in every case, when I asked them what they knew about the business they invested in, they simply tucked their thumbs underneath their suspenders and shrugged.

The second category is the greedy investor. Janet was introduced to me through a mutual friend. She was a middle-aged woman in the real estate business. Her income came mostly from second trust deeds that she purchased from desperate and overextended homeowners. When I asked her to invest $25,000 in ZZZZ Best, her first question showed me that she was a perfect target. Instead of asking why a profitable company would need to borrow money or what I would do with the money once I got it, she asked what her profit would be. Although this may seem reasonable and insignificant to you, the con man picks up on what makes you tick. Are you more interested in return or risk?

When Janet heard that I was willing to pay three points a week on a $25,000 investment, she thought about how an extra $750 a week would change her lifestyle. And when I asked her to bring her friends into the deal, she was more than willing. Things went fine for the first year. She received her weekly payments and thought the party would never end. But like all Ponzi schemes, the end did come, and Janet lost not only her money but her friends as well.

Throughout this book I have talked about greed and gullibility. The promise of high returns has blinded the objectivity of more than one investor. Con men know that with the promise of a high or outrageous return, there is also an understood risk. But allow me to ask this question: If you lose your principal (the amount you originally invested), have you made a profit? Of course not. Then you must realize that a promised high return is only as good as the character and integrity of the person offering the deal. And we know that during the ZZZZ Best days I possessed neither.

This brings us to our final category: the friend of the perpetrator. The most painful type of financial rape is that which comes from the hand of someone we love and trust. Much to my shame, this type of victimization started off with me stealing my grandmother's jewelry at age sixteen to meet payroll, and ended with me conning my best friend's mother out of $70,000.

I can't tell you how many people have called in to my radio show to describe how their best friend or son or sister-in-law had gotten them into an investment that went bad. When initially presented with the investment, these people did little or nothing to confirm the specifics of the deal, and as a result they became victims. I recommend the following three steps of due diligence when and if you are approached by that trusting someone:

1. Do they appear desperate? Is there a sense of urgency that transcends their circumstance? Opportunities are not bail-outs. Be suspicious if funds are immediately required without ample time for investigation.

2. Are they insulted by the thought of you "checking things out"? This does not apply to those of you who are investing in the person and not the object. There are situations in which the investor doesn't care if he or she ever sees the money again; the investor just wants to help a friend or loved one in need and can afford to absorb the loss. But for those who can't, there needs to be a line drawn between business and friendship. The opportunity must stand on its own merit, minus the relationship.

3. Are they willing to be accountable to you after the investment? Remember, it's *your* money and you have the right to know how it was spent and when you will get it back. *You* set the parameters. The recipient of your funds must be willing to adhere to the conditions you set for the investment.

I don't want to create paranoia, but we do live in desperate times. And although there are many honest people who would never think of defrauding a friend or loved one, there have been too many cases in which relationships have been abused. Be objective and think things through carefully. Don't think fraud can't happen to you.

Conclusion

Throughout this book I have attempted to answer the how and the what to the fraud question, but I have not yet answered the *why*. I would like to answer this relevant question by quoting one of my favorite authors, C. S. Lewis. The opening chapter of his book *The Abolition of Man* is titled "Men Without Chests." In it, Lewis analyzes the moral dilemma America is facing:

"I opened a book the other day but I will not name it. I shall call it The Green Book." [Lewis did not like to criticize other people and rarely responded to his own critics.] "But be sure the book really exists. It was written by two authors. I shall call them Gaius and Titius."

He continues, "When I opened that book it was teaching children about ethics and morals and values. And Gaius and Titius do not believe there is any such thing as absolute values, so how they were teaching the children was this way.

"When you take your boy for a walk, and you take him in front of a waterfall and your little boy looks at the waterfall and says to you, 'My, Mother, that waterfall is sublime' (forgive the term; remember, it is an Englishman's example. The word *sub-lime* simply means that the boy was in awe of the waterfall), you've got to pause long enough, say Gaius and Titius, to look at your son and say, 'Now listen to me, son, there is no such thing as a sublime waterfall. All that it is, is water falling. And because that waterfall looks so massive and awesome, you feel so shrunken in front of that gigantic profusion of water that you stand there, look at it, feel dwarfed, and say, 'My, isn't that sublime.'

"What actually happens, say Gaius and Titius, is that the waterfall seems so great, you seem so small and your glands within your body begin to secrete certain juices. Those juices, when they are secreted, give to you a feeling which scholars interpret and psychologists tell you is a feeling of viewing sub-limity. But there is nothing sublime out there—it's only the glands secreting juices which give you a feeling which some people say is the feeling of sublimity."

Author, ethicist, and scholar Dr. Ravi Zacharias anchors what Lewis was saying in this modern-day illustration: "The Air Florida jet takes off from Washington airport. Seconds into the air the pilot knows it's in trouble. Moments later it plummets into the icy waters of the Potomac. Bodies are spilling out from every window and emergency exit. People are dying in icy, watery graves. One woman is able to swim away from the airplane and, with no strength left, suddenly notices a chopper on top of her that lowers a ladder. She grabs hold of one of the rungs of the ladder, relieved that rescue is in sight. The chopper begins to gain a little more altitude and to her utter shock she doesn't even have enough strength to hold on to the rung. She lets go of it and crashes back into the water.

"A man by the name of Lenny Skutnick is walking by the water when this happens. Thankfully he did not read Gaius and Titius. Otherwise what he thought was a noble deed would have been nothing more than a set of glands that were secreting certain juices which psychologists interpret as a feeling of nobility. If you jump in and save somebody, your glands secrete juices which make you feel good all over.

"On the other hand, he could have jumped in and drowned her and come out of the water with a different set of glands secreting a different set of juices, which people would have called a feeling of shamefulness and guilt—although there is no such thing as nobility, it's only in the glands. There's no such thing as shamefulness, it's only in the glands and it's all in the secretions. Nobility and shamefulness are not realities out there. It's all in the body—within itself."

Now don't miss the punchline given by Lewis: *"If I believe these men, they tell me mathematics is real, therefore my brain is real. Food is real, therefore my stomach is real. But they tell me my emotions have nothing whatsoever to do with reality. They are going to produce a generation of men with brains, men with stomachs, men without chests—no heart!"*

May I suggest to you that this generation of men without chests has already been produced, and that the $400-billion-a-year problem of consumer fraud is merely the fruit of a society that has lost the objective standard of right and wrong and replaced it with selfish pragmatism? You might discount the solution I'm about to give as the soppy babblings of some disillusioned Christian, but in my experience on Wall Street and the almost eight years I spent in jail with thousands of prisoners—many of whom showed no remorse for their crimes and planned on committing them again upon release—I am absolutely convinced that the only way to prevent fraud is to change the heart of the perpetrator before the crime is committed.

And I know of no other way to accomplish that feat than through divine intervention, which I call conversion.

Bibliography

Adamson, Deborah. "Financial Planners: Who Do You Trust?" *Daily News*, June 16, 1996, p. 1.

Alliance Against Fraud in Telemarketing. "Swindlers Are Calling." Brochure. 1990.

Better Business Bureau. "Obtaining a Patent and Invention Development." March 1990.

Better Business Bureau. "Penny Stocks." 1996.

Better Business Bureau. "Preventing Credit Card Fraud." Pamphlet. 1996.

Better Business Bureau. "Tips on . . . Financial Planners." Better Business Bureau Consumer Information Series, 1992.

Better Business Bureau. "Tips on . . . Health Insurance." Pamphlet. 1996.

Better Business Bureau. "Realizability Report." May 23, 1996.

Blechman, Andrew D. "Four Students Arrested in Computer Scam." *Los Angeles Times*, Ventura County edition, May 18, 1996, p. B3.

Brennan, Robert F. "Protect Yourself Against Malpractice by Your HMO Doctor." 1996. Via E-mail at: rbrennan@directnet.com

Burnell, Fritz. "Quantity Ordered Changing After Invoicing." June 13, 1996. http://acc-pac.com/wwwboard/plus/faq.html

Campola, Tony. See p. 43

Caton, C. J. *MLM Fraud: A Practical Handbook for the Network Marketing Professional.* Publisher unknown, 1991.

Commonwealth Fund. "A Survey of Patients in Managed Care and Fee for Service Settings; Three City Survey Finds Working Americans Dissatisfied." 1996. Web site: http://www.cmwf.org

Conn, Charles Paul. *Promises to Keep*. New York, N.Y.: The Berkley Publishing Group, 1985.

Consumer Action. "Preventing Telemarketing Fraud." VI1(E). January 1994.

Craig, Julia. "Fraudulent Telemarketing." *Criminal Law News,* vol. 16, no. 1.

Credential Services International. Newsletter. Vol. 9, no. 3.

Davis, Karen. "Managed Care Plans May Not Get Better as They Grow Bigger." 1996. Web site: http://www.cmwf.org

DeLange, Brett. "Debt Collection Company Ceases Attempts to Collect Illegal Charges from Idaho Consumers." Web site: microsoft internet explorer

Direct Selling Education Foundation. "Pyramid Schemes: Not What They Seem." Pamphlet. 1991.

Elliott, Emerson J. "The Condition of Education 1995." Web site: microsoft internet explorer

"Ex–Real Estate Salesman Convicted in $10 Million Fraud." *Los Angeles Times,* July 16, 1996, p. B4.

Federal Trade Commission, Food and Drug Administration, and National Association of Attorneys General. "The Facts About Weight Loss Products and Programs." Pamphlet. 1996.

Federal Trade Commission. "Job Ads, Job Scams and 900 Numbers." Pamphlet. 1996.

Federal Trade Commission. "Land Sales Scams." Pamphlet. November 1992.

Federal Trade Commission. "The Skinny on Dieting." Pamphlet. March 1996.

Federal Trade Commission. "Timeshare Resales." Pamphlet. 1996.

Ferris, Jackie. "Disease or Behavior? Researcher Can Blend Best of Both Approaches." Web site: www.arf.org

"Fraud and Abuse in the Financial Planning Industry." Web address: webmaster@state.pa.us

Glionna, John M. "Real Estate Watchdog Is Asleep." *Los Angeles Times,* Valley edition, August 12, 1996, p. B1.

Hall, Len. "Fugitive in $2 Million Real Estate Scam Caught After 8 Years." *Los Angeles Times,* Orange County edition, June 23, 1996, p. B10.

Information Technologies. "900 Numbers Participant List." 1996.

"Introducing Internet ScamBusters!" NETrageous, Inc., web@netrageous.com.

Jacobs, Durand F. "Problem Gamblers and White Collar Crimes." California Council on Compulsive Gambling, 1987.

Jarvis, William, M.D. "Quack Buster." Buzz, Inc., 1996. Web site: www.BUZZMISSION. html

Joyal, Bob. *How to Find the Best Home at the Best Price.* Calabasas, Calif.: The Home Buyers Center, 1996.

Kling, Arnold. "Watch Out for These Scams." Web site: http://www.homfair.com/home-fair/scams.html.

"Learning from the Master." *The News,* October 15, 1994.

'Lectric Law Library. "Phony Invoice Schemes." Web site: http://www.lectlaw.com.

Marohn, Stephanie. "Designing Healthy Women." *Alternative Medicine Digest,* no. 12, pp. 40–42, 74, 1996.

Martin, Renee C. "Forgery Prevention Tips." 1996.

Miller, Greg, and Tom Petruno. "For Investors, the Internet Has Promise, Perils." *Los Angeles Times*, June 3, 1996, p. A1.

National Consumer Law Center. "MCI Settlement Outreach Program." Report. May 8, 1996.

National Futures Association. "Investment Swindles: How They Work and How to Avoid Them." 1996. swindles.txt@gopher.gsa.gov

Olmos, David R. "Blue Shield, In Bold Move Will Waive Specialist Referrals." *Los Angeles Times*, July 1996, p. 1, 13.

"Online Investment Schemes: Fraud and Abuse in Cyberspace." *NASAA Investor Bulletin*. Web site: http://www.gnn.com/meta/finance/feat/archives/invest/nasaa.html

Pehler, Arthur L. "Card Fraud Alert." *Telecard World Magazine*, 1996.

"Penny Stock Frauds." Better Business Bureau literature. 1996. Web site: http://www.cbbb.org

"Phony Job Opportunities." Internet Assistant for Word, Information Technology Division.

Pressman, David. "Patent Basics." Nolo Press. Web site: http://www.smartbiz.com/sbs/arts/piyl.htm

Printech. "Fraud Protection Paper." 1996. Web site: microsoft internet explorer

Reno, Ronald A. "The Diceman Cometh: Will Gambling Be a Bad Bet for Your Town?" *Policy Review: The Journal of American Citizenship*, March–April 1996, p. 1.

Richman, Sheldon. "Why the State Took Control of 'Education.'" 1996. Web site: http://www.sepschool.org

Ronaleen, Roha R. "Make Big Money Working Part Time at Home." *Kiplinger's Personal Finance Magazine*, vol. 49, no. 10, 1995, p. 1.

Rosenfield, James R. *Direct Mail Marketing*, vol. 57, December 1994, p. 32.

Schwarz, M. Roy, M.D. "Medical Marketing and Media." 1996. E-mail: webmaster@cpsnet.com

Securities Division. "Penny Stocks: A Guide for Beginning Investors." July 1996.

Spragins, Ellyn, Jeremy Kahn, and Annetta Miller. "How to Choose a Doctor at Your HMO." *Newsweek*, June 24, 1996, p. 63.

"A Survey of Patients in Managed Care and Fee Settings." Web site: http://www.cmwf.org.

"Technology." *Los Angeles Times*, May 30, 1996, p. D2.

"Time Magazine Asks: HMO's? No!" *Time*, January 22, 1996, p. 1–2.

Tucker, Robert. *Quacks of Old London.* 1996. Web site: http://www.telport.com/dkossy/london.html

Tucker, Robert. "John R. Brinkley and Goat-Gland Science." Web site: http://www.tele-port.com/dkossy/brink.html

"United States Postal Inspection Service, Hot Tip on Playing Foreign Lotteries by Mail: Don't Do It!" 1996. Web site: http://www.usps.gov/websites/depart/inspect/

"United States Postal Inspection Service, Receipt of Unsolicited Merchandise." 1996. Web site: http://www.usps.gov/websites/depart/inspect/

"United States Postal Inspection Service, Six-Cent and Other Short-Paid Postage." 1996. Web site: http://www.usps.gov/websites/depart/inspect/

Van Derbeken, Jaxon. "Officer Linked to 'Pyramid' Scheme." *Los Angeles Daily News,* May 8, 1996, p. 10.

Wright, Don. *Scam!* Elkhart, Ind.: Cottage Publications, 1996.

Young, Paul N. "Arbitration Urged for Investors Burned by Brokerage Firms." *Personal Investing News,* March 1995.

Zamichow, Nora. "The Lords of the Lot." *Los Angeles Times,* July 1996. Web address: archives@latimes.com

Zarkaras, Alex. "Education Adrift." 1996. Web site: microsoft internet explorer